Curriculum Inquiry

John I. Goodlad and Associates:

Margaret P. Ammons

Edith A. Buchanan

Gary A. Griffin

Henry W. Hill

Alicja Iwańska

James A. Jordan

M. Frances Klein

Robert M. McClure

Maurice N. Richter, Jr.

Kenneth A. Tye

Louise L. Tyler

Elizabeth C. Wilson

CURRICULUM INQUIRY

The Study of Curriculum Practice

McGRAW-HILL BOOK COMPANY

New York   St. Louis   San Francisco
Auckland   Bogotá   Düsseldorf   Johannesburg   London   Madrid
Mexico   Montreal   New Delhi   Panama   Paris   São Paulo
Singapore   Sydney   Tokyo   Toronto

Thomas H. Quinn and Michael Hennelly were the editors for this book. Christopher Simon was the designer. Teresa Leaden supervised the production. It was set in Caledonia with display lines in Optima by Monotype Composition Co.
Printed and bound by R. R. Donnelley and Sons.

Library of Congress Cataloging in Publication Data
Main entry under title:

Curriculum inquiry.

  Includes index.
  1. Curriculum planning—Addresses, essays, lectures.
I. Goodlad, John I.
LB1570.C925   375'.001   79-10109
ISBN 0-07-023530-9

123456789 RRDRRD 7985432109

To
Jimmy Jordan
and
Ole Sand

Contents

Curriculum Inquiry

Introduction: The Study of Curriculum Practice

JOHN I. GOODLAD

This book is about curriculum practice, with the prime focus being the study of practice. What the study of curriculum practice involves should become clear as the reader proceeds. This is not a manual or guidebook for curriculum development. Nonetheless, if what follows provides some insight into the dimensions and complexity of curriculum practice, it follows that the book has practical value. A major goal is to help theorists, researchers, and practitioners increase their understanding of what the curriculum field embraces.

As we shall see, succeeding chapters are held together by a common framework; they are not simply a collection of individual views about various pieces of what is embraced by the word "curriculum." This conceptual framework is laid out in the first two chapters and revisited in the final chapter. In most of the intervening chapters, some part of this framework is described or interpreted in order to help the reader see the relationship of this part to the whole. However, this may not be adequate orientation for the reader. And so my major purpose in writing this Introduction is to provide some background information and commentary—to make more explicit some relationships among these chapters which might not otherwise be clear.

Five identifiable sets or phases of personal involvement in the field of curriculum, several proceeding concurrently, are reflected on subsequent pages. First, there was a period of conceptual work with selected colleagues at the University of Chicago. Second, there was utilization and refinement of this work as curriculum consultant to a large school district on the Atlantic seaboard. Third, there was further use and modification of the initial conceptualization in curriculum development at the University Elementary School, UCLA. Fourth, there were explorations into the utility of this conceptualization as a research tool by graduate students at UCLA and by me. Finally, there was further refinement of the conceptual formulation for the purpose of guiding a comprehensive study of curricula in a sample of elementary, junior high, and secondary schools. All of this took place over a period of more than two decades; some of what follows reports work still in progress.

Development of a Conceptual System for Curriculum

In 1947, I enrolled in Education 260, *Basic Principles of Curriculum and Instruction,* at the University of Chicago because I knew nothing about the subject and soon would be required to display some knowledge on the qualifying examinations for the doctorate. The course was taught by Ralph W. Tyler. My performance was less than impressive. Although I emjoyed the course, I was not aware of it having on me an impression of any unusual significance and I found little or no use for it in my subsequent employment at Emory University in Atlanta, Georgia. But then, some five or six years later, I found myself drawing upon concepts such as scope, sequence, and integration which apparently had found a roosting place in my brain. I even began to teach a warmed-over version of what has become known as the Tyler Rationale, employing his syllabus as the basic text.*

*Ralph W. Tyler, *Basic Principles of Curriculum and Instruction,* University of Chicago Press, Chicago, 1950.

For the most part, I treated curriculum planning as though it were a rather puerile exercise in ideas, antiseptically removed from institutions and the people who work there. And then, for reasons that are completely obscure today, I prepared for a curriculum conference at the University of Georgia (1956) a paper which placed alongside the substantive elements of curriculum some of the sociopolitical aspects which increasingly were becoming apparent to me and which are inevitably encountered in any "for real" foray into the practice of curriculum. I was at last beginning to relate and weave together formal, academic learnings and those of the so-called school of hard knocks, a school that involved me in curriculum planning with individual teachers, school district curriculum committees, and state task forces.

Later that year, now on the faculty of the University of Chicago, I set about assembling a small group of young scholars to work together on conceptualizing the curriculum field in such way as to combine the ends-means components described by Tyler with these process elements. My colleagues in that endeavor were: Margaret P. Ammons (education), Alicja Iwańska (anthropology), James A. Jordan (deceased—philosophy), and Maurice N. Richter, Jr. (sociology). Our work was to be conceptual rather than theoretical or empirical and our purpose was to construct an ordered view of the domains of curriculum and possible interconnections or relations among them. With the invaluable assistance of Maurice Richter, I pulled together some of our thinking several years later in a limited edition, *The Development of a Conceptual System for Dealing with Problems of Curriculum and Instruction* (University of California, Los Angeles, 1966, out of print.)*

Although this work was entirely ideaistic—we constructed not a single piece of curriculum and ventured as a group not at all into actual practice—we found ourselves grappling as

*Supported by the Cooperative Research Program of the Office of Education, U.S. Department of Health, Education, and Welfare. Contract No. SAE-8024, Project No. 454.

ERIC Document No. ED 010 064, available through National Cash Register Company, Bethesda, Maryland.

much with the political, social, and transactional processes of praxis as with normative matters of product and substance. It is clear that curriculum development is a significant human activity and that any reasonably adequate conceptualization of the whole simply must encompass the acts and actors as well as the ideas in the ongoing dramas. The study of curriculum is the study of this practice and how practice might be improved.

My shift in institutional affiliation to the University of California, Los Angeles, in 1960, brought the collaboration somewhat abruptly and abortively to a close. We had not finished even a draft of a report, although written elaborations of concepts and many position papers filled several boxes prepared for shipment to the West Coast. And now, we were scattered and all deeply involved with the demands of our new jobs. The monograph produced six years later was only a summary outline of our thinking—to be fleshed out later, we hoped. Chapter 1 and, to a lesser degree, Chapter 2 deal with the phenomena we sought to encompass in a conceptualization of what the curriculum field includes.

At one time, I had hoped to include with a more developed version of the conceptual system for curriculum some of our position papers which helped to clarify the domains, levels, and processes it seeks to encompass. With this purpose in mind, I examined hundreds of pages of notes and papers on such curricular topics as the translation of educational goals into objectives (Richter), criteria for evaluating lists or sets of educational goals (Ammons), the role of values in the decisions of school board members (Jordan), praxiological considerations in curriculum (Iwańska) and so on. All of the elements of the conceptualization that emerged were there. But many of the topics were developed in fragmentary fashion; some were not rounded out at all. Also, some of the key ideas appear in better form in the initial 1966 version of the conceptualization than in our notes.

Out of it all I selected three papers which appeared to me to make contributions to curriculum thought in their own right, with or without reference to the conceptual system. Together, they reveal some of the inquiry that carried us to the formulation published in 1966. These papers, revised by the authors, appear here as Chapters 10 and 12 (both by Iwańska) and 13 (by Jordan).

The substantial body of writing by Ammons and Richter influenced the conceptual system to considerable degree. It proved not possible for me to select out of the corpus of their writing chapter-length papers which would stand alone and complete as chapters for this volume. But Ammons and Richter are included in the list of associated authors, nonetheless, because their work influenced and is represented in much of what follows.

Use and Refinement in a School District

Meanwhile, at about the time of the transition from Chicago to Los Angeles, I became involved on the East Coast with one of the most comprehensive, ambitious undertakings in curriculum planning ever undertaken by a single school district, so far as I know. The ensuing four years of close involvement and several additional years of a more peripheral association provided a much needed and appreciated opportunity to test in the political-social and professional-technical domains what had been up to then almost exclusively in the domain of ideas. There is little doubt in my mind that this long-term consulting relationship served to both delay and, ultimately, influence significantly the writing of the monograph referred to above. If process and substance are given reasonably equal treatment in the conceptual system that emerged, it is this experience that brought the two into balance.

Elizabeth C. Wilson, in Chapter 9, provides us with a fascinating account of the people, ideas, and events comprising the real-life drama of curriculum practice with which I had the good fortune to be associated.

Curriculum Development at the University Elementary School

The teaching of Ralph Tyler at the University of Chicago in the late 1940s, work with the colleagues named above and others at that University in the late 1950s, and association with Elizabeth C. Wilson and her colleagues in Montgomery County, Maryland, during the 1960s influenced substantially my subsequent thinking and writing in the field of curriculum. But, mostly, these experiences influenced my teaching and involvement in other instances of praxis—notably intensive curriculum planning at the University Elementary School of the Graduate School of Education, UCLA.

Soon after coming to the UES as its Director (1960), my colleagues there and I joined in what became a continuing process of dialogue about and change in the organization and programs of the School. The teachers sought some kind of organizing framework to guide and relate an emerging array of changes in the School's structure and curriculum. With some reluctance, I agreed to conduct a year-long seminar on principles of curriculum development concurrent with the ongoing work of several task forces made up of the faculty sub-groups responsible for each unit or phase of the School.

Five of the authors of subsequent chapters were, at various times and in varying ways, associated with this work. Three of them wrote chapters for this book about some aspect with which they were closely associated at the UES. Robert M. McClure, in Chapter 5, describes and analyzes the sustained efforts of each faculty sub-group to define a goal-oriented framework to guide curricular decisions and instructional practices. Edith A. Buchanan, in Chapter 6, documents the efforts of a sub-group in early childhood education to justify its members' decisions with and for children. M. Frances Klein, in Chapter 7, describes the effort of a small group of teachers to introduce greater rigor into processes of instruction and evaluation. All three used the conceptualization of curriculum discussed above and in Chapter 1 to guide their research and analyses.

What comes through clearly in all three chapters is that agreeing on and justifying curricular decisions to guide learning and teaching is exceedingly difficult even under the best supporting circumstances. Even the most experienced, thoughtful teachers do many things because that is the way they have been done over time, not because they have thought their way through to a defensible posture. And it is clear that teachers make curricular and instructional decisions, perhaps most of the time, with little or no regard for decisions intended to influence them made by persons, such as legislators, in far-off places.

Using the Conceptual System for Research

We get further insight into decision-making processes in curriculum from the studies of Gary A. Griffin and Henry W. Hill reported in Chapters 3 and 4, respectively. The former used the conceptual system discussed in Chapters 1 and 2 to find out whether decisions actually are made at all three levels—societal, institutional, and instructional—described by the conceptualization. The latter employed the conceptualization in examining certain aspects and impacts of societal decisions.

Griffin concluded that institutional curricular decisions— that is, decisions made by the staff for their educational institution (perhaps in collaboration with community representatives)—are not well-attended to in practice. McClure's research, reported in Chapter 5 suggests a reason: it is exceedingly difficult for those operating the institution to come together effectively as a decision-making group. Buchanan and Klein echo this explanation. Given the present organization of school time and the level of teaching as a profession, to expect school staffs to prepare curricula may be quite unrealistic. Nonetheless, an ongoing process of coping with curricular issues appears to be essential to self-renewal in schools.

Presumably, there are appropriate and inappropriate decisions, or more or less desirable ones, for the actors at societal, institutional, and instructional levels. It is chaotic and wasteful for each group to repeat the work of some other. It is frequently unfortunate and sometimes illegal for one group to ignore the work and decisions of another. Hill's research delved into some of the attendant problems and issues. He reports specifically on curricular laws pertaining to instruction passed by legislators and their knowledge, along with the knowledge of school superintendents, school board members, and teachers, of such legislation. His work points ultimately to the importance of the question of who should make what curriculum decisions and the difficulty of coming up with any clear-cut answers to it.

Frances Klein and I developed a mutual interest in exploring the nature of curriculum work beyond the borders of the United States. A catalyst for me was the opportunity, in the summer of 1971, to serve as a member of the faculty assembled in Gränna, Sweden, to conduct the International Seminar for Advanced Training in Curriculum Development and Innovation. Subsequently, Klein received a grant from and was selected an Academy Associate of the National (U.S.A.) Academy of Education to work with me in conducting a survey of curriculum centers in selected countries. These centers are relatively new institutions created in many countries to advance the work of curriculum development for elementary and secondary schools.

We sought to determine the kinds of curricular questions and problems dealt with by the centers and whether they were similar to or identical with those posed by Tyler. We sought also to see whether the conceptual system discussed in this volume was of any use in describing and drawing conclusions about the major loci of curricular activity in the countries surveyed. We concluded that Tyler's questions have relevance to all the centers in describing the work to which they are committed. Utilization of Goodlad's conceptual system revealed an overwhelming domination of curriculum development and influence at the societal level. As in Griffin's study, the institutional or school level appeared to be disproportionately inactive and underutilized. The results of our survey appear in Chapter 11.

Refining the Conceptual System

It is gratifying that the conceptual system has been viewed by others as useful for curriculum development, empirical research, and various other kinds of inquiry. It has received attention, also, because of its shortcomings. Louise Tyler and

Frances Klein observed that it appeared to downplay the role of learners, placing them in an apparently passive or instrumental role.

I agree. But the validity of their observation depends on whether the conceptual system is employed descriptively or prescriptively. If the former, then I am forced to conclude that it is all too accurate. Although much lip service is given in this country and elsewhere to the importance of taking into account the needs and interests of students, such is done only in rare instances. Neither in this country nor in the countries surveyed and reported in Chapter 11 are there systematic efforts to study and use data on student experiences with curricula in seeking to develop or revise curricula.

Responding to the prescriptive possibilities of the conceptualization, Tyler and Klein added the personal or experiential level. Tyler and I discuss the experiential in Chapter 8 from the perspective of the meaning derived by students in their encounters with programs provided for their learning. Curriculum development could begin here and be supported and nourished rather than determined by the other levels.

A recent refinement of part of the curricular conceptualization occurred as a consequence of embarking on a detailed study of a sample of elementary, junior high, and secondary schools in the United States.* Two of my colleagues in this endeavor, Kenneth Tye and Frances Klein, and I searched for a framework to guide our efforts to describe school curricula. We employed the levels of the conceptual system but found it necessary to break them down into further subdivisions. This framework and its use are described in Chapter 2.

Association with the work on which succeeding chapters are based and both writing and editing what follows resulted in some further modifications and refinements of the initial conceptual system. Some minor modifications appear in

* Funded by the Danforth, Jennings, Kettering, International Paper, Mott, Rockefeller, and Spencer foundations, the JDR 3RD Fund, the Needmor Fund, the National Institute of Education, Pedamorphosis, and the U.S. Office of Education; administered by the Institute for Development of Educational Activities, Inc. See John I. Goodlad, "What Goes on in Our Schools?" *Educational Researcher,* 6, No. 3 (March 1977), 3–6.

Chapter 1 (Figure 1.1) but these involve merely adding some elaboration omitted from the original. In Chapter 14, the conceptual system for curriculum is revisited and revised in the light of my experiences with it over a couple of decades and such use and reactions of others that have come to my attention.

In summary, the conceptual system and work most directly related to its initial formulation are best represented in Chapters 1, 2, 10, 12, 13, and 14. Although Chapter 9 is essentially a description of the system's use in curriculum development, the work it describes confirmed for me the significance of the political-social domain of curriculum. Applications in the University Elementary School setting are recounted in Chapters 5, 6, and 7. Additional inquiries employing the conceptual system as a tool are reported in Chapters 3, 4, and 11. Chapters 1 and 8 add modifications and refinements, and Chapter 14 attempts a brief reexamination of the conceptualization as a whole.

About the Authors

As stated at the beginning of this Introduction, succeeding chapters are not designed to provide a dozen or so individual perspectives on the curriculum field. Each author had in common with all the others some encounter with a conceptual system, designed by me in collaboration with several others, for purposes of describing what constitutes the field of curriculum and guiding both curriculum development and curriculum inquiry. The several authors either helped construct this initial conceptualization or then used it in some way.

Not all of the writers of this volume know all of the others. I am fortunate in knowing them all. We have worked together, in various groupings and on a variety of projects, over a long period of time. We have shared experiences that have shaped our lives and our careers. I introduce them in reverse alphabetical order, out of deference to those who are only too accustomed to being listed last or toward the end of most lists.

Elizabeth C. Wilson has taught the humanities in both private and public educational institutions. During a period of rapid change in education and schooling, she served as Director of Curriculum for the Montgomery County, Maryland, school district. In this position, she engineered one of the most ambitious and comprehensive curriculum development efforts ever attempted. Today, she is retired from full-time employment but maintains her educational interests through consulting and writing engagements.

Louise L. Tyler has served as director of research for a school district, has taught at the University of Chicago and Chicago Teachers' College and has been visiting lecturer or professor at several other colleges and universities. As professor of education at UCLA, her present position, she taught several of the other contributors to this volume. She probably is best described as a curriculum theorist, with a special interest in the educational implications and use of psychoanalysis.

Kenneth A. Tye currently is Program Officer for the Los Angeles-based research office of the Institute for Development of Educational Activities, Inc. (| I | D | E | A |), an affiliate of the Charles F. Kettering Foundation. He, too, has been a public school teacher and administrator and has lectured at several colleges and universities, including UCLA. His scholarly interests are in educational leadership (with special attention to the principalship), curriculum, and global education.

With a formal background of preparation in sociology, Maurice N. Richter, Jr., has spent his career to date as a university-based teacher and scholar. His interests center on sociological theory, the sociology of science, and the sociological study of social inequality and social change. It was he who introduced Parsonian and other sociological concepts into our curriculum work at the University of Chicago. Currently, he is Associate Professor of Sociology at the State University of New York, Albany.

Robert M. McClure is Senior Professional Associate, National Education Association. In this capacity, he manages the NEA's programs in instruction and professional development. He has taught at all levels in the public schools. His professional and scholarly work has focused on helping practitioners, particularly teachers, become more competent and potent in making educational decisions. His scholarly work has been in curriculum and related fields.

The career of M. Frances Klein has brought her from the Englewood Elementary School in Florida to a professorship at Pepperdine University in Los Angeles. Not surprisingly, her scholarly work has focused on school programs, particularly at the elementary level. One of her special interests is the development of criteria for the development and evaluation of curricular materials. Currently, she is studying curriculum practice in elementary and secondary schools.

James A. Jordan (deceased) had an unusual career as athlete and scholar. Indeed, his abilities in football (Georgia Tech) made possible the collegiate basis for the academic career that followed. He was successful in combining teaching and scholarly interests at Emory University, where he completed a doctorate in humanistic studies with a strongly philosophical orientation. He returned to Emory University after our group at the University of Chicago disbanded and was on the faculty of the Institute of Education there at the time of his death.

Alicja Iwańska joined our group at Chicago out of sheer curiosity; she had no background in the field of curriculum per se but was intrigued. Her coming was timely—sheer serendipity. Today, she is professor of sociology and anthropology at the State University of New York, Albany. She is author of two books on Latin America and of monographs on Poland, Chilean women, and American farmers. Her numerous sociological and anthropological articles have been written in English, Spanish, and Polish.

My relationship with Henry W. Hill goes back to a time before the work at Chicago described here—to when he was a graduate student at Emory University, where I taught. Much later, he took his doctorate at UCLA and became associated with some of the work described here. Although most of the authors have spent part of their careers in elementary or secondary schools or both, Henry Hill never left the school setting and expects to retire there. He is presently principal of Kincaid Elementary School in Cobb County, Georgia.

Half of the authors (Buchanan, Griffin, Hill, Klein, McClure, and Tye) completed their doctorates at UCLA, where they did their curriculum studies with Louise Tyler, or me, or both. Gary A. Griffin, like the others in this group, came directly from experiences in schools and with children. Today, he is Associate Professor of Education at Teachers College, Columbia University. His teaching, scholarly work, and consulting are in curriculum planning, educational change, and supervision.

A major part of Edith A. Buchanan's teaching experience was at the UCLA Elementary School. Her chapter stems directly from the work there. She taught also in the UCLA Laboratory for Teacher Education. Now, she is Professor of Education at California State University, Dominguez Hills. Her primary field of teaching, writing, and consulting is early childhood and primary education.

Margaret P. Ammons, like Henry Hill, took her master's degree at Emory University while I was teaching there. She went on to complete her doctorate at the University of Chicago. Subsequently, she joined the faculty of the University of Wisconsin, where she taught elementary education and curriculum and contributed significantly to the teacher education program of that institution. Today, she heads the teacher education program at Agnes Scott College in Decatur, Georgia.

About the Dedication

The book is dedicated to Jimmy (James A.) Jordan and Ole Sand, both of whom died tragically in accidents within a short time of each other. I am pleased that one of Jimmy's papers appears here. The rest of his substantial contribution to the contents is described on preceding pages and in Chapter 1.

Ole Sand was friend to many of us. Indeed, he encouraged several of the authors to go on to doctoral studies and assisted them in their choice of institutions and subsequent careers. Had he lived, he would have critiqued many of the chapters—and they would have been the better for it, in both style and substance.

About the Genesis of the Book

One of the coauthors, Henry Hill, must be held largely responsible for the fact that this book was written. I had about given up on my earlier resolve to expand into a book the 1966 exposition of the conceptual system in curriculum when Henry Hill drew to my attention the fact that several studies had employed the conceptualization. He suggested that these be more widely disseminated. It was he who submitted to the Program Committee of the American Educational Research Association a proposal for a symposium.

And so six of us appeared at a subsequent AERA Conference with a clutch of brief papers. We so enjoyed our almost private session on the final afternoon (while conferees were on or rushing for planes to go home) that we decided to expand these papers into a book. For most of us, enjoyment ended right there; such is the (bitter) fruit of obligations assumed in haste and good humor, to be regretted "back home."

The expanded papers were about ready to go to press in monograph form when Louise Tyler raised some of the kinds of questions for which she is well known (such as, "Why don't you include the original conceptual system?") and I went back to the drawing board. The result was a long delay and a mightily expanded manuscript. The outcome is, I hope, that a relatively extensive body of related material has been brought together in one place.

Curriculum has been and is a field of shifting emphases, often excesses—from societal needs, to the whole child, to subject disciplines and back around the clock again. And it has been and is disappointingly noncumulative. So-called theoretical work has tended to be abstraction, not theory; so-called practical work has tended to be situationally and personally experiential, not practical.

I have long argued for some middle range conceptual work, short of a theory or theories but more than lists of practices—conceptual work sufficiently used and tested to demonstrate some reasonably accurate reflection of practice. It is in a spirit of conceptual inquiry and the related conduct and study of curriculum practice that this book is offered to those willing to take the time to read it.

1

The Scope of the Curriculum Field

JOHN I. GOODLAD

Curriculum practice is what curriculum makers work at. Curriculum inquiry is the study of this work in all its aspects: context, assumptions, conduct, problems, and outcomes. Such inquiry embraces at least three kinds of phenomena. The first is *substantive* and has to do with goals, subject matter, materials, and the like—the commonplaces of any curriculum.[1] Inquiry is into their nature and worth. The second is *political-social*. Inquiry involves the study of all those human processes through which some interests come to prevail over others so that these ends and means rather than others emerge. The third is *technical-professional*. Curriculum inquiry examines those processes of group or individual engineering, logistics, and evaluation through which curricula are improved, installed, or replaced. All of these are addressed in this and subsequent chapters.

Although it is possible to concentrate on the study of any one of these three sets of phenomena, comprehensive inquiry into praxis necessarily encompasses all three. They may be conceptualized separately for purposes of study, but they are inseparable in practice. Curriculum inquiry is incomplete until it goes beyond the pieces to study the relationships among them and thus to encompass the whole. To do this requires the existence or development of a conceptualization of the curriculum field. Otherwise, one will not know what to study or whether, in studying it, one is myopically preoccupied with a piece or understands that piece as part of a larger whole.

Two decades ago, at the University of Chicago, I brought together a philosopher, a sociologist, an anthropologist, and a student of curriculum, in addition to myself, to begin work on such a conceptualization. A preliminary formulation was published in 1966.[2]

Only 500 copies were printed, the intention at that time being to use feedback from the initial distribution in preparing a revised, fleshed-out version. That task still lies ahead. Meanwhile, the original has been discussed in most subsequent reviews of the literature in the curriculum field and has been used for research purposes, particularly the study of practice. This volume reports and analyzes some examples of this use. Many of the succeeding chapters describe an inquiry based on one or more components of the conceptual system and conducted within the perspective of the whole. Several describe the use of the conceptualization to guide practice, practice which was, or could be, subjected to study. And some chapters elaborate on the original conceptualization, concentrating on elements or levels identified before and fleshing them out so as to enable better and deeper understanding.

The writer debated whether to include the initial conceptualization is this volume and decided against doing so. Feedback has revealed both some largely avoidable misunderstandings and the need for revision. In particular, the use of it by my coauthors has been most instructive. Consequently, the intent in this chapter is to summarize the major features of the original and, in doing so, to offer some clarifications designed to avoid the earlier misinterpretations and to define the scope of the curriculum field within which practice and, therefore, the study of practice may be delineated. The concluding chapter revisits the initial conceptualization and puts forward some revisions.

TOWARD A CONCEPTUALIZATION OF CURRICULUM

The problem of the practitioner is to gain perspective, to see connected things as related. The problem of the theoretician is to stay sufficiently close to practice to avoid assuming his own, probably preferred, world of action. It has been my belief that the prime criterion to be satisfied by any reasonably adequate conceptual system in the field of curriculum is that it would both provide perspective for the practitioner and portray practice for the theorist. I see it as a bridge between the conduct of practice and the effort to develop concepts and theories.

By conceptual system, I mean a carefully engineered framework designed to identify and reveal relationships among complex, related, interacting phenomena; in effect, to reveal the whole where wholeness might not be thought to exist. Such a system consists of categories abstracted from the existential phenomena. The system is designed to describe and classify categories which can be readily discussed and manipulated at consistent, clearly identifiable, levels of generality and which can be developed from different perspectives.[3]

My colleagues and I at the University of Chicago first turned to previous work that attempted to deal both with practice and with a rather broad array of phenomena. The writings of Bobbitt,[4] Bonser,[5] Charters,[6] Harap,[7] Draper,[8] and others in the 1920s and 1930s were found to be close to ongoing processes of curriculum but geared more to providing direct assistance than to describing or accounting for practice. Tyler's[9] rationale, now well known, proved particularly useful in pulling together into a related set of questions matters which often had been addressed disparately before. Although his questions were phrased prescriptively, a slight rephrasing makes them useful for guiding descriptive research:

1. What educational purposes does the educational institution seek to attain?
2. What educational experiences are provided to attain these purposes?
3. How are these educational experiences organized?

4. How is the attainment of these purposes or the value of these experiences being evaluated?

Tyler identified at least the major commonplaces of curriculum—the elements about which curriculum makers must make decisions, on which researchers must focus, and to which theorists must pay attention in formulating their theories and conceptions. These have to do with ends and means and the relationships among them. Smith, Stanley, and Shores[10] dealt with these, too, both implicitly and explicitly, and also provided considerable insight into some of the sociopolitical and technical-professional aspects inescapably involved in curriculum practice.

We lacked the resources for systematic observation of practice (see Chapter 2 for a description of later work of this kind) and so drew upon our own direct experience as well as upon that of practitioners in the seminars we taught together. Since then, I have been endeavoring to learn more about curricula as they are practiced in school settings.[11] Insights gained have served, in turn, to illuminate and flesh out what a comprehensive view of curriculum practice and the study of it might include.

The ultimate purpose of curriculum development—both practical and theoretical—presumably is to improve the knowledge, skills, and attitudes of human beings. The intent is to enhance one's ability to find meaning in one's life. There are, then, potential learners who will respond to something called a curriculum, a curriculum they will perceive quite differently from the way it was perceived by all those who had something to do with producing or developing it. In its movement from wherever it had its beginnings to where these learners encounter it, this curriculum changed profoundly from whatever it was at the outset. To call it *a* curriculum is a mistake; it was many curricula, each successive one changing more profoundly than a larva changes in becoming a moth.

Of course, there are curricula which have no distant beginnings. They arise out of the immediacy of an interaction among students, the spontaneous creativity of a teacher, or the driving thirst to know of an independent learner. Some curriculum theorists believe that these are the only curricula of worth. However, when one views curriculum planning from the perspective of public institutions serving social commitments, one soon realizes that spontaneous though such curricula may appear to be, they usually emerge out of interpretation of what is desired by unseen, remote decision makers. Consequently, one reasonable definition of curriculum is "a set of intended learnings."[12] It does not encompass those complex personal problems experienced by those for whom curricula are intended, but does permit consideration of learners as a data source in selecting what is to be taught and learned in educational settings.

Curricula of intentions are developed in different locales, usually with different actors at each locale. My colleagues and I classified these at what corresponded to levels of remoteness from those learners for whom the curricula were intended and named them the *societal*, the *institutional*, and the *instructional*. Each of these is discussed later in a section on the study of curriculum practice.

Not surprisingly, this classification resembled the sociological one developed by Parsons.[13] After all, he was studying essentially the same phenomena, albeit in broader terms. And there was, in the little group I had brought together to conceptualize the curriculum field, a sociologist who was thoroughly familiar with Parsons' work.

In retrospect, the use of the term "levels" appears to have been subject to misunderstanding. Some readers of the little publication summarizing our work interpreted these hierarchally. Also, the two-way arrows which were designed to suggest communication between levels (see Figure 1.1) sometimes were seen, surprisingly, only as one-way—from societal to instructional to learners. The perceived relationship is linear, with the instructional level presumably dependent upon and subservient to the societal. The resulting problems are compounded when the conceptualization is converted from describing existing practice to prescribing what ought

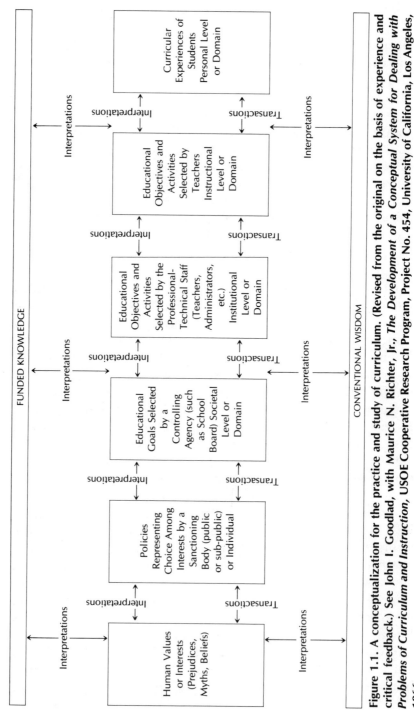

Figure 1.1. A conceptualization for the practice and study of curriculum. (Revised from the original on the basis of experience and critical feedback.) See John I. Goodlad, with Maurice N. Richter, Jr., *The Development of a Conceptual System for Dealing with Problems of Curriculum and Instruction*, USOE Cooperative Research Program, Project No. 454, University of California, Los Angeles, 1966.

to be, as Griffin points out so well in Chapter 3. This may be how much curriculum development goes on, but it is not the way it could be or the way everyone wants it to be.

The problem arising out of the difference between what we had in mind and what some readers perceived was further exacerbated by our use of the word "rational" in such reference as we made to the possible normative and prescriptive uses of the conceptualization. Although one member of our group viewed "efficiency" as inherent in any notion of rationality, this view never secured our agreement. By rational, most of us meant only the simplest of definitions: namely, imbued with reason or understanding. Having conceptualized, we thought, an intellectual approximation of existing sociopolitical reality, we advocated no revolutionary overthrow of the system whereby curriculum decisions are made. We proposed, rather, that it be improved or enriched through the infusion of rationality; that is, that decision makers seek the best possible reasons for what they do. At a minimum, they should turn as often as possible to relevant knowledge, rather than to single studies or hearsay, and should both be aware of what is being done at other levels of decision making and seek some coordination of effort. Also, since popular opinion cannot be ignored in public education, there should be some systematic effort to appraise the conventional wisdom, perhaps through surveys. Mere responsiveness to the most vocal elements is inadequate.

We used as illustrative the observation that curricular decisions usually deal with ends and means. We failed to point out that activity does not always arise out of purposes; often there is activity before or without purpose.[14] Further, since we used Tyler's four questions as illustrative of those curriculum makers seek frequently to answer, we picked up the criticism of all those who object to Tyler's work in curriculum on the grounds that it is derived from an industrial or engineering model.

It is now relatively easy to see how we might have avoided at least such misunderstanding as stemmed from our perceived identification with one side of a long curricular debate. This debate has been oversimplified, but rather usefully so, as a fundamental difference in viewpoint between humanists and behavioral empiricists. (Actually, these two views and positions of a more centrist character were represented in our group.) But both adherence to and rejection of the essentially Western (linear) industrial model of human behavior referred to earlier and, specifically, of curriculum planning are so strong in our society that avoiding misunderstanding in any attempt to conceptualize what is and then employ essentially this same configuration in suggesting how what is might be improved is virtually impossible.

Our use of the word "levels," the vertical depiction of these, the arrows between levels (seen by some, interestingly enough, as pointing only one way!), failure to define "rational," and employment of the ends-means paradigm put us into the linear, rational mode, with rational assumed by critics to mean "efficient." Some of these problems are corrected here and in Chapter 2. But most must await a revision of the initial conceptualization.* Perhaps a prescriptive and a descriptive conceptualization, carefully separated and distinguished from each other, will be needed, since differing but complementary modes of inquiry are required for constructing each. The same general configurations will prevail, however, because the absence on the prescriptive side of a category required to encompass practice or vice versa would be difficult to explain or justify.

A descriptive conceptualization is built from observation, taking on increasingly firm shape as the evidence accumulates. Comparisons of pupil effects under varying naturalistic circumstances also are valuable since they raise serious questions about possible malfunctioning of the curriculum. A prescriptive form is built up from both normative and empirical modes of inquiry, from which criteria for judging

*Figure 1.1 represents a modification of Figure 4 in the initial conceptualization based on some further reflection and feedback from constructive critics. I am particularly grateful to Louise Tyler and M. Frances Klein for their development of the personal level or domain. In Figure 4 of the initial conceptualization, students appeared to be merely the passive recipients of curricula designed in remote places. Of course, a *descriptive* conceptualization probably is accurate in conveying considerable passivity and limited degrees of freedom for students to transact curricula.

the adequacy of practice are developed. For example, Griffin's study, reported in Chapter 3, revealed relatively little institutional curriculum planning activity. This gives evidence to reduce the comparative significance of this category, from a quantitative perspective, in any descriptive conceptualization. But it is my view that there must be much greater decentralization of authority from the societal to the institutional domain of decision making, with a corresponding increase of activity at the latter.[15] Consequently, a prescriptive conceptualization developed by me would place greater stress on the institutional than is revealed by such descriptions of practice as are available. It must be remembered that any prescriptive model carries with it the value orientations of whomever created it.

Over the years, I have drawn upon the work of our Chicago-based group in teaching, research, and consulting activity. And, during these same years, I have had the good fortune to be associated with colleagues who have found something of interest in both the initial conceptualization and my later critiques of it. Some have used it for research purposes; others in seeking to improve certain aspects of practice in which they were engaged; others to study practice purporting to follow the conceptualization to some degree. Samples of such work are reported in subsequent chapters.

My initial interest was in examining the processes through which society and its educational institutions ultimately express their interest in educating the people. I eschewed extensive analyses of students, while including them as a category, not classified, in the conceptual system (Figure 1.1). Clearly, however, there is a curriculum of the personal or experienced, just as there is of the societal, institutional, and instructional domains. This has been developed elsewhere by Tyler and Klein.[16] It is included among the domains described in Chapter 2 and given further attention in Chapter 8.

Although research is needed to determine the kinds of decisions made at societal, institutional, and instructional levels, as well as how those for whom plans are intended are brought into the process, it is obvious that curriculum making occurs at all of these levels. It is obvious, also, that decisions at, for example, the societal level, such as requirements regarding the teaching of health and physical education, affect what teachers do at the instructional level. And the reactions of teachers to such decisions affect subsequent societal decisions. We do not know very much about these relationships, except that they exist. Ultimately, one would hope, curriculum inquiry will provide helpful insights into them.

My colleagues and I noted in practice the existence of interpretations as well as transactions or negotiations from level to level (pp. 29–39 in the initial conceptualization). Negotiations regarding curricular matters sometimes are part of collective bargaining, for example, and influence the outcomes of transactions. To avoid crowding the diagrams, we did not include words to describe these processes along with the two-way arrows. Perhaps this inclusion now in Figure 1.1 will help to make clear that the conceptual system assumes transactions and interpretations flowing back and forth between levels and not a linear process, with one level subservient to "a level of higher authority." To suggest such linearity would be to deny what actually goes on. At the same time, however, it is important to point out that there probably is more linearity than many teachers would like and less than some legislators might prefer. Determining what should or might otherwise be calls for prescriptive, rather than descriptive, use of the conceptual system.

Figure 1.1, as well as the diagrams in the original, suggests still another corrective for or protection against the dominance of one level of decision making over another. As stated earlier, curriculum makers employ both funded knowledge and conventional wisdom in arriving at decisions, not always differentiating between the two. Teachers use knowledge of the children they teach or of the learning process in diverging markedly from state or other guidelines and requirements. Sometimes, they are ignorant of relevant laws enacted by legislators, as we shall see in Chapter 4. Likewise, pressure from parents causes local school officials to ignore or bend directives coming from elsewhere. We have very little knowledge of how these various pressures and data sources influence decisions. But it is obvious that they do, and that curriculum practice is far from being neat, orderly, or rational. The development of a conceptual system to assist in at least describing such practice as it exists would appear to be useful activity.

One concluding comment about the use of the conceptual system briefly described and discussed here is in order. As noted earlier, some readers of the initial version concluded from it that planning curricula begins at the societal level with, for example, legislators or school boards, and ends up with what they decreed being presented in some concrete form to students. In practice, however, the process could and does begin anywhere. It could and sometimes does begin with a teacher and a group of students. To repeat, the two-way arrows between levels and the deliberate eschewing of one-way designations were intended to convey this observation. But, on the other hand, this does not mean that such a teacher would completely ignore the existence of decisions made by others and intended for him or her. A teacher might decide to integrate subjects specified separately in courses of study or choose methods and time periods other than those recommended. It seems to me that such decisions are likely to be more enlightened, more intelligently executed, and, on the whole, better when made in the light of relevant decisions by others, knowledge, and popular opinion or public expectations.

One purpose of a conception of the whole—or at least a reasonable approximation of it—is to help practitioners develop and use a broad, comprehensive perspective on their work. Another is to give direction to curriculum inquiry, the study of curriculum practice.

THE STUDY OF CURRICULUM PRACTICE

Let us return to where this chapter began. Curriculum planning goes on wherever there are people responsible for, or seeking to plan, an educational program. When state legislators pass laws regarding the teaching of the dangers of drug abuse, the inclusion of physical education, or requirements outlining the time to be spent on given subjects, they are engaging in curriculum planning. When local school boards decree that reading will be taught according to a hierarchy of specific behavioral objectives, they are involved in curriculum planning. When school staffs decide to use television broadcasts as a basis for interesting students in current events, they are engaged in curriculum planning. When individual teachers decide to use selected library books for enriching the language arts offerings, they are involved in curriculum planning. When students decide which books they will read in a literature course, they are involved in curriculum planning. The study of curriculum practice includes all of these activities in its scope.

For any group or class of students there are, clearly, several intended curricula: one built of legislative acts decreed by a state legislature; one approved by a local school board; one made up of the school's courses of studies and accompanying instructional materials; one presented by the teacher (see Chapter 2). The students respond to planned curricula and to unplanned curricula, in ways both intended and unintended. There is, then, a *personal* curriculum, unique to each student. The study of curriculum practice includes this, too.

Curriculum inquiry is the study of this work. It embraces substantive, political-social, and technical-professional issues, problems, and processes. The balance of this chapter is devoted to a brief discussion of these components of curriculum inquiry. Subsequent chapters discuss, selectively, aspects of the substantive, political-social, and technical-professional in curriculum practice and the study of practice.

The Substantive in Practice

The substantive takes us into all those matters of goals—what is taught, how what is taught is arranged or evaluated, what evaluation procedures are used, and so on—which have been grist for the mills of curriculum planners, theorists, and researchers for many years. But, as stated at the outset of this chapter, the focus almost always has been on what *ought* to be, not what *is*. For example, an analysis of Tyler's rationale reveals that his four questions are couched in the language of *should* and *ought*. His syllabus is a guide to curriculum construction or engineering. Not surprisingly, most of the doctoral dissertations employing his rationale use analytical procedures to suggest curricula appropriate for various countries, institutions, or subjects.

But, as proposed on preceding pages, it is useful to modify his questions so that *is* or *are* questions are asked: What are the (actual) goals of this school district? How is this curriculum organized? Thus, curriculum inquiry is, in part, anthropological and sociological. Also, it is at times experimental, but experimental in an analytical sense. Hence, to find out the relative merits of one curriculum pattern over another, the researcher finds patterns in existence which offer some outward manifestation of difference, describes and analyzes them according to differences and similarities (as one details the difference between shake, shingle, and slate roofs), and then attempts some evaluation. This kind of work offers some promise of producing theories, since the frequent coexistence of certain characteristics (such as amount of time devoted to a topic) and certain qualities (such as student interest) suggest relationships and, therefore, the possibility of predicting outcomes from knowledge of time use and students' attentiveness.

As stated earlier, we are some distance from such theory building, since the necessary empirical work is skimpy. One of our purposes in this volume is to turn attention toward the empirical, beginning with some mapping of the terrain of interest. What are children and youth taught in school? How much time is devoted to what topics? When and for what time periods do topics reappear? What is done with them the second or third time that was not done the first time these topics were introduced?

However, as Chapter 2 makes clear, questions such as these arise out of the vantage point of the external observer. There are other perceptions. What do teachers perceive the curriculum to be? Students? School board members? Parents?

The curriculum is in the eye of the beholder. And so there are many curricula perceived simultaneously by different individuals and groups. The task of the researcher is to choose his perspective and then, initially, to describe what he sees. Disparities in perception are part of the data in seeking to understand the curriculum, not as a puerile thing of carefully construed ends and means, but as a significant ongoing entity in the lives of all involved in it.

As a concluding note in this discussion of the substantive, it is important to point out that curricula do not remain for long within the realm of ideas alone. Enthusiasts for a given product of ideational activity desire to have it make a difference somewhere and so seek to inject it into the political-social domain of practice. The study of how such curricula fare there and of the differences between pure varieties and those injected into the vagaries of more immediate practice constitutes part of the inquiry process. As the study of practice probes back into analysis of a given curriculum, the theoretic and the practical come very close together.

The Political-Social in Practice

One of the blessings of dealing only with the substantive components of curriculum is relative isolation from the arenas of ultimate use. The development of ideas is not easy, of course, but any voyage of commitment seeking acceptance of these ideas in sociopolitical decisions can be soul searing. Ideas must endure intense competition where much more is at stake than simply their validity.

The term "political" is not used here in any pejorative sense. It pertains to those processes through which differing views of what is desirable are placed in public competition and, usually, achieve at least a temporary status of primacy. Views range from those representing short-term parochial interests to those embracing noble images of the future. In curriculum planning, governmental leaders choose, for example, between alternative views of the creation of man and of how capital should be distributed. Their choices place restrictions on the freedom exercised by local school boards in determining the ends and means of schools under their jurisdiction. Likewise, the choices of both legislators and school board members have far-reaching implications for what boys and girls study in the lower schools.

State and local authorities sometimes go so far in specifying their choices that few degrees of freedom in decision making remain for school administrators and teachers. Some of the degrees of freedom remaining for these decision makers frequently are usurped by administrators, leaving little alternative for teachers other than to teach pre-prepared lessons. For them to be held accountable for achieving progress with diverse groups of students under such circumstances is to place teachers in unenviable circumstances of considerable responsibility and little accompanying authority. The kinds of curriculum decisions made by various individuals and groups in the political hierarchy of decision making is a potentially productive realm for curriculum inquiry. Such inquiry could provide a useful knowledge base for policy decisions about who should make what kinds of decisions pertaining to the ends and means of education and schooling.

Chapter 3 represents an attempt to determine the extent to which various parties in the decision-making hierarchy are, indeed, involved in processes which might be judged appropriate for them in our society. The central problem, an important one, in the particular study of practice reported there is simply to find out something about the curricular preoccupations of several different groups of actors in curriculum practice. Chapter 4 looks specifically at the way in which some state legislators in their law-making role involve themselves in curricular specifics pertaining to classroom or instructional activity. The study of all of this is part of curriculum inquiry.

Likewise, various groups of educators, often in collaboration with parents or other community representatives, seek to arrive at consensus about curricular commonplaces. Chapters 5 and 6 document in considerable detail the complexity of this process and suggest, by virtue of what they reveal about social groups at work, why it is so frustrating and, frequently, so nonproductive. Almost everyone wants to share

in curriculum planning, especially for one's own children—
at least until one becomes involved in the complexities and
inevitable compromises. But the demands on one's tact,
ability to compromise, patience, and general goodwill are
extraordinary. This is a much-overlooked fact of life in
curriculum practice and deserves careful study. Perhaps it is
better (and it certainly is easier) for school staffs, for example,
to develop criteria and techniques for choosing among curricular alternatives already available than to seek to build
curricula from scratch.

The Technical-Professional in Practice

It is clear that technical operations requiring specialized
knowledge and skills enter into all levels and aspects of
practice. State and national governments employ professional-technical staffs to gather certain essential data and to
implement policy. The superintendent of schools in a local
district provides school board members with information
regarding curricular practice and, personally or through others, seeks to maintain and improve what is taught in the
schools. These individuals are from time to time called upon
to report on the economy, efficiency, humaneness, or relevance of educational programs within their sphere of authority.

Usually, however, in referring to the technical, we have in
mind the work of individuals and groups making up the staffs
of educational institutions such as schools or colleges. They
are faced with achieving several goals simultaneously, giving
appropriate attention to the full range of learnings intended
for grades or other units in the educational system, making
daily work interesting or at least palatable for the students,
and so forth. It is intended that teacher and administrator
education shall focus on the specific knowledge and abilities
required to perform these technical-professional functions.

In recent years, psychological considerations have tended
to outweigh philosophical ones, with how to plan the curriculum more efficiently tending to override questions of
whether existing ingredients are worth having at all, let alone

deserving of the time required to arrange them differently. We need a great deal of information about the demands confronting technical-professional staffs, how these are met, what abilities appear to be most used, what data sources and data are brought into play in the process, and so on. Many of the succeeding chapters provide some insights into aspects of the technical and professional in curriculum practice.

The Conceptual System as a Guide to Inquiry

Curriculum practice and its study are enormously complicated by the fact that the substantive, the political-social, and the technical-professional are not neatly separable or identifiable entities. The making of curricula is the making of decisions. Normative decisions involving choices among values or interests, empirical decisions calling for data, personal ambitions, group loyalties, characteristic and entrenched ways of behaving, choices between what is preferred and what can be afforded, all of these and more are inextricably interwoven.

We have seen from the conceptualization summarized earlier that these complex curriculum decisions are made close to, very remote from, and at several intervening distances from those the process is intended to affect—students, real or imagined. Seldom are students consulted or involved directly, although real or imagined data about their characteristics, interests, problems, and needs are invoked again and again by those presumably planning for them. Legislators at federal and state levels pass laws and vote funds which determine whether certain topics appear in the lessons of students in the schools and the preparation of materials for such lessons. State legislators sometimes determine how much time will be devoted to them and whether they will be taught daily or on an unspecified schedule. Local school board members further prescribe the curriculum, frequently specifying which books may or may not be used.

Although these *societal* lay decisions—federal, state, and local—take place in a political context, they are no less substantive than those made at other levels by professionals.

And they certainly embrace matters of praxis, particularly involving questions of financial economy. Professionals are not loath to seek to influence these societal decisions.

Taken together, the decisions of federal, state, and local lay bodies, in large measure, prescribe the curriculum of schools and systems of schools—the *institutional* level of decision making. School personnel must *interpret* or translate the more general societal decisions into more specific curricular meaning. There is much less of this kind of activity than is often assumed; curriculum elements frequently come from sources existing quite outside of the formal hierarchy of public schooling such as textbook publishers. In fact, it is fair to say that the ends and means of curricula frequently are determined by publishers and not by the elected representatives of the people, although the process is a cyclical one, with the identification of who is influencing whom being exceedingly difficult.

At the institutional level, much more is involved than simply interpreting for or by professional-technical staffs the meaning of societal-level decisions, as we have seen earlier. A *transactional* process, as well, is involved whereby professionals bargain for additions to or changes in what they perceive to be the meaning of the intended learning formulated more remotely. Traditionally, the transactional agent has been the superintendent, but recent years of growing teacher militancy have seen erosion in his authority. Now, teachers frequently include curricular matters in the bargaining package and have forced superintendents and, often, principals to be identified with societal agents, as employers rather than colleagues.

Once societal intent has been translated into curricular specifics and transactional processes are temporarily dormant, professionals in schools are in a position to know the degrees of freedom in planning available to them. However, such clarity and stability rarely are achieved. Further, it appears that the kind of curriculum planning occurring beyond the school, more than curriculum planning within the school itself, is destined to guide or direct the instructional activities of individual teachers. Consequently, translating the institutional curriculum and negotiating with the principal and staff as a whole are not excessively time-consuming activities of individual teachers at the *instructional* level of decision making. At this level, they tend to work relatively autonomously in their classrooms, perhaps either negotiating with students directly or assuming that they have the students' proxy by the law of required attendance.

We see, then, that there are decisions involving political negotiations, curricula substance, and praxis at societal, institutional, and instructional levels in the hierarchy of schooling. Griffin's chapter testifies to the existence of all three. It suggests, also, the probability that the institutional level may be the least active. My own studies, conducted with colleagues, tend to support this conclusion.[17] Perhaps the principal, teachers, students, and parents of local schools should constitute a more powerful decision-making unit, interesting itself in the political as well as the other aspects of curriculum decision making. It is possible that, in this way, schools would be reconstructed to become more potent educational entities.

Institutional planning is enormously difficult and demanding, as we see in Chapters 5 and 7. Strengthening this weak link in the curriculum planning process may be exceedingly important in the search for better ways to improve student learning. A promising place to begin is with naturalistic studies of the extent and nature of these staff processes, with as much attention to what does not go on as to what does.

Since curriculum planning involves different types of decisions—political-social, substantive, and professional-technical—differing data sources must be brought into play in the search for tenable answers and solutions. If curriculum planning were fully rational—which, of course, it is not—*funded knowledge* from a host of fields and contexts would provide the prime data source. But the existence of knowledge does not assure its use. There is disagreement over what constitutes valid knowledge, and the level of education possessed by a society has something to do with the extent to which that society values knowledge as a basis for choosing among alternatives. Even when data appear to be very hard, there are those who reject them because they believe in their right to have opinions in all realms. They do not want their opinions to be upset by the availability of data.

The data brought into social and political decision making usually are classified more realistically as *conventional wisdom* rather than funded knowledge. Politicians seek both to shape and to appeal to conventional wisdom. Consequently, even their most enlightened decisions usually fall short of serious recourse to funded knowledge, especially when it is relatively far removed from, or not congruent with, the conventional wisdom. Nonetheless, they frequently do seek to bring valid knowledge into decisions, especially when the goal is to raise the level of conventional wisdom through educational processes. The kinds of data sources used, the data extracted from them, and the uses of these data are an important subject matter for curriculum inquiry.

We would hope that professional educators would draw almost exclusively from funded knowledge in curriculum planning, but this is not the case. If their decisions outrun conventional wisdom to a considerable extent, adhering to them will be fraught with difficulty, as most administrators know full well. Therefore, schools and school systems tend to be conservative institutions, preserving what is already central to the thinking of the majority and, therefore, safe. We should not be surprised to learn that schools tend to blunt or flatten out the most controversial and potent thrusts of innovations.

Curriculum decision making draws upon data pertaining to societal conditions and trends (usually compiled by economists, sociologists, political scientists, and futurists); popular opinion (usually compiled by survey researchers and pollsters); child development, the nature of learning, youth problems, and the like (usually resulting from the work of behavioral scientists, especially psychologists); knowledge in the various subject fields (accumulated by specialists in the disciplines commonly taught in or considered for the schools); and matters of efficiency (provided by economists, systems analysts, planners, etc.). Philosophical analyses pertaining to the nature of truth, knowledge, the good life, and the good society are much less often sought out, although their importance receives abundant verbal testimony. In regard to matters of value, our rich heritage of logical thought and normative discourse tends too often to be ignored in favor of individual or group opinion.

Ironically, the most neglected data source in making curriculum decisions is the experience of the students who are at the viewing and receiving end of all these complex processes. The developmental characteristics of children and youth traditionally have been studied in the planning of curricula, but these are data from human development, not from the personal domain of curriculum practice. Measuring pupil effects in the form of academic achievement also is standard practice, and such data are useful for curriculum revision. But studies into the totality of a student's curricular experiences, *as seen through the eyes and mind of the student* over the course of a day or week are rare, indeed. Likewise, we know little about what any given group of students has been exposed to over twelve to thirteen years of schooling, let alone how they feel about it. Admittedly, this aspect of curriculum inquiry presents exceedingly difficult problems. This personal domain of curriculum and the study of it are explored in Chapter 8.

Curriculum planning takes place continuously as a society envisions possibilities for improving upon present conditions, translates its perception of the gap between present realities and envisioned possibilities into goals, and assigns responsibility for achieving these goals to educational institutions. Sometimes these goals involve only improvement upon functions already being performed. Such goals are conservative, calling upon citizens for improved performance along already accepted lines. Sometimes, however, goals are radical, calling for new ways of behaving and the utmost in personal effort and sacrifice. A major goal in curriculum planning is to choose funded knowledge over conventional wisdom in all of these decision-making processes. Careful study of ongoing practice might, as a minimum, make us more self-conscious about how we currently make curriculum decisions.

THE MAKING OF CURRICULUM POLICY

As stated earlier, presumably the ultimate purpose of curriculum planning is to improve the knowledge, skills, or attitudes of identifiable learners, to help individuals get greater meaning and satisfaction from their lives. Subsequently, we have tried to provide a glimpse of the enormous complexity involved. Curriculum planning touches the whole of human existence. In this and subsequent chapters, we stress the importance of trying to understand this complexity through its observation and analysis.

Certainly, the pursuit of such understanding is, in itself, a worthy end; but it must serve other ends, too. It should enlighten practice, particularly the making of policy. More and more countries are discovering that more education is not necessarily the answer to all problems. In fact, too disproportionately large a commitment to schooling, for example, may leave urgent social problems dangerously unattended. And such a commitment certainly means neglecting other educational avenues and choosing the welfare of tomorrow's adults over today's. There are, then, policy choices of great import in deciding whether to place education above other "goods" and whether to educate this group or that in various ways. In making such policy decisions, knowledge of what exists is as important as projection of what should be. In fact, there is no separation of the two in policy matters.

Policy researchers would disagree on the nature of policy research and how it should enter into the formulation of policy. Nonetheless, several major steps seem to be involved. The first is clarification of a problem which is only sensed, sometimes by a few intuitive spokesmen. In curriculum, the problem may seem to be a decline in mathematical competence, perhaps as revealed in college admission test scores. The usual conclusion in such circumstances is that students need more mathematics. But this is a shotgun approach to the problem. A more definitive diagnosis is required and this may mean examining the existing curriculum in detail. Perhaps there are too many gaps in the mathematics curricula of individual students. Perhaps teachers do not understand what they are teaching. Perhaps pedagogical procedures create a distaste and a lack of motivation for mathematics. Such data usually are in short supply.

But even the availability of extensive knowledge about what is going on—knowledge which we assert is essential—does not provide a policy decision. Normative processes pointing to what is desirable constitute a parallel step and these, too, require a kind of research. Part of it is documentary, a search of the literature to identify points of agreement among those who have thought deeply about the problem and to sort out the comparative strength of competing views. The purpose is to put up for consideration alternative models, based on research and experimental practice, which might replace with profit certain existing practices. Thus, the "new" mathematics was deemed by many in the 1950s and 1960s to be preferable to most of the math then being taught in schools.

The juxtaposition of what exists and what might be better still is inadequate for policy decisions and subsequent action. Perhaps what emerges as desirable from inquiry so flies in the face of conventional wisdom that it will be rejected out of hand. Such has been the experience of many who have mustered substantial support for sex education, for example. A third step of analysis is called for, in which the nature of the gaps between what is and what seems desirable is examined with great care to determine sheer magnitude, approximate time and cost of closing them, possible points of least and most resistance, and the like.

With all of this done, it becomes possible to lay out a plan and possible timetable for proceeding. The plan may suggest the preparation of new materials initially but extensive provision for teacher education at a later date. Unfortunately, this is where much policy planning stops, even if it goes this far in any systematic way. Subsequent steps include the mapping of specific strategies for effecting change and the detailing of roles, actions, and activities for various groups to be involved. This, too, calls for pulling together extant knowledge, this time on the nature of change and innovation.

The process described above sounds overly prescribed and

orderly and will be either compelling or distasteful for many persons, depending on their dispositions toward rationality, creativity, or intuition. But it need not be excessively any one of these. The whole must be characterized by a healthy skepticism toward rationality in general and tempered by the same kind of creative intuition that human beings always have found to be productive as well as protective from rigidity. Too much dependence on prediction and the translation of predictions into rigid work plans can lead to the kinds of difficulties experienced by the aircraft industry, for example. But failure to follow steps such as those outlined here, and, particularly, to seek out relevant data, opens up the entire process to opinion alone and, since one man's opinion often is regarded as being as good as another's, especially in the curriculum field, not much of the deliberation involved rises above conventional wisdom.

Curriculum planning, at this point in time, is so amorphous and so nonscientific that we have little to fear from the intrusion of rationality. We need to recognize the fact that curriculum planning is a human process which can be improved through seeking better reasons for what we do. Part of the improvement lies in studying the process and providing, as a result, data to be taken into account in this significant realm of human conduct and practice.

This volume is intended to increase interest in such activity. However, it is necessarily limited to the description and analysis of only pieces of the action. We do not get, from the assembled chapters, a picture of elements and processes within and among all domains of a single set of sociopolitical realities—a state legislature, a local board in that state, a school under that board's jurisdiction, teachers in that school, and students in their classes. Such composites are required for more effective approaches to the determination of curricular policies for educational institutions.

NOTES

1. By "commonplaces" is meant areas of ground constituting the focus of discourse in regard to which each discussant must take a stand. One of

these is subject matter. Just as the learning theorist takes a position with respect to the transfer of training, the curriculum theorist discusses the role, adequacy, or validity of subject matter. Similarly, practical curricula in the sociopolitical realm are marked by particular selections of subject matter. See Carl Tjerandsen, "The Adequacy of Current Treatments of General Education in the Social Sciences," unpublished doctoral dissertation, University of Chicago, 1958.

2. John I. Goodlad (with Maurice N. Richter, Jr.), *The Development of a Conceptual System for Dealing with Problems of Curriculum and Instruction*, Cooperative Research Program USOE, Project No. 454, University of California, Los Angeles, 1966.

3. Ibid., p. 1.

4. Franklin Bobbitt, *How to Make a Curriculum*, Houghton Mifflin, Boston, 1924.

5. Frederick G. Bonser, *The Elementary School Curriculum*, Macmillan, New York, 1920.

6. W. W. Charters, *Curriculum Construction*, Macmillan, New York, 1924.

7. Henry Harap, *The Technique of Curriculum Making*, Macmillan, New York, 1928.

8. Edgar M. Draper, *Principles and Techniques of Curriculum Making*, D. Appleton-Century, New York, 1936.

9. Ralph W. Tyler, *Basic Principles of Curriculum and Instruction*, University of Chicago Press, Chicago, 1950.

10. B. Othanel Smith, W. O. Stanley, and H. J. Shores, *Fundamentals of Curriculum Development*, World Book, New York, 1957.

11. See, for example, John I. Goodlad, M. Frances Klein, and Associates, *Behind the Classroom Door*, Charles A. Jones, Worthington, Ohio, 1970, rev. and retitled, *Looking Behind the Classroom Door*, 1974; and John I. Goodlad, M. Frances Klein, Jerrold M. Novotney, and Associates, *Early Schooling in the United States*, McGraw-Hill, New York, 1973.

12. Goodlad, *The Development of a Conceptual System*, pp. 11–12.

13. Talcott Parsons, "General Theory in Sociology," in Robert K. Merton, Leonard Broom, and Leonard S. Cottrell, Jr. (eds.), *Sociology Today*, Basic Books, Inc., New York, 1959, pp. 3–38.

14. James G. March, "Model Bias in Social Action," *Review of Educational Research*, vol. 42, no. 4, Fall 1972, pp. 413–429.

15. John I. Goodlad, *The Dynamics of Educational Change*, McGraw-Hill, New York, 1975.

16. Louise L. Tyler and M. Frances Klein, "Not Either-Or," Paper delivered at the Annual Meeting of the American Educational Research Association, New Orleans, February 25, 1973.

17. See, for example, Goodlad et al., *Behind the Classroom Door; Early Schooling in the United States;* and Goodlad, *The Dynamics of Educational Change.*

2

The Domains of
Curriculum and
Their Study*

JOHN I. GOODLAD,
M. FRANCES KLEIN, and
KENNETH A. TYE

A FRAMEWORK TO GUIDE CURRICULUM INQUIRY

The Problem of Definition

The English language is remarkably flexible. It changes with the times. Such is the case with the use of the word "curriculum." For most people, it has meant and still means a course, or body of courses, offered by an educational institution. From Chapter 1 it should be evident that there are other kinds of curricula—such as those actually experienced by students—and, therefore, other definitions.

*For proper understanding of this chapter, it is necessary to differentiate the work of the coauthors. The first half of the chapter is frequently in the first person because it recounts the experiences of John Goodlad and is written by him. Beginning on page 59, there is a conceptualization of curricular domains written by him but developed with M. Frances Klein and Kenneth A. Tye. The use of that conceptualization for research purposes, beginning on page 65 and continuing through page 72, is described by the latter. Although Frances Klein did not participate in writing this chapter, she contributed significantly to the thinking underlying it.

But attempting to give the word some formal definition does not begin to suggest the scope of what falls under the rubric "curriculum" when words such as construction, planning, or development are added to it. For example, curriculum development can mean the careful arranging of step-by-step "sets" in a planned sequence designed to produce a reading skill in pupils. Equally legitimately, it means the total array of efforts of a nation to develop programs of study for students at elementary, secondary, and tertiary levels of the formal educational system. And this, in turn, can include both the sociopolitical processes involved and the fruits emanating from them in the form of intended learnings for students. The study of curriculum might and does include activities at the former, specific level and at the latter, broad or general level, and a great deal in between.

Nowhere is this range and variability more apparent than in graduate education courses with titles that include the word "curriculum." One such course might focus almost exclusively on the decision-making roles of legislators, school board members, superintendents, and parents; another on the implications of various educational philosophies on what should be taught; another on psychological principles supporting the arrangement of subject matter; another on the structure of knowledge, the nature of meaning, and how these discipline curriculum planning; still another on the precise delineation of objectives and how to evaluate them.

Who is to say that one of these courses deserves the word "curriculum" attached to it and the others do not? That one is right and the others are wrong? Yet this is the box we get ourselves into in attempting some single, proper definition of curriculum, a questionable activity in which curriculum specialists have far too long engaged. We need definitions, of course, to carry on productive discourse, but attempts to arrive at a single one have inhibited discourse. If someone wishes to define "curriculum" as a course of studies, this is legitimate—and certainly not bizarre. Let us begin there and see where it takes us. If someone wishes to begin with curriculum as "the experiences of students," let us see where this carries us. But let us not begin by throwing out each definition and seeking only to substitute another that merely reflects a different perspective. We can readily see what a short distance this has taken us.

My colleagues and I, in writing the chapters of this volume, have endeavored to use curriculum as a generic term—that is, common to, or characteristic of, an entire group of things and activities. All or any matter mentioned in preceding paragraphs is included. For various purposes, one may choose to define a specific subtype or class of curriculum within the whole. Thus, there are, for example, a formal curriculum prescribed by state or local authorities; an operational curriculum seemingly being presented at a given moment; and a curriculum experienced by students. In choosing to call one of these *the* curriculum, it is important to remember that there are other curricula and especially that the word "curriculum," in its full generic sense, can embrace all of these. It also can embrace the sociopolitical and technical-professional processes of creating these various curricula. Likewise, all of them are appropriate subject matter for curriculum inquiry.

The Theory-Practice Interplay

Just as there is no single definition of the word "curriculum," there is no single theory. The pursuit of *a* curriculum theory is fraught with the same problems as the pursuit of a definition. Given the terrain to be encompassed, the very idea of such a theory boggles the mind. The best we can hope for, I think, are relatively short-range theories, the most readily attainable stemming from inquiries into the nature of knowledge and knowing. Theories from these sources will not help us much in seeking to understand the sociopolitical aspects of curriculum. We have made little progress in either realm of theory making. Most current writing labeled "theory" is talk about theory rather than the systematic building of theory.

Meanwhile, curriculum practice in all its diversity goes on. It has gone on for a long time—since God provided an apple tree and warned Adam and Eve against its fruit, and since the earliest people initiated their young into tribal ways through example and ceremony. And it has gone on without benefit of formal definitions and articulated theory. Presumably, our interest in these latter matters stems from a desire to improve curriculum practice, as is the case in other realms of human endeavor.

Humankind has developed two basic modes of thought to guide and improve practical activity. One of these is the theoretical-deductive; the other the empirical-inductive.[1] Perhaps because of the complexity referred to earlier, the former approach has not been very productive in the field of curriculum. It has become highly abstract and speculative, turning in on itself rather than out to the world that theory should help explain. Ideally, theory and practice should feed each other, the latter providing the "stuff" for inquiry and the former returning useful insights.

Practice, in turn, tends to be expedient. Since people are at center stage throughout, experiments are neither favorably regarded by practitioners nor easily carried out. Consequently, the empirical-inductive mode of thought has suffered from a dearth of cumulative evidence about recurring phenomena.

Human advancement occurs most rapidly when there is a productive interplay between the two modes of inquiry. But, with both relatively empty of useful materials, the body of knowledge produced by curriculum as a field of study is limited, indeed.

It has been my contention for some years that curriculum inquiry must move back to basics, and there is nothing more basic for study than what people practice or do, good or bad, right or wrong. By examining what legislators do to influence student learning, what happens to their decisions, and what use, if any, they make of such knowledge in subsequent decisions, we get one view of part of the world of curriculum planning. Similarly, we need to look at what administrators and teachers do to develop a total program for, say, the students in a specific secondary school, and so on.

We do not require an initial theory to study such activity but, if we are predisposed to theories and happen to have one, we should look for data running counter to as well as supporting the theory. We should not hurry to arrive at generalizations and conclusions,[2] nor should we eschew the formulation of some tentative working hypotheses. In time, there will be opportunities for some productive interplay between our quasi-theories and what ongoing practice begins to tell us.

At long last, studying the phenomena of practice as they occur is becoming recognized and even extolled by opinion makers in various subdivisions of the education field. Schwab created quite a stir when he castigated curriculum specialists for the abstract, pseudoscientific character of much of their discourse and directed their attention to the practical.[3] Jackson spent a year observing and trying to figure out what makes up life in the classroom.[4] Sarason tells us that we may not get very far with new "oughts" and "shoulds" in curriculum unless and until we have some considerable understanding of the institutions for which they are intended.[5] Bronfenbrenner argues effectively for viewing the total ecology of the child's life (the total curriculum?) in seeking educational interventions designed to make significant, developmental differences.[6] A field of educational praxiology (the study of action and conduct) is beginning to emerge, admittedly more of talk than reality (see Chapter 12).

While this increasing interest in the careful examination of educational practice in a search for guiding principles is encouraging, the problems of moving forward are formidable. Dewey reminded us quite a few years ago of the need for theory to begin and end in practice.[7] But theorists and researchers have turned only rarely to analysis of what exists. Instead, they have favored experiments—usually, short-term and with small samples, partly because of financial restrictions—into what could exist under certain circumstances. What exists became a control rather than itself a subject for investigation.

For more than twenty years, the fashionable model for such research has been the now well-known input-environmental response-output paradigm. Most established scholars and large numbers of their students learned it and practice it, often fervently—and it certainly has its uses or it would not have attracted so many good minds. Many of them are now in positions of influence with, for example, federal funding agencies. Almost subconsciously, they apply the criteria of, first, a theory, then hypotheses, then clear statements of precise purposes, to all proposals for research and development. Breaking new ground with unconventional proposals such as ones in the praxiological realm—proposals more likely to end than begin with theories—is exceedingly difficult.

It probably will be some years before we will move substantially from short-term inquiries that simply accept the premises from which they are derived to inquiries which depart from and, indeed, challenge the universality of their present syntax. Schwab effectively addressed the rhetorical, sociopolitical, and substantive issues involved some years ago.[8] My presidential address on some of these matters to an audience of the American Educational Research Association in 1968 was applauded by only a few.[9] But the times are changing. It is likely that the words and cautions of March[10] and Cronbach,[11] both impeccable empirical researchers, regarding the limitations of our conventional research modes will be heard by many.

Some of our brightest young scholars are willing to depart from the conventional paradigm but are put off by the perceived costs of significant naturalistic studies. And, until they become a little more confident of the scholarly approval of older peers in the university setting, for example, they are cautious about undertaking inquiries into complex educational practices for which promising explanatory theories are as yet lacking.

Confronted by these problems years ago in my own work, as discussed in Chapter 1, I decided that a necessary, unglamorous first step was to develop some kind of initial conceptualization of what curriculum as a field of practice and, therefore, a potential field of study consists of. Instead of defining it, I would look for it. Instead of formalizing a theory, which necessitates excluding as well as including phenomena, I would anticipate the possibility of finding one.

As is the case today, there was not an army of donors standing ready to outfit even a one-person search party.

The approach implied does not mean that one goes in without a beginning map, without tools, or without hunches. But to individuals thoroughly caught up in the conventional alternative of well-formulated theories and hypotheses and, frequently, little or no experience with the field of practice "out there," it probably looks this way. And the more they insist on prestated theories and hypotheses, the more they both interfere with the open-ended inquiry involved if understanding is to be gained and reveal their own lack of appreciation for badly needed alternative modes of inquiry.

In my own early efforts to lay out the curriculum domain, substantial experience in and with schools and the formal preparation provided by a major research-oriented department of education were available to draw upon. I had some knowledge of state and local curriculum planning activity, a good deal more of what teachers seek to do, and some of what they actually do. There were books, articles, and people representing various disciplines available for assistance. At that time, all of the foregoing—and not the opportunity to examine practice rigorously—necessarily became the substance from which a beginning conceptualization was shaped. As subsequent chapters should reveal, that conceptualization proved useful in studying the domains of practice it sought to identify.

Websters's (Third New International) Dictionary defines "domain" as "a distinctly delimited sphere of knowledge or of intellectual, institutional, or cultural activity." Following this definition, then, the domain of curriculum includes both the field of knowledge embraced by the term "curriculum" (as one uses the terms sociology, history, biology, and the like) and the human processes and products of curriculum making. Unfortunately, curriculum is not yet "a distinctly delimited sphere of knowledge." Consequently, the human activity from which the field takes its substance and derives its postulates is not at all defined and clear, either.

The central purpose of this book is to lay out much of what this activity (praxis) encompasses so that the scope of the study of curriculum praxis is defined. From this, in turn, it becomes possible to identify the elements likely to constitute theory building. Without such elements as building blocks, theorizing becomes specious; in Dewey's words, ". . . it becomes speculative in a way that justifies contempt."[12] However, we are not attempting to produce a theory or theories. Our goal is much more modest: we simply want to engage in some of the preliminary work having to do with mapping the terrain or domains of curriculum. This should aid efforts to develop useful curriculum theory.

As we have seen already, this terrain is varied and far-flung. Consequently, instead of dealing with curriculum as a single domain, we have divided it up into several. These come, initially, from the conceptual system partially described in Chapter 1 and more comprehensively delineated elsewhere.[13] The present chapter attempts both a further refinement and overview of these domains and an introduction to what is involved in their study. Chapter 3 presents research on the existence of several of these domains in practice and discusses their practical usefulness, with special reference to normative considerations. Many of the succeeding chapters focus on a selected domain, for the most part reporting decision-making processes involved and research on these processes. We believe that our total discussion embraces, at least at a general level, most of what is involved in the field of curriculum.

To repeat, our intent is to draw attention to the *study* of curriculum planning processes and products, to the ongoing nature of praxis in all domains, and to the delineation and, ultimately, understanding of the phenomena. What curriculumists have tended to do is to jump over descriptions and analyses which have been found necessary in other fields and, indeed, to proffer prescriptions of what ought and should be, normative judgments not enlightened by adequate awareness of what is. Schwab bluntly pinpoints the research need:

My own incomplete investigations convince me that we have not the faintest reliable knowledge of how literature is taught in the high schools or what actually goes on in science classrooms. There are a dozen different ways in which the novel can be read. Which ones are used by whom, with whom, and to what effect? What selections from the large accumulation of biological knowledge are made and taught in this school system and that, to what classes and kinds of children, and to what effect? To what extent is science taught as verbal formulas, or as congeries of unrelated facts or as so-called principles and conceptual structures, or as outcomes of enquiry? With what degree and kind of simplification and falsification is scientific enquiry conveyed, if it is conveyed at all?[14]

CURRICULUM INQUIRY: THE PROCESS DOMAINS

From Chapter 1, it is apparent that one branch of curriculum inquiry would involve the study of decision-making processes at all the levels depicted in Figure 1.1: societal, institutional, instructional, and personal. Methodology is derived from such fields as political science, sociology, anthropology, and psychology—indeed, most of the behavioral sciences. While theoretical constructs from these fields undoubtedly are useful, they are not sufficient and, for some purposes, could be dysfunctional. For example, the paradigms educationists borrow from psychologists usually employ the familiar in-dependent-dependent variables model, with pupil effects dependent upon some experimental (independent) variable. But, perhaps, at a minimum, pupil effects should be examined as an existential condition which, in turn, influences teacher morale, parent satisfaction, and economic support, and triggers all sorts of interesting actions and reactions. More boldly, this paradigm might be temporarily set aside, the intent now being to begin with some "playful" hunches about the phenomena,[15] deliberately eschewing theories and hypotheses.

We have seen also from Chapter 1 that there is, to a degree, an hierarchical character to the existing decision-making structure constituting the several domains of practice. Legislators do not intend for the educational bills they pass to stop with their own peer group. Legislation is intended, on the contrary, for other levels of decision making, as guides to school boards and, especially, to teachers. Often, enactments are not intended to encourage discretionary behavior;

specific content and instructional time periods are prescribed (see Chapter 11).

No level or domain of decision making functions independently of restraints, or of directives as to what values are to prevail. However, the body politic presumably sanctioning the role of legislators and school board members does not speak with a single voice. There are many sub-publics which may be categorized by regions, socioeconomic class, levels of educational attainment, age, occupation, and so on. Individuals belong to several of these and are torn by conflicting interests. Various sub-publics differ with respect to what they believe the schools should do. Controlling agencies such as school boards, appointed or elected to do presumably what the electorate wants, frequently respond to narrow, vested, highly vocal interest groups. The generalization probably holds that such bodies respond more to segments of the conventional wisdom than to funded knowledge in making the societal decisions entrusted to them.

Practical curriculum makers in the United States are very much attuned to the democratic concept of participation (see Chapter 9). Faced with choosing between a curriculum built out of choice from competing ideas drawn from scholarly inquiry and a curriculum emerging from sociopolitical compromise, they tend to favor the latter. This reality is somewhat dumbfounding to these scholars who, unhappy with the products of such compromises, commit themselves to curriculum making as though it were solely a search for truth and a process of humanizing the fruits of this search.

In a democratic society, the twin conditions to be striven for are extensive open participation enriched by deliberate recourse to sources of knowledge, including the curricula of ideas, and truly responsible representation at the level of controlling agencies. Since societal decisions inevitably place restraints on all other domains, it is important that they be highly rational—that is, that they be made for the best possible reasons. Unfortunately, however, the distance between the local school house and the state capitol is great— greater psychologically than geographically. Many education bills introduced frequently go unnoticed by the citizens.

Those passed and written into the education code more often than not are unknown to, or elicit no response from, teachers (see Chapter 4).

Societal-level decisions are in some ways the most potentially dangerous decisions, simply because the public interest does not extend far beyond one's own child and school, and yet one's own child and school are affected by them. Perhaps it is fortunate, therefore, that many of the decisions made in far-off places have no practical effect and, apparently, the potentially restraining sanctions often are impotent or difficult to employ.

Nonetheless, who participates in societal decisions, how these decisions are made, and what consequences they have are extraordinarily important matters for systematic inquiry. Undoubtedly, the results would be revealing and suggestive in relation to dealing with the important normative question of who should make what decisions. Such data would have practical utility in regard to allocating accountability to all those persons, in addition to teachers, who make or should make decisions affecting the education of our young.

The fact that many decisions by controlling agencies fail to get into the delivery system, fall out along the way, or are ignored on reaching their targets contributes significantly to the very real autonomy of other levels or domains in the entire decision-making structure. Ambiguity regarding realms of decision-making authority also is an aid to autonomy (as well as an asset to those who know how to use power for their own ends). The respective authority and responsibility of state and local boards is ill-defined. Although local boards are erratic in their use of power and freedom, they benefit from powerful traditional rhetoric regarding local control. Lack of definition of state vis-à-vis local authority opens up considerable opportunity for extensive spheres of autonomy at the institutional level. However, Griffin's findings (Chapter 3) suggest that this may be the least active domain, that school staffs do not currently appear to be potent in exploiting the freedom they have.

Observation suggests that decision makers in the formal sociopolitical structure, as well as most reformers, have in

mind the individual teacher as the target. Even while condemning the school as ineffectual, it is the teacher, not the
institution, they have in mind. Perhaps this is because we
have difficulty in conceiving of the school as a culture with
its own modes, implicit rules of operating, established roles
and reward systems, and the like. Or, subconsciously, we
think of the teacher as relatively weak and ineffectual, an
Ichabod Crane, and so seek to direct restraints at the teacher,
effectively inhibiting institutional-level authority. Partly in
defense, teachers do organize, but as a collection of individuals belonging to an association or union, rather than as a
collective, school-based body, perhaps including parents and
students, organized around the school and its improvement
as a guiding concept.

Acceptance of the school as the key entity for curricular
improvement by the principal, teachers, students, and parents
raises to a level of operational significance an array of
troublesome issues and problems. As suggested above, citizens tend to become far more exercised about close-at-hand
matters—personalities of teachers, content of textbooks, report cards, and the like—than about legislative bills pertaining
to educational policy. Parents are more conservative regarding their own child's schooling than toward general educational matters. Participation in school affairs is not at all
evenly distributed; there are individuals who make a career
out of "school-board watching." Consequently, there are
many informed, able, busy citizens who would prefer to keep
their neighbors out of the schoolhouse, leaving both authority
and accountability to the staff. Also, there are those who fear
the parochialism of too much local control and participation.
They fear that personal and small-group interests will prevail
over those broader concerns of a democratic society and the
welfare of humankind.

We have very little data pertaining to some of the assertions
put forward above. Likewise, we have little data on alternative
modes of community participation in school affairs. Even a
typology showing an array of modes and a detailing of assets
and liabilities appearing to be associated with each would be
helpful, as would be some measures of parent and teacher

satisfaction apparently associated with each. Such data will not in themselves answer any of the normative questions coming to mind, but they certainly would provide useful information in seeking to determine appropriate and inappropriate areas of community involvement.

There is, for example, a technical-professional realm for which the staff must have appropriate authority and responsibility and for which they must be held accountable. But this realm is ill-defined; there is not available "a distinctly delimited sphere of knowledge," although a sizable body of lore (some from funded knowledge, some from specific pieces of research, a good deal from accumulated experience) is scattered about. But in some areas of critical interest, such as raising low reading scores from the fifteenth to the thirtieth percentile, teachers are perceived to be impotent and vulnerable. What cannot be clearly articulated as professional terrain becomes everybody's meadow in which to bivouac.

Schooling tends to be one of those spheres of human activity for which the modus operandi appears to be, "Since we don't know, legislate." Consequently, teacher education and the practice of teaching are, to a degree, controlled by a host of legislated requirements pertaining to accreditation, certification, and mandated curricula which conspire, both legally and psychologically, to inhibit creative planning at the institutional level. People with minimal technical-professional backgrounds, remote from data pertaining to students and their lives, in their wisdom remove to a higher level of incompetence some of the decisions school staffs should make collectively and individually. And yet, ironically, the teacher is still held accountable for the outcomes.

Although these and other restraints on institutional decision making are serious ones, school staffs have freedom and opportunity for creative curriculum development extending far beyond what they presumably employ. The culture of the school appears not to be organized for self-renewal;[16] much of its energy goes into self-preservation. The institutional domain is as much sociopolitical as it is substantive. The politics of campus life often are as bitter and intense as those of the professional political arena and, as the late Senator

William Benton once said, there are no ground rules. In recent years, attacks from without have been so many and so intense, and new panaceas for reform so demanding, that school staffs often have evolved a defensive posture of seeming internal harmony instead of that buoyant, self-critical ambience so characteristic of self-renewing individuals and groups. A staff turned in upon itself is not a healthy one.

Even when these sociopolitical problems are at a modest level of intensity, coping with the substantive issues is formidable. The University Elementary School described by McClure in Chapter 5 is relatively free from societal-level restraints, and the faculty is experienced and professionally prepared beyond the norm. Nonetheless, the teachers experienced a host of difficulties in seeking to define an institutional curriculum to guide daily instruction.

In many ways, the institutional domain brings into the decision-making arena the full range of substantive, political-social, and technical-professional interests, problems, issues, and complexities. Perhaps this is why it appears to be the least well developed and productive of all the domains. We need to know much more about the school as the depository of curriculum decisions made elsewhere, as a social system, and as an agency for serving societal and community educational interests.

There is a growing body of lore presumed to be relevant to the instructional domain of decision making.[17] Seeking to improve the competence and performance of individual teachers has been a long-term—indeed, almost the exclusive—focus of preservice and in-service education throughout recorded memory. While acquiring available technical-professional knowledge and skills on the part of teachers is a necessary condition for improved student learning, it is not sufficient. Many of the restraints already discussed conspire to inhibit and distort utilization. There is evidence to suggest that there are school and even "professional" norms derived from other than funded knowledge that effectively restrain teachers from doing what they have been technically prepared to do. Getting insight into all these matters would be a useful outcome of the careful study of school practice.

The personal or experiential domain of curriculum, involving that which students experience, has not been taken seriously by curriculumists, rhetoric to the contrary notwithstanding. They have contented themselves with reviewing the possible implications of human development concepts for curriculum planning and with puerile statements about student involvement. But just how students might participate effectively in the decision-making process has been confined to general prescription and a few, admittedly often useful, case reports. Even extensive interest in individualizing learning has focused primarily on the instructional domain rather than the personal.

Do students at various levels want to be more involved? Do they feel more strongly about some areas of potential participation than they do about others? How do they respond to the present instructional program? Are they aware of goals and do they care about them? Do their central preoccupations and what goes on at school interface in significant ways, or do the two pass each other by? We do not have useful data about such matters. It is not sufficient for curriculum specialists to have insight into human development and learning. They require the particulars of student reactions and experiences if they are themselves to be students of the personal domain of curriculum practice.

Knowing more about all these sociopolitical and technical-professional processes and their effects would be exceedingly useful. But this knowledge will not come easily or soon. It is a domain in which opinion is highly valued and jealously protected. As one school board member put it, "Having hard data from research would take all the fun out of it." The problem of securing research funds is compounded by the fact that inquiry in this domain is expensive.

Securing an adequate supply of researchers for such work will be exceedingly difficult. Schools of education have fragile links with the contributing disciplines, and university structure still is not conducive to sustained interdisciplinary work. The most thoroughly prepared researchers from the best schools of education will have difficulty in deviating from the research models they have learned well. Some of the leadership must come from opinion makers in education and curriculum whose own research careers may be mostly behind them but whose views still influence the field.

CURRICULUM INQUIRY: THE SUBSTANTIVE DOMAINS

The conceptual system summarized in Chapter 1 employed here as a guide to inquiry and used by the writers of most subsequent chapters emphasizes processes. This is not surprising, since curriculum development is a form of human action and conduct and curriculum inquiry is its study. But such activity produces substance or product. Curriculum inquiry is the study of this, too. Indeed, process and product are so entwined that they can be separated only for conceptual or heuristic purposes. Both are domains of praxis.

There is, however, a realm of practice—not included in Figure 1.1 and the discussion so far—that appears, at least on cursory examination, to be more in the realm of the theoretic. This is the development of curricula of ideas; it usually stops short of the sociopolitical marketplace of decisions, actions and compromise. It represents the hard work of scholars, teachers, and others who put together what they think is best for students of various ages in given programs of study. It, too, is a curriculum of intentions.

Although curricula of ideas are constructed to reflect funded knowledge, developers often address themselves to problems likely to be encountered if and when their products are launched into the arenas of sociopolitical action. Extant religious beliefs, myths, prejudices, and the like, and their possible impact on any efforts to implement the curricula, are discussed and safeguards built in to the degree possible. But only a few of the vagaries "out there" can be anticipated.

Curricula spawned in the 1960s—SMSG, PSSC, BSCS, CBA and so on—are examples. It would be a mistake to regard such curricula, even when not implemented, as not part of practice and, therefore, not proper subject matter for inquiry. They involve, in Schwab's words, "deliberation and tactic."[18] Persons who build these curricula, like persons who build curricula out of ongoing interaction with students, employ theory in their deliberations but produce curricula, rarely theories. They work in realm of the practical.

Some years ago, seeking to classify this aspect of the practical, I used the word "ideological."*[19] "Ideational" or "ideaistic" would be equally suitable and I often use all three synonymously. Curricula emanating from this kind of curriculum development are viewed as ideal or exemplary in the eyes of their creators. But much of what was viewed as ideal by those who made them is rubbed off, compromised, or corrupted as ideological curricula are moved into the sociopolitical and technical-professional processes of adoption and implementation.

One of the many interesting questions for inquiry is this slippage that occurs when one of these ideological or ideaistic curricula is adopted for use in an educational system. There is a tendency in our society to blame some supposed change or innovation for falling standards. But even when approved as policy, as in the adoption of "new" mathematics, key elements of the change do not always find their way through to students. The study of the practice of curriculum should embrace such phenomena.[20]

When one begins to think of different kinds of tangible, substantive curricula, the caveat regarding the definitional problem, sounded at the beginning of this chapter, becomes particularly relevant. It immediately becomes apparent that there are several distinctly different curricula even in an educational system committed to single, specific programs in mathematics, science, history, etc. We suspect that this is true, but perhaps to a lesser degree, in highly centralized systems as well (see Chapter 11). Several years ago, in beginning a conceptualization of these curricula for purposes of a project in studying curriculum practice,[21] my colleagues

*There is danger in using the word "ideological." I have in mind preoccupation only with ideas arising from basic knowledge, although most certainly there is a give-and-take struggle over what ideas are to prevail. To some people, however, ideological means adherence to a particular set of ideas to the blind exclusion of others. Perhaps using the alternative spelling, "idealogical" would help circumvent this problem. However, in the final analysis, any curriculum, whether ideal or representative of sociopolitical compromises, reflects ideologies.

in the research program of the Institute for Development of Educational Activities, Inc., M. Frances Klein, Kenneth A. Tye, and I followed the conceptual system summarized earlier in coming up with five: ideal, formal, perceived, operational, and experienced.

All of these domains involve some kind of product, tangible or of the mind. It should be possible, we conjectured, to compare how each commonplace (e.g., goals) is dealt with at the level of prescribed policy (the formal curriculum) with, for example, how each is operationalized in the classroom (the operational curriculum). Data regarding the ingredients of these several curricula should be of great interest and usefulness to parents, curriculum workers, and educators, as should be the differences encountered from level to level. Before recounting our exploratory look into these matters as an example or case study in curriculum inquiry, it is desirable to provide brief descriptions of each.

Ideological Curricula

As stated earlier, ideal curricula emerge from ideaistic planning processes. Although good ideational work anticipates the problems of adoption and use, products usually are designed to serve a varied marketplace of decisions and actions and stop short of the give and take of sociopolitical processes. Except for trial testing, implementation is left for someone else. Consequently, it is rare for the elements of some ideal curriculum to be carried through to students in their original form. Even if the content remains reasonably intact, the methodological structure of a discipline may be distorted through the pedagogy employed.

One determines the contents of ideological curricula by examining textbooks, workbooks, teachers' guides, and the like. To a degree, predictions can be made regarding the fate and success of such curricula by applying criteria pertaining to how the materials were tested, what kinds of students used them during the stage of formative evaluation, what kinds of pedagogical behaviors are called for, and so on. In recent years, considerable work on the development of such criteria has taken place.[22] To make a difference, such curricula must find their way successfully through the process of policy making and instruction described earlier.

Formal Curricula

Formal curricula are those which gain official approval by state and local school boards and adoption, by choice or fiat, by an institution and/or teachers. For such approval to be secured or granted, there must almost necessarily be some sort of written documents: curriculum guides, state or local syllabi, adopted texts, units of study set forth by a curriculum committee, etc. The formal curriculum could be a collection of ideal curricula, simply approved and passed along without adaptation or modification. The important consideration is that it is official; it has been sanctioned.

Our research interest here is similar to that in the ideal but is somewhat more crucial. It is in the formal curriculum that society's interests usually are embedded. When the socio-political process has functioned, when the societal decisions have been made, a formal curriculum remains, for better or for worse. The process continues, but the product is the artifact left for analysis. Presumably, in the analysis one finds those beliefs, values, attitudes, and the like which society or some dominant group in society wishes the young to acquire. Statements of goals are merely statements of aspirations and are subject to various interpretations. But what is laid out to be learned constitutes an interpretation. One gets closer to what is intended for the schools by examining what is to be studied by students than by examining statements of aims or objectives. Whether or not what is intended gets to students and what they do with it are quite different from goals or objectives and important foci for inquiry.

Perceived Curricula

Perceived curricula are curricula of the mind. What has been officially approved for instruction and learning is not necessarily what various interested persons and groups perceive in their minds to be the curriculum. Parents differ widely on what they think their schools teach and differ perhaps even more widely in their reactions to what they perceive. Undoubtedly, these perceptions generate changes and frequently are taken into account in curriculum revision. But, at any given moment, the most significant perceptions probably are those of the teachers.[23] If they perceive the daily time spent on art or music to be minimal, they are in the best position to effect adjustments.

Consequently, we are very interested in ferreting out what teachers perceive the extant curriculum to be and what attitudes they have toward what they view as reality. Their disposition (e.g., degree of satisfaction) toward these perceptions should provide the researcher with significant insights into "school" as seen through the eyes of this group of primary participants.

Then, with data available regarding both parental and teacher perceptions, it is possible to make various comparisons. Problems pertaining to school-community relations could be the result of parents' wanting something other than what the school provides. But they also could be products of poor communication. The schooling enterprise functions in the absence of a solid knowledge base and in the presence of a great deal of opinion.

Operational Curricula

What teachers perceive the curriculum of their classrooms to be and what they actually are teaching may be quite different things. At the point of instruction, it is difficult to separate the what and how. Teaching is relatively immune from diagnostic scrutiny, and so there is little feedback from others; only a few teachers voluntarily seek continuing evaluation from their students. We know little about the extent to which teachers engage in self-diagnosis, how penetrating their analyses are, or how the results are used. Teachers tend to be shocked when they see themselves in action on film or videotape. Some studies suggest that teachers acquire early a rather limited repertoire of pedagogical modes and stay with them.

The operational curriculum is what goes on hour after hour, day after day in school and classroom. There is no way of knowing, for sure, what this is. The operational, too, is a perceived curriculum; it exists in the eye of a beholder. The technique of modern social science is for trained observers to watch and record, frequently using short time intervals so that the variety and amount of behavior taking place can be verified among observers and quantified. There exists a substantial literature on observational methodology.

However, dissatisfaction with classroom observation as a research tool continues. To get reliable measures, it is necessary to focus on a part of the whole such as interaction patterns, to predetermine precisely the relevant components, to prepare easy-to-use check sheets, and to mark elapsed time accurately.[24] Critics maintain that the most essential elements and dynamics often are lost in the process. On the other hand, the technique of trying to maintain detailed anecdotal records and thus to capture these dynamics confronts the observer-recorder with an overwhelming task. An enormous amount of training is required to produce interobserver reliability. Whatever the choice of method, there are severe liabilities.

To get a reasonably large sampling of operational curricula necessitates the use of techniques that can be accommodated to the demands of quantification. But until inquiry encompasses a range of types of schools and some sampling of each type, curriculum inquiry will not lead us to useful conceptualizations and theories. The cost of engaging in such work constitutes a formidable deterrent.

Experiential Curricula

Difficult as it is to get some dependable data on the operational curriculum, the one experienced by students is even more slippery. Watching students tells us very little of what is going on in their minds. Asking them raises many questions of validity. Dare they trust us to care seriously about their answers? Dare we trust their answers? Even if we get some insights into what appears to be happening now, what difference will it make later? If the students have learned some facts or principles, does it matter that they hate the subject and, perhaps, the teacher? One does not get far into thinking about the experienced curriculum, let alone inquiring seriously into this domain, before being over-whelmed by the myriad of problems of "deliberation and tactic."

As stated earlier, the literature on general human development simply is not sufficiently explicit for curriculum development purposes. We need data on interactions, for example: what appear to be the most compelling kinds of school experiences for various students at different ages; whether the curriculum as subject matter makes much difference to daily satisfaction in school; whether matters beyond the classroom make much difference and, if so, what and how; and where student aspirations and school offerings come together and most widely diverge. Instead of viewing school as good or bad, desirable or undesirable, we may be able to arrive at more definitive judgments with respect to what functions schools should and should not try to perform for various student subpopulations simply by learning something of what students derive from and think about operational curricula.

Studying Domain-to-Domain Discrepancies

This brief introduction to five different domains of curriculum is sufficient to illustrate the problem of deriving any single definition of curriculum and the complexity of studying practice comprehensively. It also illustrates the importance of employing similar commonplaces and concepts for curriculum discourse, analysis, and development among and across all domains. Otherwise, there is no way, for example, of tracing the slippage from any ideal formulation to what reaches the student, or of working backwards from what the student perceives to what the formal curriculum intended for him or her. And it illustrates how extraordinarily difficult it is to engage in this kind of detective work even when the conceptual work has been carefully done. It is no easy task to sort out as related what the student is learning, what the teacher is teaching, and what the curriculum maker intended for both even when this relationship may be present to a high degree. Curriculum inquiry gets into largely uncharted territory in the operational and experiential domains.

The balance of this chapter is devoted to a report of work in progress, a study of the practical in curriculum.

Comprehensive pilot testing of concepts and instruments in schools had just been completed at the time of writing this chapter. In spite of the recency and vividness of this experience, it is impossible adequately to portray the complexity of the hundreds of decisions made along the road to this trial run, the hard work, the frustrations, and, indeed, the humbling character of studying curriculum practice. It is easy to write and talk about the need to build curriculum theory out of the stuff of onging practice; but, first, there is a lot of pioneering work to be done in simply mapping the terrain.

STUDYING THE DOMAINS: AN EXAMPLE OF CURRICULUM INQUIRY

Twenty-five data collectors arrived in a community to spend six weeks interviewing, observing, and administering questionnaires to students, teachers, administrators, parents, and selected nonparents. This was a pilot test, a putting together in one place, of all the preceding work of conceptualizing a research design and preparing instruments. The purpose was to study the daily operation of a triple of schools (elementary, junior high, and secondary), with major focus on curricula.

These twenty-five individuals were selected on the basis of their experience in data collection; their sensitivity to and understanding of schooling; and, above all, their good judgment and ability to work well with others. They had been trained in data collection for several weeks. They had learned the intent, substance, and organization of the study, and the

skills of interviewing, observing, administering questionnaires, working in teams, and managing classrooms. They
were trained through simulating interviews, viewing video
tapes, and actually observing in schools and classrooms.

To guide data collection in the curriculum domains, instruments and schedules were developed from a conceptual
grid prepared by a small group of curriculum specialists and
based on elements to be tracked through the various domains
discussed earlier in this chapter. Two sets of considerations
guided the formulation of the grid: curricular commonplaces
and qualitative factors which affect these commonplaces (see
Figure 2.1). The curricular commonplaces were those usually
selected by curriculum specialists: goals and objectives,
materials, content, learning activities, teaching strategies,
and evaluation. Grouping patterns and the use of time and
space were added.

Those of us who developed this framework realized that
the nine elements did not provide sufficient guidance for the
development of instruments and schedules. There are factors
which may have great impact on curriculum but which cannot
be considered elements or commonplaces. For example, it is
often stated that if teachers and students have some influence
or authority over curricular decisions, the satisfaction they
experience and the learning the students achieve are likely
to be greater than if they are not involved in decisions.
Consequently, involvement in decision making and seven
other qualitative factors identified from exhaustive reviews
of the literature were included in the framework developed
to give guidance for the collection of data. These were:

1. Decision making: degree of influence and input of
various groups in decisions about curriculum elements.
2. Rationale: reasons given for the ways in which a given
curriculum element functions or is implemented.
3. Priorities: those aspects of the curriculum element
given greatest emphasis in time spent or importance attached
to it.
4. Attitudes: satisfaction regarding the curriculum element.

5. Appropriateness: degree to which the curricular choice is suitable for the intended purpose.

6. Comprehensiveness: the extent to which all possible variations on the particular curricular element are provided.

7. Individualization: degree to which the curriculum element is adapted to individual differences.

8. Barriers/ Facilitators: factors which impede or promote attention to a given curricular element.

A cell was included for each of the curriculum elements in order to allow for the generation of items which would lead to an adequate description of what was observed in each of the schools and classrooms studied.

By utilizing the grid shown in Figure 2.1, specific research questions for the curriculum component of the study were generated. For example, in the matter of goals and objectives, the following kinds of questions were raised of each domain (i.e., formal, instructional, operational, and experiential):

1. What are the goals and objectives and how are they stated? (description)

2. Who chooses them? (decision making)

3. Why were they chosen? (rationale)

4. Which are considered the most important? (priorities)

When all perspectives, curricular elements, and qualitative factors were applied to the subject areas (e.g., science, arts, foreign language, reading, homemaking), it became obvious that there were in excess of 500 potential questions to be answered in order to get a comprehensive picture of a school's curricula. We were in the classic dilemma of descriptive research.

The inclusion-exclusion criteria previously employed implicitly were now sharpened and made explicit. Several important questions were generated to guide instrumentation:

1. What would parents, policy makers, and educators most want to know?

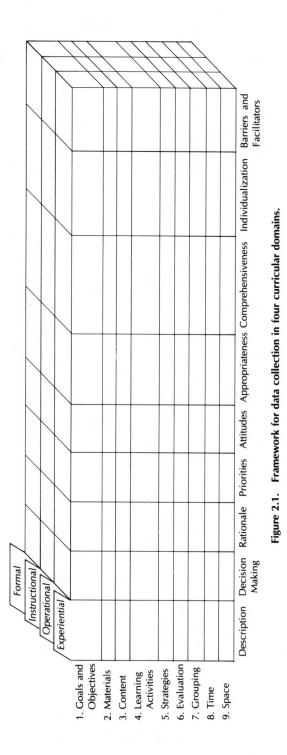

Figure 2.1. Framework for data collection in four curricular domains.

2. Which data sources (e.g., teachers, students, parents) will give the most accurate data?

3. Which questions best allow for tracking through the dimensions of the curriculum?

4. Which questions can be operationalized sufficiently to get data which adequately elaborate the elements included in the framework?

5. Which questions are most likely to yield quantifiable data?

Wherever possible, questions were translated into closed items to be included in questionnaires or observation schedules. Other questions were left initially in open-ended form in questionnaires or on interview schedules. Instruments and schedules were then pretested in order to check on readability, clarity, and discriminating ability. Such pretesting resulted in rewriting or, in some cases, eliminating items. Also, initial responses to many open-ended items resulted in our being able to develop, subsequently, closed-ended responses, saving both response and analysis time. Some items were left in open-ended form simply because we anticipated richer responses from this mode. Through these processes, we cut in half the number of questions to be answered.

Questionnaires and interview schedules contained comparable items for each data source: parents, principals, teachers, students for grades 4 through 12, teacher aides, and district officials. Because of the reading problems with younger children, interview schedules were developed for grades 1 through 3.

The operational curriculum was documented through anecdotal records and an observation schedule in selected classrooms—two classes at each grade level in the elementary school and sixty percent of all subject offerings in secondary schools. Data from the anecdotal records were to answer such questions as "How much of the school day is spent on instruction?" or "What are the rules and regulations of the classroom?" The observation schedule was used by observers to mark for such things as who made various decisions. The plan of data collection called for documentation of the experiential curriculum in two different ways. First, students were asked on questionnaires and in interviews about their perceptions of what they were taught (e.g., How easy? How interesting? How important? What else would you like to learn?). Student outcomes were documented in two ways. Affective outcomes (e.g., attitudes toward school, learning, peers, teachers) were measured as part of data collection. Cognitive outcomes were documented from existing achievement test scores in each school and were supplemented with data on students' knowledge of global systems, a cognitive instrument prepared for the curricular substudy on global education.

We recognize that the use of existing achievement test scores places a major limitation on conclusions regarding student outcomes because of class-to-class variations in the administration of such tests. Further, in terms of across-school data, it is difficult to make comparisons because schools use different standardized tests. Ideally, we would have constructed and used our own measures, but this was beyond our financial resources.

In the pilot testing described here, we collected data in the following subject areas: reading, language arts/English, mathematics, social studies, natural sciences, the arts, physical education, foreign languages, career or vocational education, and special education.

To describe the curriculum of the school as has been set out above is a significant, complex undertaking. However, we are examining the specifics of the curriculum as only a part of a larger study of schooling which views the school as a social system, interacting internally through its own components and externally with its environment. Other substudies paralleling the curriculum substudy, in which are embedded many curricular relationships, include descriptions and analyses of classroom climate, the adult social system, and school-community relations.

Study of classroom climate assumes that both teacher behavior and pupil-teacher interactions are critical to the development of a climate that supports or impedes learning. We are examining the relationships between curricular elements and various aspects of the surrounding milieu. The following questions suggest relationships to be examined:

1.   What is the relationship between student involvement in curriculum decision making (amount and kind) and their perception of the behavior of teachers?

2.   What is the relationship between student perceptions of the appropriateness of curriculum offerings and their self-concepts?

3.   Do instructional elements (clarity of objectives, teaching strategies, etc.) have any relationships to the climate of the classroom?

Study of the adult social system conceptualizes school staff interactions as occurring within several "spaces" which contain the school world. These are: (1) material space (facilities, materials, equipment); (2) people space (personal characteristics, purposes for interaction); (3) time space (events which make up the work life, history of the school as it relates to change, future of the school as it relates to possible change); (4) task space (professional orientation, accountability procedures, formal and informal organization for work—including unionization, problem-solving processes, problems faced by the school); and (5) affective space (feelings about and evaluations of the other four spaces). There are numerous relationships to be examined between these matters and the curriculum. Curriculumists will be interested in the relationships between what goes on in these spaces and the elements or qualitative factors of curriculum as perceived by teachers, students, observers, and so forth. Examples are:

1.   What are some of the relationships between the history of the school as it relates to change and the present formal/ perceived/operational curriculum of the school?

2.   What are some of the relationships between the clarity of curriculum goals in the school and the problem-solving and communications processes by which school business is conducted?

3. In what ways, if any, does material space appear to affect the attainment of the school's goals?

The school-community part of the study views school-community relationships as occurring in six categories: (1) perceptions of what goes on in the schools, (2) expectations for the school, (3) communication patterns between school and community, (4) community involvements in the school, (5) community influence in the school, and (6) community resources available to and utilized by the school. In a time when there is much rhetoric and some action in terms of community involvement in curriculum decision making, we clearly need to know how people see their schools. Here, descriptive data become important. Again, relationship questions should be important to curriculumists. Examples are:

1. How do parental and community curriculum expectations for the school vary from those of teachers and administrators?

2. How do parental and community perceptions of how they should be involved in curriculum decision making vary from the perceptions of teachers and administrators in this area?

3. What is the gap between community resources available to the school and community resources used by the school?

There is one other data source built into this study which should be of interest to curriculumists. Prior to actual data collection, school staffs are asked to identify data they would like to have collected about their school. Our experience to date suggests that there will be very few concerns expressed by faculty members which are not already addressed by present instruments. However, two additional, significant questions pertaining to the curriculum were raised by staff members in the pilot schools, and short survey instruments were designed so that appropriate data could be collected. The elementary school had an open-plan building. Teachers were organized into teams and students moved among teachers. Teachers at that school wanted to know how children felt about this organizational plan. High school teachers wanted to know how their students viewed the future. The study staff designed student survey instruments to give appropriate data to teachers. Knowing the kinds of data about their programs wanted by teachers should be of interest and use to curriculum workers.

The total study is designed not to test a theory or several predetermined hypotheses about schooling and curricula but to provide, first through description, a reasonably comprehensive picture of a practical arena where rather ordered processes of teaching and learning presumably occur. From such a data base, it will then be possible to examine a series of significant questions (or hypotheses) regarding this enterprise: (1) Is a wide range of goals being sought through daily practice? Or, stated as an hypothesis: A week of instruction in schools reveals attention to only a relatively narrow range of goals. (2) Does instruction provide for varied modes of student learning? Or, as an hypothesis: Classroom instruction tends to utilize only a very limited array of learning styles and modes.

To make such judgments, normative principles or standards must be invoked. Consequently, one phase of the study involves reviewing the literature for relevant research findings and consulting panels of specialists in order to identify desirable alternatives. Comparing descriptive data with normative postulates will both suggest directions for improvement and, given the size and nature of the gaps, suggest some of the kinds of difficulties involved in moving from where we now appear to be to where we might want to go with educational improvement.

Our present intention is to study in depth a small number of schools presumed to be different. We are deliberately picking schools that appear to differ markedly in geographic location, size, socioeconomic levels of students, and so forth (see Figure 2.2). One of our basic assumptions is that there is not one American school but many. They probably will be alike in some respects but quite different in others. Perhaps we will be able to come up with a typology of schooling. Should we be developing and requiring *a* curriculum for all

SCHOOL SIZE

		LARGE	SMALL
SOCIOECONOMIC STATUS OF STUDENT POPULATION	MIDDLE S.E.S.	1. metropolitan—all or predominantly white. 2. metropolitan—all or predominantly nonwhite. 3. rural—all or predominantly white. 4. rural—all or predominantly nonwhite. 5. metropolitan—racial mix. 6. rural—racial mix.	1. metropolitan—all or predominantly white. 2. metropolitan—all or predominantly nonwhite. 3. rural—all or predominantly white. 4. rural—all or predominantly nonwhite. 5. metropolitan—racial mix. 6. rural—racial mix.
	LOW S.E.S.	1. metropolitan—all or predominantly white. 2. metropolitan—all or predominantly nonwhite. 3. rural—all or predominantly white. 4. rural—all or predominantly nonwhite. 5. metropolitan—racial mix. 6. rural—racial mix.	1. metropolitan—all or predominantly white. 2. metropolitan—all or predominantly nonwhite. 3. rural—all or predominantly white. 4. rural—all or predominantly nonwhite. 5. metropolitan—racial mix. 6. rural—racial mix.

Figure 2.2. A beginning typology of schools to be studied.

the different schools in the typology or should we be preparing differing curricula? If the latter, should the goals for all be similar or should both ends and means be varied and open to local option? It is our hope and intention that this exploration in curriculum inquiry will enrich curriculum development by adding some knowledge of what exists to the customary processes of explicating what should or ought to be.

It is assumed here that curriculum theory stems from and seeks to enlighten both ideological and political-social or technical-professional practice. The theorist sets up the commonplaces to be addressed. These, presumably, correspond to those dealt with also in the practical domains. In the past, the theorist has been interested primarily in the ideological domain, pursuing issues in the selection and ordering of subject matter apart from all those even more difficult and troublesome issues pertaining to the arenas where groups or individuals pursue their vested interests. This is legitimate, important work, but its limitations must be recognized. Unfortunately, it has not served notably to bridge the gap between theorists and practitioners. Likewise, the makers of ideological curricula too often have worked with limited knowledge of sociopolitical realities, preparing materials without adequate recognition of the needs, problems, and interests of those for whom they were intended. Theories and conceptualizations of curriculum, to be maximally useful, must embrace the full range of the practical. Consequently, determining that range and the specifics within it is exceedingly important inquiry.

NOTES

1. James B. Conant, *Two Modes of Thought*, Trident Press, New York, 1964.

2. Lee J. Cronbach, "Beyond the Two Disciplines of Scientific Psychology," *American Psychologist*, February 1975, p. 121.

3. Joseph J. Schwab, *The Practical: A Language for Curriculum*, National Education Association, Washington, D.C., 1970.

4. Philip W. Jackson, *Life in Classrooms*, Holt, Rinehart & Winston, New York, 1968.

5. Seymour B. Sarason, *The Culture of the School and the Problem of Change*, Allyn & Bacon, Boston, 1971.

6. Urie Bronfenbrenner, "Experimental Human Ecology: A Reorientation to Theory and Research on Socialization," Presidential Address, Division of Personality and Social Psychology, American Psychological Association, 1974.

7. John Dewey, *The Sources of a Science of Education*, Horace Liveright, New York, 1929.

8. Joseph J. Schwab, "The Structure of the Natural Sciences," in G. W. Ford and Lawrence Pugno (eds.), *The Structure of Knowledge and the Curriculum*, Rand McNally, Chicago, 1964, pp. 31–49.

9. John I. Goodlad, "Thought, Invention and Research in the Ad-

vancement of Education," Presidential Address, American Educational Research Association, Chicago, February 8, 1968.

10. James G. March, "Model Bias in Social Action," *Review of Educational Research,* vol. 42, no. 4, Fall 1972, pp. 413–429.

11. Cronbach, op. cit.

12. John Dewey, op cit., p. 56.

13. John I. Goodlad (with Maurice N. Richter, Jr.), *The Development of a Conceptual System for Dealing with Problems of Curriculum and Instruction,* Cooperative Research Program USOE, Project No. 454, University of California, Los Angeles, 1966.

14. Joseph J. Schwab, *The Practical: A Language for Curriculum,* National Education Association, Washington, D.C., 1970, p. 30.

15. March, op. cit.

16. John I. Goodlad, *The Dynamics of Educational Change,* McGraw-Hill, New York, 1975.

17. See, for example, Michael J. Dunkin and Bruce J. Biddle, *The Study of Teaching,* Holt, Rinehart & Winston, New York, 1974.

18. Joseph J. Schwab, "Foreword," in William A. Reid and Decker F. Walker (eds.), *Case Studies in Curriculum Change,* Routledge and Kegan Paul, Boston, 1975, p. vii.

19. John I. Goodlad, "Curriculum: The State of the Field," *Review of Educational Research,* vol. XXX, June 1960, pp. 185–98.

20. See Reid and Walker (eds.), op. cit.

21. This study, begun in 1973, is entitled, "A Study of Schooling in the United States," and is administered by the Institute for Development of Educational Activities, Inc. (| I | D | E | A |), an affiliate of the Charles F. Kettering Foundation. Financial support has been provided by an array of private and public agencies.

22. See, for example, Louise L. Tyler, M. Frances Klein, and Associates, *Evaluating and Choosing Curriculum and Instructional Materials,* Educational Resource Associates, Inc., Los Angeles, 1976.

23. For a study into the assumptions that sixty elementary-school teachers brought into instruction, see Anne M. Bussis, Edward A. Chittenden, and Marianne Amarel, *Beyond Surface Curriculum,* Westview Press, Boulder, Colo., 1976.

24. Ned A. Flanders, *Analyzing Teacher Behavior,* Addison-Wesley, Reading, Mass., 1970.

3

Levels of Curricular Decision Making

GARY A. GRIFFIN

The purpose of this chapter is to describe curricular decision making according to a particular framework: John Goodlad's conceptual system,[1] which was significantly influenced by the work of Ralph Tyler. The discussion has two points of focus. First, there is a summary of a research study which attempted to ascertain where, in five school systems, certain curricular decisions were made. Here, considerable emphasis is placed on the framework itself and some reasons for its appeal are put forth. The second part of the chapter deals with the practice of curricular decision making in light of the findings of the study and how this practice might be illuminated by other data sources. The chapter concludes with a perspective on and some questions about praxis.

A STUDY OF PRACTICE IN CURRICULAR DECISION MAKING

The Conceptual System—A Framework for Description

As indicated in Chapter 1, over a period of years Goodlad and his associates developed a framework for describing the curricular enterprise in school settings. This framework has as a central theme the illumination of theoretic inquiry and curricular practice. That is, the system seeks to *contain* practice to a reasonable degree as well as posit, from the more removed and less hotly involved position held by curriculum students and theorists, areas for study and, one hopes, theoretic activity. It is the former enterprise that this study of curricular decision-making addresses. The principal research question addressed by the writer was, "Who, individuals or agencies, appear(s) to be making decisions regarding curriculum in selected school systems?" The answer to this question becomes a datum regarding the degree of descriptive accuracy of the Goodlad conception of decision making in curriculum.

It is necessary to recapitulate Goodlad's notion of levels of decision making here to clarify later discussion (see Chapter 1). The *societal* level of decision making refers to those decisions made by persons or agencies removed in time and place from the individual learner. For the purposes of the study to be reported, the societal level was indicated to be boards of education (local or state), state departments of education, federal agencies concerned with educational policy and procedures, and the like. The *institutional* level of decision making refers to school faculties, central office persons, curriculum committees, and others in the school system working together within the framework provided by societal decisions to provide more concrete guidance to teachers and students. The *instructional* level of decision making refers to individual teachers, or teams of teachers responsible for identifiable students, deciding alone or with students what shall occur in specific educative settings.

It is also important to note that the Goodlad conceptual system uses as its decision content those issues actually resolved at these levels, the four categories of decision noted by Ralph Tyler in his well-known *Basic Principles of Curriculum and Instruction*.[2] Abbreviated to headings, the four categories are decisions related to purpose, decisions related to student experiences, decisions related to organization, and decisions related to evaluation.

From the discussion so far, one can see that if the Goodlad

conceptual system were in perfect correspondence with practice as a descriptive tool, the broadly stated decisions regarding what all students and teachers will engage in will be seen to be made by boards of education and like bodies; the more specific decisions, usually framed as sets of alternatives for teacher selection and for guidance of classroom practice, will be made by committees of professionals or so-called middle management persons in school systems; and specific decisions about what certain identifiable students will learn, do, or prove about themselves will be made by teachers and, perhaps, students in classroom settings.

Naturally, this abbreviated description leaves much to be desired with respect to the attention—or lack thereof—paid to other considerations within the conceptualization. It does, however, provide some indication of the appeal of such a mode of description and study. The appeal is the same to be found in the conceptually neat and elegant classification scheme provided by Tyler. It is important to consider this generalized attractiveness in order to understand the discrepancy between the system and the description of practice it is meant to contain.

As has been mentioned, the Goodlad/Tyler work is neat and elegant. It is seductive, intellectually and pedagogically, to those who maintain that man is a rational being and that groups of such rational beings will also behave rationally as groups. That is, put into educative deliberation, it is most reasonable to assume that there are (or should be) decisions made at various levels of an institution which are not in conflict with one another, that persons acting as decision makers should be aware of and should influence decisions made by others at different levels, and that the decisions should reflect some deliberate consideration of what might be called "commonplace decisions" regarding curriculum. Another argument for the elegance of the system is that it is based, or appears to be, upon a conceptualization of schools and school systems as hierarchically organized human groups in which, ideally, there is immediate and remedial attention to dysfunctionality when decisions are either abrogated or are in collective disharmony. (Consider the consequences of a decision to package soup in twelve-ounce cans by one decision group and the decision to calibrate the soup-dispensing machine at fourteen ounces by another decision group. The noneducational analogy is deliberately drawn to indicate the potential for disaster when school persons adopt production models as either prescriptions or descriptions.)[3]

Another compelling concept which underlies the system is the notion, at least at the societal and institutional levels of decision making, that cooperative decisions *are* made, and, further, that mechanisms in the institutions provide for such cooperation. After all, we do *believe* in collegiality and working together toward mutually desired ends, don't we? More of this later. And, as one last appeal for the acceptance of the system, there is the complicated notion of consent that is so implicit. Although nominally careful to consider that various levels of decisions and decision makers will inform others (about transactions which take place), there remains the belief that, rational school people being collectively rational, the persons at various levels will come to consent to decisions made at some distance from them. Particularly crucial here, it appears to me, is the idea that students will consent to the parameters of behavior changes, learning opportunities, patterns of organization, and evaluation practices and procedures made by either societal persons or institutional persons. A certain passivity is implied, although probably not intended, which is pleasant and soothing to those of us trying to make our ways carefully and constructively through the chaotic conditions found in our private and public worlds.

What is intended by the preceding paragraph is to offer some reasons for the attractiveness of the conceptualization apart from the ones which come to mind from a more pedagogically oriented view.[4] Important in this attraction is the seeming ease with which the system offers us the opportunity to see our disparate works as being important, if not central, and directly related to the works of others in mutually reinforcing ways. Appeal to our sense of pedagogical isolation is difficult, if not impossible, to ignore.

Purpose of the Study

The purpose of the study reported in the following pages was to determine the degree to which the Goodlad conceptual system accurately depicts the levels of curricular decision making which the system indicates as being reflective of reality.[5] As has been stated previously, the system is meant to be mutually informing between theoretic inquiry and practice. If not, or at least if substantially not, then the system loses its force as an intellectual and pedagogical tool. (It should be stated that the study of the reflective accuracy of the system was encouraged by Goodlad and that he offered considerable assistance in its conduct.)

Setting and Procedures Used in the Study

Five school systems were selected to participate in the study. Their selection was determined partly because of willingness to bare their decision-making apparatus, structure, and behavior, and largely because of the differing organizational and demographic characteristics they possessed. Differences regarding degree of urbanism, complexity of organization, nature of student groups, numbers and characteristics of teachers, history of curriculum-planning operations, and innovative practices were considered potentially important discriminating variables to be considered. Consequently, the school systems could be classified as urban, suburban, or rural; highly complex or relatively unencumbered organizationally; large, medium, or small in number of students; inactive to highly active in curriculum-planning activities; static to explosive in efforts to innovate; and with teacher groups possessing mostly baccalaureate degrees to those with a large number of graduate degrees.

In all, 407 persons participated in the study, ranging from 36 in the smallest system to 158 in the largest. In order to "place" the persons in the Goodlad conceptualization, each respondent was classified as a societal, institutional, or instructional decision maker. For each of the levels in each of the school systems, the respondents numbered at least 50 percent of the total number possible at the societal level, 25 percent of the total number at the institutional level, and 20 percent of the total number at the instructional level. These designations of number were an attempt to secure responses from each level which would, as statistically accurately as possible, reflect decision-making behaviors of others in the system who did not participate in the study.

The question of what the respondents would attach reports of their decision making *to* was thought to be a simple one to answer, at least initially. Because Goodlad accepted the Tyler framework as a large part of his conceptualization, it was decided to use decisions regarding purposes, experiences, organization, and evaluation as ones to which respondents would indicate their degree of participation. As is often the case in such apparently "easy" resolutions in research, an immediate crisis revolved around the lack of any systematic attention previously given to the various decision categories. It was discovered that the curriculum literature tended to flee from specification and closet itself in generalities little more precise than noting that such decisions must be made, but with very little indication of what those decisions might look like in actual practice. It became necessary, therefore, to formulate as complete a listing of curricular decisions as possible, and, further, to offer examples of such decisions which could give the respondent the opportunity for quick and verifiable identification with his world of practice.

The result of this deliberation was a collection of forty-three discrete curricular decisions, each accompanied by a highly specific example of its possible manifestation. (Illustration: The decision stated "Selects Objectives for a Lesson" was exemplified by "the objective with this fifth-grade class today will be 'to recall five Civil War generals.' ") In each of the areas of decision making noted by Tyler, decisions were stated from general to specific to illustrate the Goodlad conceptualization's designation of societal, institutional, and instructional. The decisions were validated by expert opinion as to (1) the degree to which they were agreed to be, in fact, curricular decisions, and (2) the degree to which they reflected the Goodlad conceptual system. The forty-three decisions formulated withstood this scrutiny and were included in a questionnaire.

The questionnaire asked each respondent to indicate the role he or she played in making each of the decisions. As the persons responding had been classified according to placement within the system and the decisions had also been placed within the system, it was then necessary to determine from the responses whether or not a person designated, for instance, as instructional actually made instructional-level decisions, and, if so, to what degree he participated in the decision making. Was his participation a cooperative endeavor or did he make the decision relatively unilaterally? Further, each respondent was asked to indicate who in the system made the decision if he did not. Consequently, by analyzing the data one might determine not only who participated in decision making but who was *perceived* as participating. It was the intent of this procedure to offer cross-validation of perceptions of respondents' own behavior with perceptions of others' behavior as well as with others' perceptions of the individual respondent's behavior.

The data were collected over a two-month period by administering the questionnaire to groups of respondents in the five settings.

Findings of the Study

It will be recalled that the purpose of the study was to determine how precisely and accurately the Goodlad conceptualization reflects practice. It should also be noted that the study was undertaken because explicit in the conceptualization is the idea that a system such as Goodlad's must, to be fruitful and powerful, not only give direction to theoretic inquiry but illuminate what is going on in schools and school systems.

The analyses of the responses indicate the following decision-making practice for the five school systems studied:

1. Societal level curricular decisions are made (2 of 2) by societal level persons.

2. Instructional level decisions are made (16 of 16) by instructional level persons.

3. Institutional level curricular decisions are not made (1 of 25) by institutional level persons.

4. Thirteen of the twenty-five institutional level curricular decisions do not appear to be made clearly at any of the three levels.

5. Two of the twenty-five institutional level curricular decisions appear to be made at the societal level.

6. Nine of the twenty-five institutional level curricular decisions appear to be made at the instructional level.

7. Size and organizational complexity appear to affect the degree to which school districts are reflective of the levels of decision making tested by the study.

8. Teachers participate extensively in making curricular decisions and, more than any of the other positions studied, appear to make decisions consistently more unilaterally.

9. Decisions regarding matters of organization appear to receive the least attention of the four types of decisions considered by the study.

10. Perceptions of decision making appear to be in accord with decision-making behavior as reported by respondents.

The risk of violating the precision which characterizes most reports of studies of this sort comes into play when one begins discussing the findings and is even greater when one attempts to account for them. With full knowledge of this risk the following pages will attempt to draw some lessons from the findings, rooted in the data, and finally, to move beyond the data toward conjecture based upon other study and experience related to the curricular enterprise.

Practice and the Conceptual System

For the five school systems included in this study, the Goodlad conceptualization appears reflective of practice at two of the levels, societal and instructional, but offers only a slight illumination of the institutional level of decision making. As a tool for description, then, it appears to be largely inaccurate, if not misleading to the student of curriculum. One might bluntly conclude, therefore, that the framework provided by Goodlad is not functioning as it should and, thus, must be disregarded. This conclusion would be a dangerous one, however, in that further investigation of the nonparallel level reveals that it is very likely the most complicated, organizationally and pedagogically. If the decisions noted for that level could clearly be said to be made consistently at other levels, the solution is a simple one: revise the conceptualization so that the decisions are placed where they are made. Or, conversely, *prescribe* the appropriate levels for certain decisions, including the difficult-to-locate institutional level, and use the conceptualization as a model to determine the distance of practice from an ideal. After all, curriculum literature is largely a body of work consisting of proposals for action or descriptions of past action—why bother with moving toward encompassing accuracy?

As one can see, the argument emerging here is not one of practice *versus* theory. It is one of practice *and* theory. What are the relationships most potentially productive and powerful? What disclosures can be determined from examining one against the other, less for the purpose of condemning one and praising the other than for the intention to mutually reinforce? What tools can be developed to accomplish this enormously difficult and taxing endeavor? These three questions will be used to frame the discussion of the findings of this study of practice.

First, clearly the most powerful relations between the conceptual system and practice are the ones included under the rubrics of societal and institutional decision making. There is exact correspondence between the decisions placed at these levels and those persons who make the decisions. The usefulness of this correspondence is powerful whether one is talking about reconceptualizing the role of the teacher (from "meeter of student" to curriculum planner, for example) in describing the distance from what is going on toward indicating what new behaviors, organizational and individual, must be attached to the new role, or whether one is planning a competency-based program for the education of teachers from the viewpoint of what teachers *do*. These two examples are extremes and chosen carefully to indicate the range of *use* which can be made of an accurate conceptualization, in whole or in part. Certainly, research and theoretic inquiry of a less extreme nature can be guided by knowledge about the instructional level. For instance, if the teacher's role and responsibilities indicate great attention to matters directly related to diagnosis and prescription of and for individual learners, how can such activity be made most effective? What data sources are logically or empirically necessary for the teacher to consider? How can they be made readily available, accessible, understandable, and usable? What organizational constraints must be removed and what nurturing devices must be introduced into the school to facilitate the diagnosis and prescription? Who make the best diagnosticians and prescribers? How can diagnosis and prescription become intentionally systematic, if that is desired? One could spin out such a list of questions for many more paragraphs and pages than are necessary to exemplify the usefulness that the conceptualization has for the arenas in which it is accurately reflective, and it is hoped that many will engage in such questioning and, more importantly, inquire deeply enough to provide us with some answers.

The second question posed earlier had as its core the revelation of discrepancy between the conceptualization and practice. What to do when the systemically neat and elegant descriptive components break down? The first response, as noted earlier, may be to reject the system out of hand or to reject the data from the study as insufficient to accurately describe the practice at the institutional level. Either decision, it is felt, would be inappropriate. A more fruitful manner of dealing with the finding that the institutional level is not functioning as expected is to examine the problems of institutional curriculum planning more rigorously and, at the same time, question the system meant to describe it just as rigorously. For openers, to what degree is decision making, as such, seen as a real responsibility at the institutional level?

Is it possible that those charged with participation in planning groups, as curriculum "coordinators," or as members of an interdisciplinary team at a secondary school, do not see themselves as decision *makers* but more as decision *facilitators*? Is it a revelation to be studied more intensively that the middle level appears to be functioning sporadically rather than generally as a decision level? If the institutional level does not make the decisions considered appropriate for it, no matter the criteria for deciding appropriateness, is such practice organizationally healthy or potentially dysfunctional? If either, what must be done in the schools themselves either to maintain or to modify the institutional decision-making function? (This question and its answer puts the discussion close to the prescription versus description role of the conceptual system which will be briefly discussed later.) What is called for, then, is a vigorous examination of the institutional level from more points of view and methodological stances than the one taken in the study reported here (see Chapter 5 for some of the complexities involved). Such investigations are reported elsewhere in this book, and, indeed, the last section of this chapter focuses much of its discussion on this problem.

The third question is concerned with the tools or technologies necessary to determine the relation of theoretic inquiry and practice. The Goodlad conceptualization has proved, to a large degree, to be a useful mode to characterize what *is* going on in curriculum planning as well as to indicate the overarching concerns of a proposal of theoretic nature which can be, or might be, brought to bear upon practice. As the body of research knowledge grows, it is possible to speculate that the conceptual system may be as close to an accurate and reasonably precise description as we are able to get. There are those among us who search endlessly for *the* conceptual stance, *the* prescriptive device, *the* value position, *the* answer to pressing problems of curriculum making which will end, or at least substantially ameliorate, the hesitancy and confusion which surrounds the curriculum and its study like an only dimly perceived miasma. Is it not possible that the curriculum-planning operation in schools (and at marked distances from schools) may be characterized by several modes and frameworks for description? What, for example, would be the best conceptual net in which to snare the "open school" movement which depends, in large measure, upon the school reacting to the learner as stimulus instead of the other way around as in the past?[6] It is doubtful that the hierarchical, ends-means oriented, institution-as-organizer concept would suffice. And what about a school governed by principles of existentialism? How to capture the intellectual and emotional movement into the world from a personal perspective may elude even the most loosely structured framework for description. The point here is, of course, that it may become increasingly necessary to experiment with different constructs and conceptualizations in order to mirror, with any accuracy, what is happening in schools. Although it is certainly not a novel admonition to the profession, it appears increasingly urgent that we practice what we preach regarding individual differences in light of what we know about curriculum planning. That is, recognize the diversity of planning operations, from strict mandates for behavior of all in the institution to loose, but not necessarily sloppy, institutional structures designed intentionally to promote freedom and opportunities for idiosyncratic choice making. The result of such recognition, one hopes, will be a powerful descriptive technology composed of sometimes interlocking and sometimes isolated systems not only for description but also to draw inferences for research and build theory. The Goodlad conceptualization is one such system. As we learn more about practice it may be possible to devise others.

THE COMPLEXITY OF CURRICULUM PLANNING

As in any systematic inquiry, the answers to certain questions give rise to further questions. In this instance the question was, "To what degree does the Goodlad conceptualization accurately reflect the practice of curricular decision making?" The answer, "very accurately in certain instances and not at all accurately in other instances," calls for one to reflect upon the whys and wherefores which might explain and further illuminate what is happening "out there." The conclusion drawn by many, including this author, is that the planning enterprise in any human system is extraordinarily complex. But to rest on that conclusion is to engage in intellectual flight. What do we know or suspect that may order our thinking in such a way as to provide more insight into that complexity? What commonplaces of school life might help to explain it? What belief systems, held by practitioner or observer, appear to be implicit or explicit causes of the complexity? The remainder of this chapter will offer one incomplete set of tentative explanations of the complexity, not in any final, judgmental fashion but as a means to sort out the issues which may be resolved by the observer, the practitioner, or both.

Each with a Biography—Person and Institution

Every person and every institution has a past, rich or impoverished, that can be described in terms of such concepts as rationality, cooperation, idiosyncrasy, power, subservience, dependency, aggressiveness, urbanism, rurality, isolation, and many, many others. A principal question which must be asked of any system to describe individuals, as individuals or as groups of individuals banded together in name or fact as human groups, is the degree to which the system takes into consideration the precedent facts of life about the persons and human behaviors it is meant to characterize. We have some beliefs, a little knowledge, and some preliminary hunches about schools and school people which, added together, tell us that only recently has the classroom door opened to admit the light and fresh air of new ideas of pedagogy or, in fact, new insights into the human condition.[7] The history of our educative institutions seems to have as a central theme the isolation of individuals from the turbulence of the world outside. Although this generalization, as with most generalizations, is open to question in numerous specific instances, it is still possible to verify it in large measure. Another broad statement about schools might hint at the impact of publisher upon teachers and students with little interference from other school people on its trajectory. Still another might be a characterization of schools as increasingly complex institutions in terms of aggregates (people, time, space, materials, place, and scope) but also stubbornly resistant in terms of the necessary structural or organizational changes necessary to treat the numerical complexities with ease, efficiency, or increased power upon and for the client.[8]

These sweeping statements, true or partly true or occasionally true, give a cameo view of why the decision-making structure may not reflect rationality or, perhaps a better descriptor, systematic and corrective attention to ends and means within the institution. To what extent is it possible to expect systematic health from an organization, no matter how credibly conceived as a human welfare and improvement mechanism, if it can be described at all accurately as isolated from its surroundings, nonintervening upon powerful influence sources, and institutionally static? The problem of expectations regarding decision making becomes somewhat more manageable when such generalizations are tested and proven to be true or false. The formulation and application of criteria for organizational well-being can then proceed, notwithstanding the difficulties of such a process, and decisions regarding the structure most likely to achieve the self-conscious purposes of the organization can be rooted in data. The contention here is that the complexity of the curriculum-planning process is, in large measure, the product of adherence to organizational principles which are no longer useful or productive and which should be studied as a necessary component to revitalizing the entire of the school.

Default Behavior—Who's in Charge Here?

Follow-up study of a somewhat informal nature related to the research presented earlier in this chapter hints that the reason many decisions are made by teachers when one might expect them to be made by others in the system is that the decisions themselves escape the pedagogical net of everyone but the teacher. That is, the decision is one that is perceived as a necessary one, but the teacher makes it because no one else has attended to it. This is particularly true when one speaks of organizing the curriculum beyond the traditional designation of courses, use of a textbook series, and grade-by-grade progression of content (all of which are, naturally, closely related). The conclusion which might be drawn is that, as in the preceding section, the form and structure of decision making offers too few handles on means to assist the teachers and students in their choices regarding organization issues in the example but relatively across-the-board in others. In other words, the institution *qua* institution defaults its responsibility for guidance and, by default, places ultimate responsibility in the hands of those managing the classroom.

In other informal inquiry, it has been found that teachers and students are anxiously seeking alternate routes to solving problems, and, more importantly, also searching for the stuff of which appropriate and meaningful problems are made. In the somewhat frenzied approach to, and/or retreat from the call to, accountability, it is heartening to note the increased attention being paid to other levels, using Goodlad's term, of decision making beyond the instructional. The broadening base of the performance-based teacher education movement which dismays some and gladdens the hearts of others may pull us up short and help us to recognize the interdependence of the people in a human system and how that interdependence can be used to strengthen what we are *all* about.

Knowledge Production and Utilization—The Link is Missing

A familiar refrain that wafts into our lives and out again is that theory and practice never seem to get together. Another complaint is that the proliferation of innovations exists only at the proposal level but seldom influence what happens in school.[9] What is to blame? Is the problem real or imagined? Is there some mutually exclusive set of principles which automatically divorces practice from the rarified world of proposals to innovate and change? What can be done, if anything, to resolve this issue? These questions are indicative of some of the responses to the problem of knowledge being produced, one likes to believe, in the hope that it will somehow reshape schooling and the lack of attention that the knowledge receives from those who are in the business of schooling.[10]

For many years it was assumed that the teacher training institutions were the necessary link between the production of knowledge and its utilization. Prospective teachers were introduced to the knowledge which was supposed to guide their activities; they were then set free in the world of schools. This, it appears from recent history, is a mistaken assumption, as evidenced by the increased attacks upon undergraduate schools of education as static, unchanging, unresponsive institutions unwilling to change their ways, update their methods, or revise their content. Another assumption regarding knowledge utilization was that school system programs of in-service education would become the connective between teachers and new knowledge or proposals for change. This, too, has a history of relative ineffectiveness. Teacher organizations have begun to upgrade their members' skills and knowledge as well as to produce new knowledge. The effect of this last is yet to be determined, but it is possible to conjecture that the struggle for power, in its purest and most traditional sense, will continue to dominate teacher organization activities to the substantial exclusion of concerted efforts toward the reconstitution of members' skills and knowledge.

What these statements are meant to illustrate is the potentially dysfunctional and personally unrewarding business of being expected, by one's self or others, to perform or behave in certain ways without having the necessary systems, technologies, or knowledge, if you will, to cope. When one considers the lack of attention paid to the explanations of human behavior from disciplined psychological research, the inability to deal in an intellectually honest manner with new approaches to content, the flight from proposals regarding different patterns of staff utilization, and the resistance to concerted urgings to change the environment of schooling, it is possible to tie the negativism to the natural human fear of the unknown. If this is true, or partly true, what can be done to increase the power of knowledge, new or only experimentally tested, for alteration of practice? The answer lies, in part, in the mechanisms we can devise to tie the knowledge to practice—that is, to illustrate with considerable force the potential meaningfulness of the knowledge to what we are doing. The deliberate exclusion of one or more of the special interest groups noted in the preceding paragraph— undergraduate institutions, school systems, teacher organizations—appears not to be fruitful. Just the opposite; what seems to be needed is a powerful coalition of these groups which will clarify the role of each in the continued growth of the professional educator, not just the teacher, so that lifelong learning becomes something other than a slogan we use to describe programs for young children. It is believed that this coalition, aligned with those in the business of producing knowledge, will relieve the anxiety of the sincere educator, maximize the impact of knowledge, sustain the influence of knowledge over periods of trial, error, and adjustment, and reduce in large measure the complex business of intellectual negotiation between and among the various levels of decision making in schools.

The Nonresponsive Institution—The Responsive Professional?

Polemics aside, there is evidence that many individuals and groups are concerned about the institutionalized role they are expected, or believe they are expected, to play in the course of their work and, indeed, the course of their personal and private lives. There has been the belief that school systems and boards of education mandate quite rigorously how teachers are to act, how they must meet students, how they must attack content, how they must "fit" into a routine called schoolteaching. Whether or not schools actually do make such extensive demands is almost beside the point as long as substantial numbers of persons believe they do and, hence, act according to that belief. (There is some evidence that there are far fewer role mandates than we have suspected. The data from the study cited earlier tend to support the notion that institutional decision making in the curricular sense offers little guidance and even less command.) The response to this concern for the relation between person and institution has been, in schools and out of them, to focus attention on the individual as the decision maker—to promote the problem solving at a level of immediacy rather than at a distance from those concerned with resolving the issues personally. From a distance, such a refocusing seems reasonable. Doing "my thing" is less likely to hurt me or someone else than we supposed previous to the age of the flower children, the hippies, and the freethinking activists. But does such a conception of behavior fit into the institutional framework, recognizing the charge of purpose, of the schools? Can one do his own thing when he is in a legally mandated group setting—individualization of instruction is still most often contained within a larger collective body of persons—with desirable consequences? Is such a position regarding teacher and student behavior merely a return to the conventional wisdom that a teacher teaches best when he is comfortable so there should be no dicta to guide his actions? Is such a response likely to further complicate the decision-making structure of schools and, if so, is such increased complexity desirable? There are no answers offered to these questions, and it can be seen that they are largely rhetorical. Their purpose here is to offer one more possible explanation of the agonizing difficulty of decision making in organizations, schools, which concern themselves with benefit to humans—clients, patrons, professionals. The consequences of increased individual autonomy are enormous. The consequences of stifling such a movement when it has emerged are even greater. What appears to be called for are precise and accurate observations of the phenomenon (decentralization is one such case) with constant attention to the benefits and hazards and with concomitant attention to ways out of the muddle of institution *versus* individual toward institution *and* individual.

Belief Systems and Expectations—Disparate, Disjointed, Dysfunctional

Much of the foregoing has had as an implicit theme the power of nonparallel belief systems and expectations for producing a highly complicated and often chaotic scene in schools. The discussion of levels of decision making cannot ignore the effect that differences of beliefs of what is right or wrong, and expectations as to what is to be accomplished, will have and have had upon school programs. Inherent in such a concern are the disparate ideas and understandings about roles and responsibilities which abound in school settings. One teacher wants the freedom to be creative. Another wants to engage in what might be called rule-bound behavior. Yet another wants—and, as the others, believes to be appropriate—the alternative to pick and choose from various options with the proviso that these may all be rejected by him. And, of course, there are those of us who struggle daily with resolution of this question for ourselves and emerge with few clear-cut beliefs *or* expectations. The concern is often expressed in terms of extreme homogeneity or extreme heterogeneity. As in previous discussions, it is suggested that the dichotomization will not inform our work but will falsely and disastrously sterilize it. Is it desirable for all, teachers and others in schools, to believe and expect the same things? Or is it desirable that the school people demonstrate, in one setting, all of the disparate beliefs and expectations possible? Is it always necessary to somehow convince some people to alter their expectations and beliefs in order for them to contribute together for the common good? Is there really any effective way to achieve such agreements? Is the shotgun approach more desirable than the rifle approach? Is a smoothly functioning decision mechanism, in the sense of the Goodlad conceptualization, for instance, ultimately desirable? It will be argued that such conceptualizations appear to be prescriptive rather than descriptive and that each has a hidden agenda: the seduction of school people into adopting them rather than using them for description. Such might be the case in some instances, for, after all, who among us does not have some hint of what he believes to be the perfect world? Isn't it enough, in the long run, that such modes of description are available for our use and that the formulation of judgmental criteria to apply to our own behaviors as they are found to be related to the system becomes our own private or collective act of deliberation? It is in these acts of deliberation that the expectations and beliefs which guide our actions come into the open and become more public and powerful modes of determining our decision-making behavior. It is believed that such deliberations will clarify not only what decisions are made and by whom, but will offer additional witness to the quality of the decisions, in a technical sense, and to their effect upon our work, individually and collectively.

THE STUDY OF CURRICULAR DECISION MAKING—PRAXIS I PRAXIS II, PRAXIS III

Goodlad, in his opening chapter, uses the term praxis to encompass the "real world" decisions which go into making a curriculum operational. It is the intent of the final section of this chapter to attempt an extension of that term, using varying definitions, so that it can come to embrace a somewhat larger and more inclusive set of behaviors. It is hoped that this extension will further inform the discussion of decision making in curriculum, its study and its practice.

Praxis I—Rule Governed Behavior

Explicit in the definition of Praxis I is the notion that it is an exercise or practice of an art, science, or skill.[11] It is assumed that this exercise or practice is governed by some set of rules by which one comes to know the essentials of the art, science, or skill. Further, it is assumed that it is possible, then, to master the behaviors necessary to the execution of the particular act engaged in.

Using Praxis I as the guide to collection of data for description of curricular decision making, one might ask such questions as: What are the principles of decision making from sociology, organizational administration, and social psychology which have been proven to be most fruitful for human organizations? What are the rules, individual and institutional, which govern the proper application of these principles? To what extent does the school system being examined adhere to the principles and give evidence of observing the rules which govern them? And, what, given the evidence, will be necessary to alter the structure of the institution toward alignment with the principles and rules, if that is desired?

Such descriptive frameworks come close to the prescriptive in that there are sets of expectations, or what-to-look-fors, built into the system. The principal issue when utilizing such a Praxis I system is the confidence one has in the effectiveness and "truth" of the principles underlying the conceptualization. Of major advantage here is the expectation that one will come up with data logically related to maintenance or modification actions. Such data and resultant action become, to a certain extent, public property and open to desired examination, speculation, and dialogue.

Praxis II—A Larger Net

Praxis II is defined as the examination of customary practice or conduct which implies the universe of possibilities, some of which will be rule-governed as in Praxis I and others which will not.[12] A system for examination and description with Praxis II as its orientation would look carefully at what is going on, what people are doing, what consequences are engendered, what ends are formulated, what means are attached to achieve the ends, and so forth without analyzing the data according to a preconceived principle-oriented framework. The advantage here, as in similarly structured anthropological research, is that one gets a broad vista as his point of reference rather than the presence or absence of certain operating principles or rules. Our inclination to classify will probably lead us to the eventual development of categories, schemata, and similar devices to make sense of what we observe, but the sense making will occur as a product of the observation in the widest rather than the narrowest sense.

A major difficulty in reporting the research earlier in this chapter was accounting for the fact that the Goodlad conceptualization did not reflect practice in its entire broad sweep.

The attention to the institutional level of decision making principally and schools' decision making generally in succeeding pages was an exercise, limited in refinement and based upon inadequate data and prior experience, in Praxis II. Such speculation is engaged in readily, handily, and with great frequency by school people. It is rarely informed by data, however, as this chapter testified. The proposal for the use of Praxis II, not necessarily to the exclusion of Praxis I, is an attempt to urge the use of a broader stage with a higher and wider proscenium, to return to Goodlad's metaphor earlier, in describing and studying curriculum. The key to effective use is the degree to which such widening and deepening of our vision helps us to eventually sharpen our perception of that vision and, subsequently, act upon it.

Praxis III—Toward Greater Understanding

The definition of Praxis III comes from existentialism and refers to the "particular" type of cognitive action which crucially involves "the transcending or surpassing of what is."[13] Engaging in Praxis III involves the acts of personal creativity and intellectual diligence which pushes us toward what we know not yet to be: the discovery, if you will, of what wasn't there before—or at least did not appear to be there before. The reality, then, is yet to come and the tentativeness of engagement here is not one of commitment—we *will* come to the new reality—but is the lack of certitude regarding what we believe to be, or have been told to be, real. It is this state of engagement with the world that might be called transcendence, synthesis, sense making of a "quantum leap" order, and which may help us to account for what we see, what we do, what we choose, and, most importantly, *why* we see, do, and choose as we do.

In discussions of curriculum, its practice or the study of its practice, we often tend to ignore the possibility of Praxis III in our attention to Praxis I and/or Praxis II. Or, at best, we move into informal or idle speculation which is not the intent here. At the risk of putting an existential concept to work for a pragmatic concern, can we study curriculum from the vantage points of Praxis I and II in the hope that we may come to personal and powerful contact with Praxis III? It is possible that we have intuitively moved too quickly toward discovery without carefully and sharply noting the terrain to be covered, the ideas to be considered, the people we will meet along the way in all of their infinite and valued variety, or the consequences of the fact that we are moving through the terrain.

NOTES

1. John I. Goodlad, with Maurice N. Richter, Jr., *The Development of a Conceptual System for Dealing with Problems of Curriculum and Instruction,* Cooperative Research Program, USOE, Project No. 454, University of California, Los Angeles, 1966.

2. Ralph W. Tyler, *Basic Principles of Curriculum and Instruction,* University of Chicago Press, Chicago, 1950.

3. See, for example, Gary A. Griffin, "Needs Assessment as a Concealing Technology," *Educational Leadership,* January 1973.

4. See Herbert Kliebard, "The Tyler Rationale," *School Review,* vol. 7, no. 2, February 1970.

5. Gary A. Griffin, "Curricular Decision Making in Selected School Systems," unpublished Ed.D. dissertation, University of California, Los Angeles, 1970.

6. See Lillian Weber, *The English Infant School and Informal Education,* Prentice-Hall, Englewood Cliffs, N.J., 1971.

7. See Seymour B. Sarason, *The Culture of the School and the Problem of Change,* Allyn and Bacon, Boston, 1971; *The Creation of Settings and the Future Societies,* Jossey-Bass, San Francisco, 1972.

8. See Daniel Katz and Robert L. Kahn, *The Social Psychology of Organizations,* John Wiley & Sons, New York, 1966.

9. See John I. Goodlad, M. Frances Klein, and Associates, *Looking Behind the Classroom Door* (Revised), Charles A. Jones Publishing Company, Worthington, Ohio, 1974.

10. See Edmund C. Short, "Knowledge Production and Utilization in Curriculum: A Special Case of the General Phenomenon," *Review of Educational Research,* vol. 43, no. 3, Summer 1973.

11. *Webster's Seventh New Collegiate Dictionary,* G. & C. Merriam Company, Springfield, Mass., 1969, p. 667.

12. Ibid.

13. Maxine Greene, *Teacher As Stranger,* Wadsworth Publishing Company, Belmont, Calif., 1973, p. 163.

4

Societal Decisions in Curriculum

HENRY W. HILL

The tenth amendment to the Constitution of the United States grants to the states the right to make educational decisions. While the state legislatures in many instances have retained this authority by, for example, legislating an education code, most have delegated some of this authority to local boards of education which in turn have delegated certain powers to teachers and school administrators. This arrangement differs from that in many countries. In Scotland, for example, decision making is decentralized, and most of the authority is given to local schools and teachers. In others, such as Ethiopia, decision making is centralized in the Ministry of Education.

In this country, then, the responsibility for making educational decisions is distributed among a number of groups throughout the educational structure. Educational decisions are made by state departments of education, legislatures, school boards, superintendents, principals, and teachers. Although this diffusion of authority and responsibility is a potential strength, the fact that there are no clear and generally accepted guidelines for delegation complicates matters. There is a need for clarification of who should make what curriculum decisions at various levels in the system. These levels have been identified by Goodlad as:

... *instructional* (with decisions primarily the responsibility of a teacher or team of teachers guiding a specific group of learners), *institutional* (with decisions primarily the responsibility of total faculty groups under the leadership of administrators), and *societal* (with decisions primarily the responsibility of lay boards and legislators at local, state, and federal levels of government.[1]

The importance of greater clarification increases because of current thrusts toward decentralization accompanied by increased concern that teachers and others be held accountable for pupils' learning. Presumably, teachers are free to make certain instructional decisions within a guiding framework that includes the education code. Legislators see it as their responsibility to revise the education code from time to time through bills enacted into law. Presumably, these bills and subsequent changes in the code affect and give direction to certain decisions which teachers make. Clearly, these legislative acts affect decision making in education only if those responsible for decisions are aware of and understand the legislation.

The author conducted a study designed to gain an understanding of what selected individuals involved in education knew about legislation which is designed to influence teachers' curriculum decisions. California was the state used in the study, a good choice in view of the fact that this state leads the nation in the amount of curriculum legislation it puts on the books.

Much of this legislation applies to curriculum decisions teachers make. The California Education Code specifies objectives, learning opportunities, curriculum organization, and evaluation. The effectiveness of these laws requires knowledge of them on the part of those who make educational decisions—teachers, superintendents, principals, board members, and legislators. Knowledge of curriculum legislation would appear to be required for effective curriculum decision making. The author assumes that certain instructional-level decisions about which laws have been passed should be guided by knowledge of the legislation designed to influence that instruction. However, these decisions can be and are made without such data. Every day teachers make instructional-level decisions that could be influenced by curriculum legislation. If the teachers make these decisions without knowledge of the appropriate code item, they may be unwittingly violating state laws. Too, the legislature may be busily passing legislation unlikely to affect the educational practice for which it was intended.

The study reported here used as a framework the conceptualization of curriculum decision making formulated by Goodlad. There is a practical significance to the study in that it provided information about the communication of knowledge and contributed helpful background data for sorting out issues and problems in deciding who should make curricular decisions.

This study was limited to instructional decision making in the elementary schools of California and the legislation affecting curricular decisions in these schools. The decision makers questioned were elementary teachers, district superintendents, local board members, and members of the California Legislature.

One hundred eleven elementary school districts with student populations of one thousand and over were randomly selected to participate. A letter was mailed to the superintendent of each of the selected districts requesting permission for his district's participation in the study. The letter explained that thirty teachers were to be randomly selected from the district's faculty roster; that the board members in the district would be involved, and that the superintendent himself would be included in the study.

Twenty-one school districts agreed to participate without reservation. Upon receipt of permission and rosters of the districts' elementary teachers, thirty teachers from each of the twenty-one districts were selected by means of a table of random numbers. All of the district superintendents and board members in the twenty-one participating districts were included in the study. Also asked to participate in the study were all members of the California Legislature.

A questionnaire consisting of twenty-two multiple-choice items was administered to the four groups. Each set of eleven items was designed to test the respondent's knowledge of past and present curriculum legislation. In order to select items on which the questionnaire was to be based, the Education Code was scrutinized in order to select legislation considered important to curriculum decisions teachers make. All such were selected. Each item was then given a rating of either *very important, important,* or *not important* in teachers' curriculum decisions. The code items were divided into four categories: *objectives,* or the intent of what is to be learned; *learning opportunities,* or the what or how of learning; *organization,* or when something is to be learned; and *evaluation,* or how well it has been learned.

An example of a code item relating to *objectives* is number 8553, which requires that instruction in social studies shall include a study of the role and contribution of American Negroes, American Indians, Mexicans, and other ethnic groups to the economic, political, and social development of California and the United States of America (Question 13).

The *when* or *organization* component is exhibited by code number 5771, which provides for the administering of the Miller-Unruh Reading Program in grades one, two, and three (Question 20).

Code number 9255 is an example of the *what* or *learning opportunity* component. This states that any superintendent or principal who refuses or neglects to require the use of the basic textbooks prescribed by the State Board of Education is guilty of a misdemeanor (Question 17).

Question 16 relating to the *evaluation* component was derived from code number 10753, which states that the final grade for a pupil in absence of mistake, fraud, bad faith, or incompetency will be determined by the teacher and is final.

In order to substantiate the judgment of the investigator as to the selection of items deemed important to curriculum decisions teachers make, two judges (competent in the field of curriculum study) examined the code. The judges[2] were given copies of the Education Code and the investigator's list of code items. The judges concluded that all items referring to curriculum decisions teachers made had been included. In addition to checking the competency of the selections, they also confirmed the accuracy of the division according to curriculum function and the ratings of the items.

An instrument was then constructed from the list of code items using the following criteria: (1) code item was deemed to be very important to curriculum decisions teachers make; (2) code item was representative of one of the four curriculum functions; (3) content had to be amenable to wording that presents it as a meaningful and answerable question; and (4) the elimination of content that was biased in the direction of such socially desirable answers that it would fail to discriminate respondents.[3]

To test the validity of the questionnaire, the preliminary instrument was given to a panel of three judges selected to determine the face validity of test items.[4] More specifically, Did a correct response to the item represent adequate knowledge of the code item to make rational curricular decisions? The judges concluded that all items were valid.

The next step, then, was to determine what percentage of correct responses would represent sufficient knowledge of the Education Code on the part of the respondents for them to make curricular decisions. The establishment of this type of thing has been historically one of judgment. After fruitless attempts to seek aid from the Education Committee of the California Legislature in making such recommendations, the investigator consulted with a panel of three judges deemed competent curriculumists. Following a thorough examination of the final instrument, they agreed that a 70% correct response would represent adequate knowledge to make the necessary decisions.

For the purpose of this study, then, conclusions as to whether respondents possessed sufficient knowledge to make curricular decisions pertaining to instruction were based on a correct response of 70% or better.

TEACHERS

Of the 630 teachers randomly selected to participate in the study, 320 returned a completed questionnaire, a response rate of 51%. For the purpose of this study a response rate of 60% was considered highly generalizable; a response rate of 50% or better was generalizable; a response rate of 30% or above was slightly generalizable; and anything less was not generalizable at all. Therefore, the 51% response rate of the teachers on a questionnaire mailed out was considered good and enabled the investigator to generalize to a considerable degree about the entire population of elementary teachers in California.

Table 4-1 presents the teachers' responses by questions.

Table 4.1. Teachers' Responses (by Questions)

Question Number	Responses Right	%	Responses Wrong	%	Do Not Know	%	Special*	%
1	174	54	57	18	89	28		
2	38	12	173	54	109	34		
3	124	39	138	43	58	18		
4	27	08	50	16	243	76		
5	28	09	224	70	68	21		
6	141	44	130	41	49	15		
7	260	81	47	15	12	04		
8	146	46	72	22	102	32		
9	41	13	99	31	180	56		
10	36	11	260	81	24	08		
11	87	27	73	23	160	50		
12	176	55	35	11	109	34		
13	179	56	93	29	48	15		
14	6	02	60	19	33	10	221	69
15	210	66	55	17	55	17		
16	178	56	60	19	83	26		
17	30	09	123	38	167	52		
18	60	19	173	54	87	27		
19	92	28	69	22	159	50		
20	138	43	125	39	57	18		
21	18	06	131	41	171	53		
22	46	14	157	49	117	37		

Total population   630;   total responses   320
Percent of responses   51
Returned—no answer   5
         Total   325

*These respondents answered correctly according to the code item prior to its amendment by the 1970 session of the legislature.

The number of right responses, the percentage of right responses, the number of wrong responses, the number who did not know and, for Item 14, those whose answers were correct for items prior to AB 1783 (marked special) are indicated.

The highest percentage of correct responses was for Item 7 (81%). This item asked the amount of time required for physical education prior to 1968. Responses to questions having a correct response percentage of 50% or higher were: Items 15(66%); 13(66%); 12(55%); and 1(54%). Those having a 40% or better response were: Items 8(46%); 6(44%); and 20(43%). In the 20% to 40% bracket were: Items 3(39%); 19(28%); and 11(27%). Questions having less than 20% of total correct responses were: Items 18(19%); 22(14%); 9(13%); 2(12%); 10(11%); 5 and 17(9%); 4(8%); 21(6%); and 14(2%).

The fewest correct responses were for Item 14 which asked the presently required time for physical education (400 min.). This code item subsequently has been amended, changing the required time. It becomes evident that information regarding a code change does not reach the teacher even within a twelve-month period.

The first eleven questions in the instrument are taken from curriculum legislation in effect just prior to the passage of Senate Bill 1 (Miller Bill) in 1968.

Question 1 concerns the subjects required to be taught in the elementary schools of California. *Question 2* is actually a part of the same bill used in Question 1 requiring English to be taught as a "separate subject with emphasis on thoroughness, and as a discipline separate from the subject of social studies (beginning not later than grade 4)." *Question 3* calls for a familiarity with the foreign language program and asks for those who might be exempted from studying foreign language in elementary school. Another question dealing with the foreign language program and with Chinese in particular is *Question 4,* which asks for the California law which encourages the teaching of Chinese in communities where trade with Asiatic countries forms an important element of the economy and culture of the community. *Question*

5 asks for the percentage of time in the school week which is to be devoted to academic skills in grades one to six. Instruction and training in manners, citizenship, the principles of morality, the effects of alcohol, narcotics, and other drugs, and instruction in fire prevention are included in the California course of study according to California law. *Question 6* calls for this information. *Question 7* asks for the minimum time required by school law for physical education instruction per day. *Question 8* deals with the prohibitive laws which state that no instruction or publications used in the schools shall reflect on any race, religion, color, or national origin, nor can propaganda of any kind be used, shown, or distributed to students. *Question 9* requires knowing the distance from school permitted for school trips—by law a radius of 180 miles from the school is acceptable for field trips. Another question calling for a knowledge of the law dealing with school field trips is *Question 10*; this question asks in accordance with California law, What is the necessary equipment carried or immediately available? *Question 11* turns to the Miller-Unruh Act which requires the submission of reading tests on a per-district basis.

The second set of eleven questions is based on present legislation. *Question 12* asks for the kinds of surveys for which written permission is required. *Question 13* is related to social studies instruction and to the inclusion of California's early history and a study of the roles and contributions of certain minority groups—the American Negro, the Indian, and the Mexican-American. *Question 14* calls for a knowledge of the new requirement for the minimum time permitted for physical education in the elementary school. *Question 15* asks the law concerning reference to religion in classroom instruction. *Question 16* deals with who will determine a final grade in the absence of fraud, mistake, bad faith, or incompetency. *Question 17* is concerned with the penalty for not using state-supplied textbooks. *Question 18* asks for the mandate concerning a conference or written report to parents of failing students. Teaching facts about Communism are the subject of *Question 19*. Both *Questions 20* and *22* deal with the provisions of the Miller-Unruh Basic Reading Act. *Ques-*

tion 20 asks specifically for the grades involved in the provision for instruction to prevent reading disabilities; and *Question 22* asks for the requirement for the submission of reading test scores. Finally, *Question 21* asks about the grades for which Mathematics Specialist Program provides.

Table 4.2 indicates that 50% or more of the teacher respondents correctly answered 6 items. On 12 items, less than

Table 4.2. Teachers' Total Scores

Total Scores	Number of Respondents
0	3
1	5
2	11
3	13
4	20
5	36
6	51
7	47
8	40
9	39
10	26
11	11
12	11
13	3
14	2
15	2
Know Line*	
16	1
17	0
18	0
19	0
20	0
21	0
22	0
Mean 7.1	
Median 6.4	

*Respondent scored above 15 previously defined as the minimum score exhibiting sufficient knowledge to make rational decisions.

30% of the teachers were able to respond correctly. The information contained in the table shows a lack of sufficient knowledge of most of the code items by a majority of teachers.

SUPERINTENDENTS

The total number of superintendents agreeing to participate in the study was 21; 14 returned completed questionnaires for a response rate of 67%. This was an excellent response, but the size of the sample does not allow for a high degree of generalization in regard to the superintendents of elementary school districts in California.

The superintendents' responses to each question are shown in Table 4.3. The highest percentage of correct responses (93%) was for Item 15 which states that reference to religion in classroom instruction may be made with restriction. The superintendents' lowest percentage of correct responses (0%) was on Item 18, which requires a written report or conference with parents of a child during the first half of the instructional term. Less than 30% of the respondents answered Items 9 and 21 (29%) and Item 14 (21%). Over 70% of the superintendents were able to answer 9 items correctly, and 50% or more were able to answer 14 items correctly. The superintendents scored less than 40% on these items. This means the superintendents were knowledgeable about 9 items (1, 6, 7, 8, 13, 15, 16, 19, and 20). Table 4.3 indicates the superintendents were knowledgeable about more items than were the teachers.

As with teachers, superintendents were more knowledgeable about present legislation (mean score of 6.4) than past legislation (6.0).

Three superintendents apparently possessed sufficient knowledge of past legislation, whereas four were knowledgeable about present legislation. The majority did not possess sufficient knowledge of either past or present legislation. Again, the mean is higher than the median on both past and present legislation, indicating the responses were skewed toward the top of the curve.

Table 4.3 Superintendents' Responses (by Questions)

Question Number	Responses Right	%	Responses Wrong	%	Do Not Know	%	Special	%
1	11	79	3	21	0	0		
2	7	50	6	43	1	07		
3	8	57	6	43	0	0		
4	6	43	5	36	3	21		
5	6	43	7	50	1	07		
6	12	86	2	14	0	0		
7	10	71	4	29	0	0		
8	10	71	3	21	1	07		
9	4	29	7	50	3	0		
10	5	36	9	64	0	0		
11	6	43	7	50	1	07		
12	9	64	4	29	1	07		
13	11	79	3	21	0	0		
14	3	21	1	07	0	0	10	71
15	13	93	1	07	0	0		
16	10	71	2	14	2	14		
17	9	64	3	21	2	14		
18	0	0	12	86	2	14		
19	10	71	2	14	2	14		
20	12	86	2	14	0	0		
21	4	29	9	64	1	07		
22	9	64	3	21	2	14		

Total population—21; total responses—14; percent of responses—67.

Table 4.4 presents the total scores of the superintendents. Only 1 respondent scored 70% or better, with 17 correct responses for a 77% score. The mean of 12.4 indicates the superintendents knew slightly more than 50% of the code items. The superintendents' mean of 12.4 was considerably higher than that of the teachers (7.1).

BOARD MEMBERS

There were 101 board members in the 21 school districts participating in this study, 30 of whom returned completed questionnaires for a 30% response. This low response allows

Table 4.4. Superintendents' Total Scores

Total Scores	Number of Respondents
8	1
9	0
10	4
11	1
12	0
13	3
14	2
15	2
Know Line*	
16	0
17	1

Mean   12.4
Median   12.3

*Respondent scored above 15, previously defined as the minimum score exhibiting sufficient knowledge to make rational decisions.

the investigator to make only slight generalizations concerning the population of the board members of the elementary school districts in California. The data may be considered somewhat indicative of the knowledge of a larger population but are not capable of producing strong generalizations.

Table 4.5 presents the board members' responses to questions: the number of right responses, the percentage of right responses, the number of wrong responses, the number who did not know, and, for Item 14, those whose answers were correct prior to AB 1783 (marked special) are indicated.

The highest percentage of correct responses was for Item 15(67%), which allows reference to religion in classroom instruction, with restrictions. This was the same item on which the superintendents scored the highest. The lowest number of correct responses was on Item 10, which deals with the requirement that the teacher responsible for a group of children on a school field trip have in his possession or readily available a first aid kit.

Table 4.5. Board Members' Responses (by Questions)

Question Number	Responses Right	%	Responses Wrong	%	Do Not Know	%	Special	%
1	17	57	7	23	6	20		
2	8	27	12	40	10	33		
3	14	47	10	33	6	20		
4	5	17	6	20	19	63		
5	4	13	15	50	11	37		
6	6	20	13	43	11	37		
7	9	30	13	43	8	27		
8	18	60	3	10	9	30		
9	4	13	14	47	12	40		
10	1	03	23	77	6	20		
11	12	40	8	27	10	33		
12	19	63	4	13	7	23		
13	16	53	11	37	3	10		
14	7	23	4	13	10	33	9	30
15	20	67	6	20	4	13		
16	17	57	7	23	6	20		
17	7	23	9	30	14	47		
18	6	20	17	57	7	23		
19	12	40	7	23	11	37		
20	6	20	13	43	11	37		
21	2	07	12	40	16	53		
22	4	13	16	53	10	33		

Total population		101;	total responses			30		
Percent of responses	30							
Returned—no answer						1		
Total						31		

The responses to questions having a correct response percentage of 50% or higher were: Item 15 (67%); 12 (63%); 8 (60%); 1 and 16 (57%); and 13 (53%). Those having a 40% or higher response were: Items 3 (47%); and 11 and 19 (40%). Item 7 had a 30% response and those items having a correct response of 20% or higher were: Items 2 (27%); 14 and 17 (23%); and 6, 18 and 20 (20%). Those with responses less than 20% were: Items 4 (17%); 5, 9, and 22 (13%); 21 (7%); and 10 (3%).

Table 4.6, presenting total scores, indicates that 1 board member possessed sufficient knowledge. This score of 20 was the highest of all respondents. This response by 30 respondents suggests that board members in California do not possess sufficient knowledge of legislation affecting teachers' curricular decisions as previously defined. Of the 21 respondents, 16 had scores of less than 50% correct.

Table 4.6. Board Members' Total Scores

Total Scores	Number of Respondents
0	3
1	0
2	3
3	1
4	3
5	1
6	3
7	2
8	4
9	2
10	2
11	1
12	1
13	3
14	0
15	0
Know Line*	
16	0
17	0
18	0
19	0
20	0
21	0
22	0

Mean   7.0
Median   6.5

*Respondents scored above 15, previously defined as the minimum score exhibiting sufficient knowledge to make rational decisions.

LEGISLATORS

The potential population for the legislative group was 120. A total of 11 returned completed questionnaires. This constitutes 9% of the population. Eleven legislators returned blank questionnaires and eleven wrote letters stating their reasons for not participating in the study. One legislator wrote that he was a freshman and in all honesty did not know enough to attempt answering the instrument. Three replied they simply did not have the time to participate, while five strongly questioned the study.

The total response from the legislature, including letters, was 28. However, since only 9% completed the instrument, the investigator concluded that this is not an adequate sample and generalizations concerning the legislators cannot be drawn. The responses received were scored and are presented in Table 4.7.

The information contained in this table indicates lack of knowledge on most of the code items by this small sample of the California Legislature. However, we cannot have confidence in any generalizations because of the small percentage of responses. One legislator apparently had sufficient knowledge about present legislation but none had sufficient knowledge of past legislation. There is some evidence that these legislators did not possess knowledge of curriculum legislation prior to 1968, nor of present legislation. A comparison of the means for the past and present legislation is very similar to that for the teachers and board members.

An examination of Table 4.7, which presents total scores indicates that no legislators in this group possessed sufficient knowledge for their decisions. The majority made scores of less than 50 percent correct. The mean of total scores for the legislators (7.2) compares favorably with that of teachers (7.1) and board members (7.0); however, it is much less than the mean of the superintendents (12.4).

Four legislative respondents indicated membership on the education committee. These four scored 12, 12, 8, and 6 for a mean of 9.5 and a median of 10.0. This compares favorably with the total legislative group which had a mean of 7.2 and

Table 4.7. Legislators' Total Scores

Total Scores	Number of Respondents
0	0
1	0
2	0
3	3
4	1
5	1
6	1
7	0
8	2
9	0
10	0
11	0
12	2
13	0
14	1
15	0
Know Line*	
16	0
17	0
18	0
19	0
20	0
21	0
22	0
Mean	7.2
Median	5.0

*Respondents scored 15, previously defined as the minimum score exhibiting sufficient knowledge to make rational decisions.

a median of 5.0. Those legislators who were on the education committee exhibited a greater knowledge of the legislation than those who were not. None reached a score of 15, which had been determined as the minimum score exhibiting sufficient knowledge of the legislation. The most often mentioned source of information regarding curriculum legislation was the committee staff.

The purpose of this study was to gain understanding of what selected individuals involved in education know about legislation which is designed to influence teachers' curricular decision making. The data were analyzed to determine what *each* sample group of participants—elementary teachers, superintendents, board members, and members of the California State Legislature—knew about legislation presumably designed to influence curricular decisions made by teachers. The information provided by this study was useful for drawing conclusions about effectiveness of communication of knowledge, which is vital to good teacher decision making in the area of curriculum. The data are analyzed here to determine the degree of helpfulness of this study in contributing to the study of teacher accountability. In addition, a determination of teachers' knowledge of legislation which may impinge on teachers' curricular decisions and the effects on the decentralization of curricular decision making is made.

The findings of this study were based on the following assumptions: (1) The Goodlad Conceptual System is accepted as a rational method for classifying curricular decisions. (2) Knowledge of curriculum legislation is vital to curricular decision making.

Further, it was determined that, under the Goodlad Conceptual System, the teacher, being the person closest to the learner, should make instructional level (teachers' curricular) decisions. For such decisions to be made by any of the teachers' superordinates would be an impingement on the teachers' decision-making responsibility. However, the study has presented the argument that if the teacher lacked knowledge of curriculum legislation, such legislative action could not be considered an impingement. The premise was also presented that if teachers lacked knowledge of legislation affecting teachers' curricular decisions, the decentralization of curricular decisions, as promised by California Senate Bill 1 in 1968, existed, although illegally. A lack of knowledge by teachers may be a result of default on the part of superordinates failing to insure that teachers were knowledgeable regarding such legislation.

It was determined by a panel of judges that respondents

must score above 15, or 70%, correct responses in order to exhibit possession of sufficient knowledge to make curricular decisions.

Comparisons are made as to the total mean scores of each group of participants. In addition, correct responses are compared as to curriculum component: *What?*—the intent of what is to be learned; *when?*—the organization of the learning; *how?*—the learning opportunities to be presented; and *how well?*—the evaluation of what has been learned. The item with the highest percentage correct for each population is shown, and the decision makers are ranked according to knowledge of present legislation. Finally, a comparison of the percentage of correct responses by decision makers and curriculum components is made.

In regard to the responses from the legislature, there were not enough for a valid sampling. Results are presented along with those of the other three groups—teachers, superintendents, and board members—with a caution that the sample for legislators was not adequate.

The study indicates a lack of adequate knowledge on the part of teachers concerning curriculum legislation. No teacher exhibited the knowledge deemed necessary for informed curriculum decision making as previously defined. A mean score of 7 on the part of teachers (compared to a required score of above 15 to exhibit knowledge) indicates that they do not know curriculum legislation. However, an examination of the other decision makers—board members with a mean of 7.0, legislators with a mean of 7.2, and superintendents with a mean of 12.4—indicates that the other decision makers also do not possess sufficient knowledge to make informed curricular decisions. A comparison of mean scores by decision makers shows that teachers compare favorably with board members and legislators and less favorably with superintendents.

This would indicate that more information regarding curriculum legislation designed to affect instructional decisions is reaching the superintendents than the others involved in the curriculum decision-making process. The superintendents state that their main source of such information is bulletins from their professional organizations. Evidently, the superintendents' organization, the Association of California School Administrators (ACSA), is more efficient in keeping their members informed of current legislation than are the superintendents in passing their knowledge on to their teaching staffs and boards. It would appear, also, that ACSA keeps the superintendents comparatively better informed than the legislative staffs keep the legislators informed of past and present educational legislation. It is reasonable to question whether it should be necessary for the professional organization to play this important role. One must ask: What is the responsibility of the legislature itself toward insuring the proper dissemination of information regarding educational legislation to those most concerned by such legislation? The study indicates that lines of communication between the legislature and the teacher are rather indirect and that no formal system of communication exists or is fully operational.

Letters from the respondents indicate that all but the teachers have ready access to copies of the Education Code and have the time and staff necessary for needed research of the Code as decisions might demand. It is less than rational to expect the teacher to request code research every time he makes a curricular decision such as a field trip.

As previously stated, the data indicate more information is reaching the superintendent (although through informal channels) than the other decision makers. However, communication among superintendents, teachers, and board members regarding curriculum legislation seems to be less than adequate. It can be argued that if all curriculum decisions are made by the district office, the teacher would not need to know the relevant legislation. However, if such an instructional-level decision was made by others and transmitted to the teachers, would not the teacher exhibit knowledge of this requirement by responding correctly to questions dealing with these curricular requirements? It seems evident that the teachers lack knowledge of the code requirements about curriculum as measured by this study, regardless of the source of such requirements.

An analysis of correct responses by component indicates

all four groups know more about *what* to teach than any of the other components but less about *when*. This means the respondents exhibit more familiarity with objectives than with the organization of curriculum. Forty-seven percent of all respondents were able to correctly answer questions based on code items relating to the intent of what is to be learned or objectives. The respondents were able to answer 40% of the questions based on code items relating to evaluation or *how well* the learning has taken place. There were 33% correct responses on questions relating to learning opportunities or *how* the learning is to take place. The respondents were able to identify only 25% of the items based on organization of the curriculum or *when*.

Using a correct score of 15 as determined by the judges as being representative of knowledge necessary for curricular decision making, only 4 respondents out of 375 exhibited that knowledge.

What do selected individuals involved in education know about legislation designed to influence curriculum decision making by teachers? None of those groups selected by the study exhibited knowledge of curriculum legislation judged necessary for informed decision making.[5]

In making a comparison of populations by the item of highest percentage correct, superintendents and board members were best informed about Item 15 which pertains to religion being taught in the classroom. One might ask: Does the fact that 93% of the superintendents know when reference could be made to religion indicate this an area in which the local communities exhibit a vital interest? Teachers know more about Item 7 which asks the amount of time required for the teaching of physical education prior to 1968. Legislators scored highest on Item 16 which referred to who should make the final determination of a grade. It is of interest that teachers knew more about an item of past legislation.

Overall, superintendents rank first with a mean score of 6.4 and teachers last with a mean of 3.6. Legislators are second with a mean score of 4.2 and board members third with a mean of 3.9. Clearly, superintendents are the most knowledgeable of present legislation pertaining to instruction, there being little difference among the other three groups.

Since the study shows that teachers lack knowledge of legislation designed to influence their curricular decisions, it can be assumed that such legislation is not restrictive. Consequently, true decentralization does exist as a result of default on the part of superordinates or ignorance on the part of the teachers. However, such decentralization is illegal in that the legislature, by passing laws in any area of educational decision making, assumes for itself the authority vested in the states, thus preempting the right of any agency subordinate to the legislature to make such decisions. If a teacher is making curricular decisions without possession of legislative knowledge, it can be argued reasonably that curriculum legislation does not preempt teacher accountability. It has been the position of many in the field of curriculum study that teachers should be held accountable only for those curricular decisions they should make.

It is the position of this study that limited knowledge on the part of teachers regarding legislation designed to affect their curricular decisions suggests that legislation does not make any significant impact on their instructional decisions. The teacher simply makes such decisions as if the legislation did not exist. However, the teacher's curricular decision making may be impinged upon by such legislation as he does know (as evidenced by a mean score of 7.0 for all teacher respondents as measured by the instrument). It is agreed that teachers should be held accountable for instructional-level decisions. However, a teacher's accountability is brought into question because of curriculum legislation which impinges on his freedom to make decisions. In addition, the teacher is accountable whether he or she knows the law or not. The problem is that the legislature has engaged in an inappropriate level of activity by making instructional-level decisions rather than societal-level decisions. Therefore, for what should the teacher be held accountable—decisions he is left free to make, those impinged on by legislative action, or both?

It is an assumption of the Goodlad Conceptual System that instructional-level decisions should be made by teachers. Data gained from this study show the legislature, by the sheer force of the number of code items it has passed affecting teachers' curricular decisions (64 from 1968 to 1970), has attempted to wrest this responsibility from the teacher. The teachers, as evidenced by their lack of knowledge of such legislation, have not surrendered all of their curricular decision-making responsibility to the legislature. Ironically, much of the teachers' freedom to make decisions, which probably should be theirs to make, is preserved because of their ignorance of the law. De facto decentralization in regard to instructional decisions appears to exist. Although this decentralization exists, the basis for its existence raises serious questions about how to implement current proposals regarding teacher accountability.

In regard to the possible effects of legislation, this study sustains the position of Griffin that teachers make most instructional decisions regardless of restrictions imposed through state legislation.[6]

This study brought forth a strong emotional response from a number of those asked to participate. The investigator feels a report of his findings would not be complete without the inclusion of some of these reactions.

A central thread ran through each group of responses. The teachers wrote notes of encouragement and said the study was long overdue. One urged that legislators' scores be published in the newspapers. One teacher tore his questionnaire to pieces after completing it and accused the investigator of being part of a plot to entrap the teachers headed by "the great black father" in his district. Still another wrote that information regarding curriculum legislation was very necessary to her decision making but she had to depend on her principal and he was not capable of furnishing the leadership. Another teacher wrote that the investigator had just put the "kiss of death" on the study by citing the district superintendent's approval to participate in the study. A number of the teachers assumed the investigator was well-acquainted with the district staff and stated that the investigator should be aware the superintendent was being fired. At least one teacher wrote pleading for help with what she considered more pressing problems.

Some board members wrote that they do not need to know anything about curriculum legislation, since they depend on the superintendent for their information. One wrote that if this was not forthcoming, they would fire the superintendent, which had just been done in his district. Board members also wrote that it was a simple matter to look up the proper code when necessary to gather information for a decision.

Comments from legislators ranged from wishing the investigator good luck and stating the code was a mess needing complete revision to charging that the study was a waste of time. One legislator wrote that the study caused him to fear for the future of education.

Several legislators wrote to question the basic premise of the study—the need for such knowledge. It was also stated that the investigator showed a colossal ignorance of the legislative process.

The initial response by the legislature was so small that a personal cover letter, another instrument, and a self-addressed, postage-paid envelope was again mailed to each member of the legislature.

This additional effort was rewarded by the receipt of one completed questionnaire, two letters, and one note saying the new questionnaire now resided with the original—in the recipient's wastebasket. A few legislators wrote that they were new and did not possess sufficient knowledge to attempt to answer the questionnaire. Most of the legislators signed their names to the letters or notes.

The most unusual response was from a member of the legislature who wrote that he would be successful in filling out the questionnaire because of his ability to do six things.

1. *See problems* clearly—analyze them.
2. Consider *all* alternatives.
3. Choose the *best* alternative.
4. Put this alternative into *action*.
5. *Check* it out.
6. *Change* if necessary.

This legislator's total score on the instrument was three.

The administrative assistant to one member of the legislature wrote that his employer was submitted to constant examination and to the equivalent of "finals" on each occasion of his election. In addition, whereas the legislator was willing to assist anyone in the pursuit of academic goals, he had no time for games. Needless to say, this legislator did not return a completed questionnaire.

The results of this study raise certain questions that deserve additional research. Some of these are as follows:

1. *Why did those selected not possess knowledge deemed adequate about legislation designed to influence teachers' curricular decision making?*

The study found that only 4 individuals out of 375 involved in the study exhibited knowledge determined by the judges to be sufficient to make informed curricular decisions. The judges determined the respondents should correctly answer 70% or more of the items contained in the instrument used in this study in order to be judged as having sufficient information. Before any remedies may be planned to rectify the situation, causes relative to the lack of knowledge should be determined. Is it conceivable that these decision makers do not consider this legislation important? Is there a breakdown in communications, or is teacher training and/or in-service education inadequate in this respect?

2. *Can a model of communication be developed which would serve to increase knowledge of curriculum legislation held by decision makers?*

Once a study has shown that the decision makers do consider this legislation to be important and the causes of this lack of knowledge determined, research which would evaluate different models and techniques designed to increase this knowledge would be of practical significance. As improved communication models or techniques are designed, an updated version of the instrument along with the procedures of this study could be used to evaluate their effectiveness.

3. *How much briefing do legislators receive when they are voting on new legislation pertaining to the curriculum?*

Written comments from legislators to this investigator disagree as to the effectiveness of staff briefings prior to a vote on curriculum legislation. It would be helpful to know the level of information regarding curriculum legislation the legislators themselves possess as they vote on new legislation.

The question asked by this study—What do selected individuals involved in education know about legislation designed to influence teachers' curricular decision making?—is part of the fabric of several possible major studies in this area.

Questions of importance include:

1. In what ways does curriculum legislation impinge on the rights of decision makers at the local level?

2. Are the responsibilities of all curriculum decision makers clearly defined?

3. Do legislatures concern themselves most with curriculum decisions considered the domain of professional educators?

4. Does the legislature spend more time on determining such things as the learning opportunities of the individual child than it does on setting educational goals (values) for all its citizenry? Which should it emphasize?

5. Do members of the legislature possess adequate information regarding curriculum legislation to enable them to act effectively on new legislation?

6. What should be the role of the legislature in curriculum decision making?

7. What is the effect of curriculum legislation on the schooling of children?

8. Can the schooling of California children be improved by use of more rational curriculum decision-making models such as the Goodlad Conceptual System?

In addition to the possible impingement on teacher decision making by legislation, other studies might reveal factors which tend to restrict decision making. These might be: (1) pressures from one's peers, (2) pressure from one's superordinates, (3) pressure from the community, (4) lack of expertise in curriculum decision making by the teacher, and (5) all curriculum decisions being made at the district level.

If, again, such curriculum legislation does not restrict teacher curricular decision making, the question may be asked—Has the decision-making process been sufficiently decentralized to allow teachers to be held accountable for their decisions?

If it is found that curriculum legislation does not preempt teacher curriculum-making responsibilities, the question must be asked, Do the local board of education, the superintendent, and his staff allow the teacher to make such decisions?

Studies should be initiated to determine for what curricular decisions each of the four decision-making groups should be held accountable.

The legislature is the major societal body in the states of the United States. As such, it should bear the major responsibility for making and disseminating societal-level decisions. Using the Goodlad Conceptual System as a guide, the legislature should make value decisions regarding what is good or bad. The legislature should decide such things as: Do we teach children to share or to compete? Do we prepare our high school graduates for a vocation? Do we provide adequate educational opportunities for all our citizens?

The legislature should see to it that its value judgments are disseminated. Local boards will interpret the values disseminated by the legislature according to local needs. The school system's instructional staff will develop a curriculum for all the children in the district based on these value decisions. Individual teachers will make instructional decisions based on the needs of the individual child.

In summary, there is much confusion on the part of all educational decision makers about curriculum legislation and its use in other kinds of curricular decisions. It is the responsibility of state legislators to make the entire decision-making process more rational. This can be done by passing a more simplified education code based on societal-level decisions, assuming the responsibility for the dissemination of information regarding the code, and insisting that decision makers abide by the code. But instructional decisions should be left to teachers who are close to the problems, interests, and concerns of students.

NOTES

1. John I. Goodlad, with Maurice N. Richter, Jr., *The Development of a Conceptual System for Dealing with Problems of Curriculum and Instruction*, Cooperative Research Program, USOE, Project No. 454, University of California, Los Angeles, 1966, p. 7.

2. These judges were Adrianne Bank and Kenneth A. Tye.

3. Items were field-tested with a person not specialized in education as a field of study; if the answer was readily apparent, the item was eliminated.

4. The judges were Samuel G. Christie, Carmen Johnson, and Sol Roshal.

5. The legislative sample was not large enough to be adequate.

6. Gary A. Griffin, *Curricular Decision-Making in Selected School Systems,"* unpublished doctoral dissertation, University of California, Los Angeles, 1970.

Institutional Decisions in Curriculum

ROBERT M. McCLURE

"Schooling," as Ralph Tyler has reminded us, "is a purposeful, human enterprise with consciously willed ends." Institutional curriculum planning is critical to the school because it brings programmatic coherence to the institution. The process calls for using data from a wide variety of sources and translating the information in ways that will improve those decisions that shape the institution. Good institutional curriculum planning improves the quality of decisions made by the teacher at the instructional level.

We are not as clear as we need to be, though, about those decision points unique to the institutional level, as Griffin has made clear. If we were dealing with easily observable relationships between input and outcome, this intermediate point could simply be described as a bridge. Many organizations have manuals which give specific guidance on how to bridge the gap between direction giving and implementation. These manuals provide for the organization's middle management standardized documents which reduce the aims of top management and governing bodies into operations that middlemen (such as foremen) can comprehend, act upon, and use to give supervision to workers.

Some hold that schools either do work in this manner or should do so. Witness, for example, the growing number of state or local mandated legal requirements purporting to bring about greater teacher accountability which are based on such a simple model. The processes by which the school is shaped must be based on a human dimension, however, and not on how-to-do-it production manuals which are appropriate only in organizations which differ significantly in purpose from the schools.

Teachers, curriculum specialists, principals, and others who are made responsible by the various governing groups for conducting school, must, in order to do so, translate societal expectations into institutional directives. These acts of translating require great skill because governing publics are not required to be articulate in their setting of purposes, nor are they always consistent in the clues they give the curriculum maker (see Chapter 4).

In this chapter topics related to institutional decision making are discussed in the context of two field studies. The topics on which these studies and this chapter focus include the nature of decisions appropriately made at this level, the matter of who should make such decisions using which sources of information, and an examination of some of the problems typically confronted by curriculum planners. The first study is from a school faculty as it worked on several curriculum development activities; the second is taken from a program in which a variety of school districts worked on institutional curriculum planning. One hopes these reports are typical enough of a broader reality to make such generalizations meaningful to others.

STUDIES OF CURRICULUM PLANNING AT THE INSTITUTIONAL LEVEL

Studies which move behind the scenes of planning in order to conceptualize the acts of curriculum building at the institutional level are needed for a clearer understanding of how to go about improving the processes of curriculum development. Such studies by their nature produce tentative findings, but in their breadth and tentativeness lies their significance. Curriculum development is a field of practice whose nature is too rarely explored and reported. Studies of the practical, that is, of the field at work, can contribute to greater understanding of the theoretical nature of curriculum planning. "It is this recourse to consequences, to action and reaction at the level of the concrete case," says Schwab, "which constitutes the heart of the practical."[1]

A School Faculty Engages in Institutional Planning

The University Elementary School (UES), the setting for one of the studies[2] used to develop the generalizations in this chapter, is the laboratory of the Graduate School of Education of the University of California, Los Angeles. The University's primary purpose for the UES is research and inquiry in education. The school is typical of a public school in two important respects: it has a student-teacher ratio not significantly different; it has a staff, though sophisticated, not significantly more educated than that found in the usual metropolitan elementary school. In terms of the conceptualization described in Chapter 1 of this publication, the school does differ in one significant way. UES is not faced directly with the problem of interpreting societal-level expectations into institutional purposes for the school. These functions are spelled out by the faculty of the Graduate School of Education and are represented in the person of the director of that school, a position somewhat different from that usually assumed by a superintendent. This is not, of course, to say that the faculty is unconcerned about community wishes. Interpretations of these expectations, as will be seen later, played an important role in the curriculum project they pursued.

During the time of this study there were twenty-seven teachers, some part-time, who met weekly in three groups for the purpose of dealing with basic school problems. These groups, usually called "units," were formed to correspond to the age levels of the children with whom the teachers worked—early childhood, lower elementary, upper elementary. The faculty was divided into these unit groups to solve problems related to their part of the school and to work on total school problems in smaller, discussion-oriented settings.

At the time of the study discussed here, the faculty was at work on the first phase of a two-year curriculum project which was ultimately to produce a redefined curriculum for the school. In this first phase, the three units worked independently on the development of institutional objectives, with each objective to indicate expected behaviors for learners in relation to specific content. Each objective was to be feasible for accomplishment at this school and the set was to be complete for the age span of children with whom teachers in the group worked. No directions other than these were given to the three groups except for some suggestions as to how an objective could be developed.

Three questions emerged as being important to the study conducted by these groups:

1. What curriculum procedures were used by the three faculty groups to develop their statements of institutional objectives?
2. What group problem-solving processes were evident as they worked?
3. Which procedures and processes produced the superior curricular product?

To answer the first question, the curriculum procedures used by the groups were described. The descriptions were based on a part of the curriculum rationale developed by Ralph Tyler.[3] According to Tyler, the curriculum maker has four basic tasks, regardless of the level at which he works. The first of these is the building of objectives for the curriculum. These objectives or statements of ends should be constructed in a systematic manner that consciously uses appropriate data sources about society, organized knowledge, and students. In order that objectives be useful in the remaining three tasks, it is important that they be stated in terms of the behavior which is expected of the learner and that they indicate the content or area of life in which that behavior takes place. In addition to preciseness in statement, educational objectives should meet the criteria of significance and attainability; that is, the ends selected for learners should be the most important ones out of all that could be chosen, and learners should be able to acquire the behavior implicit in the objective.

The other three tasks flow from, and are closely related to, the statement of objectives. These tasks have to do with selecting learning opportunities and appropriate materials for learners, the organization of these opportunities, and the selection of means of evaluation in terms of the objectives.

Based on Tyler's definition of the tasks of developing objectives, a content analysis was made of the faculty groups' meetings. The amount of attention given by the groups to eight tasks was recorded and the following description of each category was used.

Society. References to the nature of a local, regional, national, or worldwide society in the past, present, or future were scored in this category. Key words or comments were: church, economics, entertainment, needed vocational skills, local or national interests, skills, expectations, goal statements by local or national leaders, parent group expectations. If the group discussed what society should be like, the score was categorized under *Values.* If the discussion concerned the effect of society on students, it was placed under *Learner.*

Learner. Discussions about the nature of a child or a group of children were scored in this category. Key words or comments were: physical, mental, or social characteristics; abilities of a given child or group of children—needs, differences, likenesses; all manifestations of behavior caused by any outer source. If the group discussed what children of a given age or ability can learn, the score was considered to be *Psychology of Learning.* If descriptions were given about the child's performance relative to a specific objective, the score was placed in *Procedures* or under *Psychology of Learning.*

Knowledge. Discussion based on information about man's accumulation of organzied knowledge was scored in this category. Key words or phrases were: any of the recognized disciplines such as art, mathematics, language, history, science; the structure, concepts, generalizations, organizing threads, or big ideas in a field of study; the work of a subject matter specialist; the ways of knowing about a field. If a group discussed one of the other data sources, society for example, as a field of study for possible inclusion in the curriculum, it was scored in this category.

Values. "Should" questions, questions that revealed a discussant's value stand, were scored in this category. Key words or phrases were: good life, society, human being; the nature of man; priorities; point of view; philosophy. Discussions that related to feasibility usually were categorized under *Psychology of Learning.*

Psychology of Learning. When groups discussed the feasibility of a particular objective in terms of the learner, that discussion was classified in this category. Key words or phrases were: a particular subject can be taught at a certain age level; maturation; readiness; attainability.

Clarification of Statements. Attempts to state objectives were grouped in this category. Discussions about stating behavior and content and about precision of statement also were placed in this section. Key words or phrases were: define the term; What content would be used to produce that behavior? What would the learner do in order for this objective to be met? Discussions that related to evaluation of an objective were classified under *Procedures.*

Procedures. Scores were placed in this category if a discussion was based on one or more of the following topics: planning learning opportunities; selecting materials for instructional purposes; organizing educational experiences; evaluating learners in terms of objectives; determining ways in which this group will develop its statement of educational objectives.

Extraneous Other. Any comment that did not fit into one of the above seven categories was classified here.

To answer the second question about problem-solving processes and to look at roles related to them, the groups were observed using a standardized instrument—the Bales Interaction Process Analysis.[4] This system focuses on the descriptive and predictive rather than the prescriptive. It allows observation about problem-solving groups in regard to the manner in which they approach their task (giving or asking for suggestions, opinions, orientation) and the ways they work through their social-emotional problems (positively by showing solidarity, tension release, or agreement; negatively by disagreeing, showing tension, or antagonism).

The third question, of course, was the most difficult to answer because a judgment about a creative product was required. To determine which, if any, of the three groups developed a statement of institutional objectives superior to the other two, five judges, competent in curriculum development work, were asked to evaluate the statements. Three criteria were applied to each objective developed:

Precision—that is, did the objective clearly indicate the desired behavior of the learner and the area of content?

Significance—that is, is the objective the most important for children in our society and at this school?

Attainability—that is, is this objective suitable for the typical needs, abilities, and maturation of these students?

The three groups developed a total of 23 objectives and each was ranked on each criterion by the judges. Reliability was determined by the number of times that 4 or 5 judges were able to agree on a high or low ranking of an objective. The reliability level was .55.

Of the three groups observed, one was judged to have

produced a superior curriculum product based on all three of the criteria. Given that each group had generally the same resources and restraints to accomplish the tasks, the question then became, "What differentiated the group with the superior product from those with less adequate products?"

The study showed that the successful group followed a defined curriculum rationale more closely than did the other two, and that it gave special and careful attention to at least two sources of data usually considered relevant to the curriculum maker—the nature of the society from which the learners came and those learner characteristics which have essential relationships to the tasks of learning. The successful group also gave consideration, although not as much, to a third source of data, organized knowledge—that is to say, that portion of knowledge that made up the subject matter to be included in the curriculum. In addition to careful attention to "living sources of information"—their students and the community in which they lived—they also paid close attention to the literature and research finds about the nature of society and the learners of the age level for which the curriculum was being planned. The successful group made greater use of this kind of information and seemed to have the ability to synthesize it, to relate it to their practical problems of planning. No other group made such a conscious effort to utilize information from both their immediate surroundings and from the literature dealing with general topics about learning and teaching.

The successful group also proceeded to validate their objectives in a more consistent manner than did the others. In addition to informal discussions about values, for example, they consciously used their own defined set of values to establish priorities, limit the total range of objectives to a manageable number, and make objectives within their statement consistent with each other. There was a strong indication that the successful group was better able to do sustained work in the basic curricular tasks than were the other two groups.

It is also interesting that the successful group spent the

most time of the three groups on the total project—they worked harder and longer.

Table 5.1 summarizes the amount of time spent by the three groups in working on the various curricular tasks as each developed a statement of institutional purpose.

Problem-solving groups, according to Bales, the developer of the instrument used in this study, typically spend about one-third of their time dealing with social-emotional problems and about two-thirds in the task areas. As Table 5.2 shows, these three groups did not. Generally, their ratio of behaviors was about one-tenth spent in attempting to solve social-emotional problems and about nine-tenths in the task areas. That group which did produce the superior product, however, did devote slightly more attention to the social-emotional area than did the others. Interestingly, social-emotional behaviors were much higher for them in early meetings than in later ones—twenty percent of all acts in the first meeting, steadily dropping to nine percent in session nineteen, their last meeting.

Table 5.2 summarizes the percentage of time each group

Table 5.1. Percentage of Time Spent by the Three Groups in Discussing Various Curricular Topics

Nature of Topics Discussed	Group Producing Superior Product		Group Producing Least Adequate Product		Group Producing Moderately Adequate Product	
	Hours	Percentage of Time	Hours	Percentage of Time	Hours	Percentage of Time
Society	1.8	9.3	.7	4.0	2.8	16.2
Learner	4.0	20.3	1.0	6.0	3.5	20.1
Knowledge	2.5	12.8	1.3	8.2	1.3	7.7
Values	2.1	10.9	2.7	16.4	2.0	11.6
Psychology of Learning	1.9	9.7	1.2	7.4	1.1	6.4
Clarification of Statements	5.1	26.0	3.6	22.4	1.5	8.3
Procedures	1.6	8.1	3.5	21.2	3.0	17.4
Extraneous Other	.5	2.9	2.3	14.4	2.1	12.3
Total	19.5	100.0	16.3	100.0	17.3	100.0

Table 5.2   Percentage of Time Spent by Each Group in Problem Areas as Identified by Bales' Interaction Process Analysis Instrument

Problem Areas	Group Producing Superior Product	Group Producing Least Adequate Product	Group Producing Moderately Adequate Product
Task			
Communication	34	39	42
Evaluation	48	47	44
Control	2	4	3
Social-Emotional			
Decision	12	7	8
Tension Reduction	4	3	3

spent in solving various problems related to the task area and the social-emotional area. There is not a significant difference among the groups in the behaviors they exhibited in working on the development of their statements of objectives. Possibly an observational system that utilized process variables other than those in the Bales system would have produced different results.

There are, though, other process factors that characterize the successful group which were not revealed by the analysis system used in this study; these observations grow from studying curriculum developers as they work. For example, the successful group developed patterns of leadership unlike the others. One technique they used which produced high satisfaction for them was to consciously shift the assigned leadership role from person to person. The chief criterion as to who would be the leader for a meeting was who had the most informaion about the topic to be discussed that day.

Another observation was that participants in the successful group demonstrated in many ways their feelings of power to influence the school. Members of less successful groups just as clearly demonstrated their feelings of powerlessness in making a difference. This difference, of course, might not have existed if the faculty had been working on another kind of curricular task. Also, there is some evidence that members of the successful group understood each other better than did members in less successful groups. For example, they recalled what each other had said in previous meetings or built on the ideas of others in the group.

Finally, members of the group which produced the superior product perceived that there was a *high relationship between institutional planning and instructional activities;* members of the less successful groups did not see such relationships as clearly.

A School System Faculty Engages in Institutional Planning

In the study of a faculty group discussed above, a single school effort has been reported. In the Field Studies Program of the National Education Association's (NEA) Center for the Study of Instruction,[5] much attention was paid to helping teachers, principals, and other professionals sort out those critical areas requiring decisions and to dealing directly with questions of who should make what decisions for a school district.

Outcomes differed among the several sites in the Field Studies Program, but there is enough similarity to describe one project's work and assume it to be useful to others.[6] The work described here was conducted in Delano, California, by a system-wide curriculum council made up of teachers elected by colleagues from their building, principals, curriculum specialists, and other faculty members.

This group identified seven decision-making tasks which provided for them the critical links between the societal and instructional levels. These task definitions were arrived at by examining the ways in which other faculty groups worked, by studying the curriculum process literature, and, most importantly, by testing their work in pilot curriculum projects. These projects were in ecology, inquiry, and values clarification—areas that cut across traditional curriculum lines. The faculty's principal reasons for developing the decision-making plan was to help the community articulate its purposes for the schools and to create a method to help teachers improve their practice.

The decisions did not have to be made in the order described here, but later experience indicated that task number one should precede the others. As Buchanan points out in Chapter 6, suggested curriculum procedures do not have to be utilized in a linear, logical-deduction fashion but should serve as a framework upon which to build, organize, and validate curricular decisions.

The first task they identified at the institutional level called for *the selection of objectives which met identifiable learner needs.* Five criteria for acceptable statements of objectives were agreed to:

1.   Applicable to all or most learners in Delano;
2.   Defined in such a way that the learner's achievement toward the objective could be assessed;
3.   Be of such importance to an understanding of the field that further exploration was encouraged;
4.   That in a stated amount of time a learner could formulate a new attitude, develop a new skill, and/or acquire additional knowledge;
5.   Be possible to derive a learning activity from the objective.

In the plan which was prepared for teacher use, the faculty group gave several examples of what to them constituted useful objectives based on their pilot project experience. From the Ecology Project, for example, an objective at the institutional level was: "Student will demonstrate an understanding of the concept that there is interaction and interdependence among living and non-living things."

Before discussing other institutional-level decisions important to this faculty, it should be noted that they never worked in isolation at one level to the exclusion of another. At the instructional level, for example, the task related to the determination of objectives was to select objectives for a lesson for an identified group of learners. An example of an ecology objective which related to the institutional example above was: "Student will demonstrate an understanding of the interaction and interdependence of living organisms." At each decision point institutional and instructional tasks were described, parallel examples given, and procedures for accomplishing the task provided. At appropriate points, parallel societal-level tasks were also identified. The dynamics of interaction among the three levels is, this faculty group discovered, the key to constructive and lasting curriculum change.

The second institutional task was *to select alternative content or processes for an area of study.* Early in their three years of work, this faculty group became convinced (chiefly because of an outside consultant—a philosopher very much in touch with the problems of teaching) that the important learning outcomes had more to do with becoming skillful in the processes of learning, enjoying the process, feeling satisfied with oneself as a learner, and so on. Specific content, much of which would be out of date by graduation day, was less important to them. This point of view, which developed as the various projects were carried out, resulted in this second task being conceptualized as one of seeking content to fulfill objectives rather than having content be the only shaper of purpose.

Decision three was *to select a range of procedures and instruments to diagnose learners in an area of study, to evaluate learners in an area of study, and to assess the program.* This task definition is a good example of this faculty's insistence that the planning procedures relate directly to the jobs of teaching and learning. Across the United States as well as in Delano, the diagnosis of learning problems is a major instructional need of teachers.[7]

This group was determined that curriculum planning should include all dimensions of evaluation, not just the typical concerns for end-of-the-course tests. Among the criteria they spelled out for the institutional plans regarding assessment materials were:

1. Do they measure the stated objectives?
2. Do they meet the standard criteria for evaluation instruments, such as validity and reliability?
3. Are they practical—can they be managed in the classroom, can we afford them, and are they worth it?

4. Are a variety of devices and procedures provided, such as interviews, anecdotal records, standardized tests?

Sequencing of content, according to the Delano Council, was less important at the institutional level than at the instructional, but they did recognize that some attention to the task was necessary. Their fourth consideration then was *to select sequence of content and/or process for an area of study.* Because of their teaching experience, the group was wary of too much attention to decisions about sequencing which did not relate to the ability of the learner to negotiate his own sequences of learning. In the Inquiry Project, for example, they interpreted this institutional task at the instructional level by commenting, "In inquiry the sequence of the lesson is determined by each child. The teacher trained in inquiry will be able to respond appropriately to the student in finding his or her own best sequence."

In their fifth task they asked curriculum planners to attend to *selecting criteria for materials* and stressed in their pilot Ecology Project such criteria as the degree to which the material illustrates desired content; its authoritativeness; the suitability to maturation level of the learners; its flexibility to serve a variety of objectives; the availability of the material; its durability; and whether or not the district had enough money to buy it.

Two related tasks were emphasized in their sixth direction to institutional-level planners—*the selection of many learning opportunities and the selection of a variety of supporting materials.* Eight general learning activities were proposed to achieve one of the ecology objectives, for example, and forty kinds of supporting materials were recommended to teachers planning instructional programs at the instructional level. Teachers, then, could choose from these sources with some assurance that the employment of the teaching strategy and accompanying material would help to bring about the desired behavior contained in the objective.

The final institutional level task proposed by the Delano Council was *to construct options for the organization of teachers and learners.* Here the planners suggested a variety of arrangements—team teaching, some departmentalization in the elementary grades, individualized learning centers in open spaces, and so on—and suggested strong and conscious relationships among organizational patterns, purposes narrow and broad, and learner preferences. In the Inquiry Project, for example, they chiefly employed small groups or individual tutoring because their objective was for the individual child to determine his own best inquiry route.

It is important to remember that only a portion of the work of this group has been reported here. As they gained experience, participants saw that separating the various levels caused an unrealistic view of decision making, and they constantly tested decisions at the various levels against each other so as to validate them for all affected parties. Each of these seven decision-making tasks at the institutional level was accompanied by corresponding decision responsibilities at the societal and at the instructional levels.

Participants in the Field Studies Program were reasonably free to develop their curriculum-planning agenda. In each site there came to be a strong emphasis on giving greater attention to institutional-level matters because participants increasingly saw the relationship of decisions made at that level to the quality of instruction. This insight came about as they made decisions at the institutional level and implemented them in the pilot projects at the instructional level.

Open-ended questioning was the principal style used by the four continuing consultants to the project. This approach was deliberately selected to cause an increasing independence from the outsiders and more dependence on local solving of problems. Two comments about this way of working. First, participants, particularly during the early phases of the project, were frustrated and distrustful because of the open-ended questioning. Teachers perceive, often with reason, that they are only being involved because it is the "right" thing to do and that their work will not significantly affect the school. When they came to recognize that the consultants had no unrevealed agendas and that their work would have an impact, the process was accepted. At the end of three years, participants attributed much of the success of their work to this approach.

Second, this is not to say that the consultants to the project were empty-headed! For example, they put many questions to the participants which caused them to deal with system-wide data in new ways, or caused them to see clearer relationships between ends and means, or helped people develop their own rationale for problem solving. Also, some training in basic curriculum development was provided on request and was deemed important by participants because they saw a direct relation to the quality of the plans they produced.

At the conclusion of the three-year project in the site reported above, a formal assessment took place to determine its effectiveness in meeting the expectations of the several partners—the national association, the local school district, and the local teachers' association. The assessment was based on three of the goals that had been agreed to at the outset— to improve the quality of instruction, to give further definition to the role of the teacher in curriculum decision making both as an employee of the district and as a voluntary member of a professional association, and to develop an ongoing organization for curriculum renewal. Whenever possible, the assessment built on one that was administered at the beginning of the project so that changes of attitudes, new insights, and levels of commitment could be described.[8]

Two of the seven categories which made up the assessment seem instructive here. In the first, several questions led to an answer to the larger question. "What opinions are held about certain elements of curriculum planning?" In the initial prestudy, there was moderate agreement on the part of participants that the school system should have specified goals, that objectives for instruction should be stated in terms of student behaviors, that procedures of evaluation should require the same behaviors as the objectives, that activities and materials of instruction should be aligned with the objectives, and that the plan of organization should be in keeping with the goals. In the assessment made at the end of the project, participants had exceedingly strong feelings that these were important elements of curriculum planning and further felt that such elements were critical to a systematic program of instructional improvement.

A second category had to do with the participants' perceptions of the effectiveness of a system-wide faculty group being engaged in institutional curriculum planning. In this case there is marked evidence that participants in the project, over the three years, came to value some system-wide work and strongly felt that such work was critical to instructional improvements at the building level and in their classrooms.

These data regarding participants' perceptions about their work imply that teachers do want to be engaged in curriculum development efforts at the institutional level, that their reticence to do so in the past may have been based on their concern about lacking preparation to do the work and their feelings that their efforts would not have an impact. These critical concerns of teachers need to be dealt with openly and systematically as they were in the NEA Field Studies Program. When this occurs, it appears that change efforts will produce more lasting results.

INCREASING ATTENTION TO THE INSTITUTIONAL LEVEL

The weakest link in the well-established chain of educational decision making is at the institutional level, as Griffin's chapter reveals. To improve the capabilities of those who operate at this level to make important decisions, such as the seven described above, would be to make significant improvement in several dimensions of schooling. For example, an in-service education program designed by a school community intended to achieve a goal to which the group had committed itself would clearly be superior to those dismal efforts so often mounted by outsiders to "do good to others." Similarly, faculty-initiated curriculum improvement projects might have some staying power even though they would lack, at least at the outset, some elegance of design.

Our system of education, though, does not encourage a significant amount of institutional decision making. Boards of education, community groups with special interests, and

their immediate staffs—superintendents, assistant superintendents, curriculum directors, and the like—are attracted to
centralized systems of decision making. Teachers, on the
other hand, prefer (perhaps because of heavy student pressure
and previous lack of impact on the system) to "close their
doors and be about the business of teaching." The product
of this system is that essential, long-range decisions emanate
from the top and filter down to individuals who have difficulty
in seeing the relationship of those decisions to their own
perceived reality.

The UES study described above demonstrates the difficulty
and frustration of working at this level. New relationships,
many of them, have to be formed; products are difficult to
develop; rewards are delayed and in many cases never
realized.

Some propositions for practice have emerged from the
studies described here. These are based on certain assumptions about curricular decision making: that critical deter-
minations about learning and teaching are made at varying
distances from the learner and his teacher; that the patterns
of decision making which control the public schools do not
differ significantly from school to school, state to state, or
region to region; and that the processes of learning and
teaching suffer because of the size of gap that exists between
where a decision is made and where it is implemented.

The first proposition is that curriculum development groups
that have a planning model will produce superior plans—that
is, plans that cause more effective teaching and improved
learning—than will groups which proceed without a design.
In both of the studies reported here participants had a basic
commitment to a curriculum rationale which shaped their
work. A construct, whether it be the "Tyler Rationale" or
some other, gives curriculum planners the confidence to
move forward and be creative. Reports about the transient
nature of innovative programs reflect the lack of guiding
principles which a rationale can provide. Of particular importance, it appears, is that groups know how to systematically
identify and draw upon information about learners, their
society, and organized knowledge and have the skill to use
this information to build a program.

Also important to success is the need for sufficient time on a sustained, prolonged basis. Those groups in the studies described here which either had demonstrably better curricular products or perceived success *all* had large blocks of time which were provided as part of the working day, not, as Ole Sand used to say, "in after-school faculty meetings in which everyone quivers in unison!"

It appears as though curriculum-planning groups would improve their products if, in their planning, concurrent consideration was given to how to implement their decisions. No other single activity influenced the Delano faculty as much as their work in pilot projects which paralleled their institutional-level planning. Similar beneficial outcomes were reported by the UES faculty as they went about testing and implementing the institutional objectives they developed.

As they proceed in planning, curriculum makers must confront and answer to their satisfaction several questions about the nature of knowledge, values, who should learn what, and so on. Certainly, one of the most critical questions is, "What is the purpose of planning a curriculum?" Is it, as it came to be in some sites in the NEA Field Studies Program, to make the curriculum more explicit, more clearly understood by those who were to implement it, more effectively evaluated? Or, is the purpose of planning to better define and provide a setting in which youngsters can freely inquire into their environment? Or, is the response somewhere between those two points? Until a group has worked through the ramifications of choice, it will be indecisive about its direction and unable to focus on a definable end.

When a representative group of the faculty works on a curricular task, it often becomes isolated and out of touch with those for whom it is planning. This is particularly true when teachers are released from any contact with students for a prolonged period of time in order to plan. In the studies referred to here, curriculum-planning groups discovered the need to go into "tentative print" soon and often and share their work with colleagues.

Curriculum-planning groups, especially those new to the job, need to first focus on live instructional problems before they move to reports of studies made by others. So often a faculty group will flounder as it attempts to draw meaning from a sociological or psychological reference. At the same time community problems or student learning disabilities are being dealt with during the course of their work outside of the planning group. It is these live situations that should produce the heart of the data for the curriculum maker. Consultants to projects in the NEA Field Studies Program (thanks again to Ole Sand) often began their contact with a group by asking that participants list the answers to three questions: (1) "What is so good about this school or school system that you'd never want to change it?" (2) "What is clearly so bad that it ought to be changed immediately?" (3) "What is causing problems, but the solution is not clear and should be studied?" The answer to the third question often provided a starting point to help people clearly define their basic concerns and to begin to work on them. In a large number of cases, these basic problems were rooted in the institutional level and their solutions were to be found there.

There is inconclusive evidence about the relationship of group process to quality of product. Nevertheless, certain combinations of people work better together than do others. There are at least two critical variables related to problem-solving groups. The first is that *competence is important*—that groups which have able curriculum developers within them will produce products superior to those which do not. Surprisingly, the second proposition may be even more important: groups which perceive that they have the power to change the institution will produce products superior to those which feel powerless.

Finally, it must be said, based on many observations made possible by these studies, that nothing substitutes for a strong individual leader within the group—one who understands the nature of the task to be accomplished, can marshall the resources of the group to accomplish it, and has the energy to bring the job to completion.

Strengthening the capacity of the teachers, the principal, and others responsible for the schooling of a given group of students will not take place without the maintenance of a school climate which rewards such activity. It will be exceedingly difficult to convince those who operate at the societal level that all but the most general decisions about purpose, content, learning activities, evaluation procedures, curricular sequence, materials, and organization of teachers and learners are best made at the institutional and instructional levels—that is, close to where the learner and teacher are at work.

There are those who argue that teachers, principals, and others will be opposed to strengthening the institutional level of decision making. There is much to support that argument. Teachers have tended to be isolated from one another through devices such as graded groupings of students, self-contained classrooms, and departmentalization. Such instructional patterns do not foster collegiality and shared decision-making responsibilities. Another proposition, then, is that teachers will be motivated to take part in institutional curriculum planning if they see a clear and direct relationship between the results of that planning and their day-to-day teaching. Teachers should approach the task of institutional planning by asking the question, "What am I going to do with the youngsters for whom I am responsible?" rather than with, "What ends are we trying to attain?"

The American system of education as it is presently operated does not promote a high degree of institutional decision making. Our schools would be better if it did. Practices that bring about decentralized group decision making are on the upsurge in industry[9] (particularly in Eastern Europe and South America), in business, and in some schools.

The old basic research in social psychology[10] and many of the new studies in organizational or institutional psychology-sociology[11] point up the positive relationship of staffs participating in goal setting and their increased productivity because they have a commitment to purposes they have helped to identify and establish. Schools are complicated institutions; their problems will not go away through the application of simple mechanistic solutions. The problems need attacking at the level at which there is a reasonable chance of solving them. It has been proposed in this chapter that some very fundamental problems of schooling can be ameliorated by skillful attack from collegial action at the institutional level.

NOTES

1. Joseph J. Schwab, *The Practical: A Language for Curriculum*, National Education Association, Washington, D.C., 1970, p. 29.

2. Robert M. McClure, "Procedures, Processes, and Products in Curriculum Development," unpublished doctoral dissertation, University of California, Los Angeles, 1965.

3. Ralph W. Tyler, *Basic Principles of Curriculum and Instruction*, University of Chicago Press, Chicago, 1950.

4. Robert F. Bales, *Interaction Process Analysis: A Method for the Study of Small Groups*, Addison-Wesley, Reading, Massachusetts, 1950.

5. Much of the material reported here is excerpted from "A Decision Making Plan," produced in 1972 by the CSI Council, Delano, California, Public Schools. Single copies, if available, can be obtained from the Council by writing to them through the Delano Public Schools. Material (all of it unpublished) about the other five sites is available from Instruction and Professional Development, National Education Association, Washington, D.C.

6. Other sites included local education associations and school districts in Anniston, Alabama; Fountain Valley, California; Easton, Pennsylvania; Palos Verdes, California; and Schenectady, New York.

7. National Education Association, "Finding Out What Teachers Want and Need," *Today's Education: The Journal of the Association*, vol. 61, no. 7, October 1972, pp. 31–35.

8. The first assessment work was done by Arlene Payne in 1968 and the report of the results of that study is no longer available. It is referred to, however, in the report, "The Analysis of Assessment Questionnaire, CSI Field Studies, Delano, California, May 1971" (mimeographed, 29 pp.), prepared by Barbara Peterson and Gary Griffin, which is available in limited quantities from Instruction and Professional Development, National Education Association, Washington, D.C.

9. David Jenkins, "Democracy in the Factory," *The Atlantic Monthly*, vol. 231, February 1973, pp. 78–83.

10. For example, Kurt Lewin, "Group Decisions and Social Change," in Maccoby, Newcomb, and Hartley (eds.), *Readings in Social Psychology*, 3rd ed., Holt, Rinehart & Winston, New York, 1958.

11. For example, Gordon L. Lippitt, Leslie E. This, and Robert G. Bidwell, Jr., *Optimizing Human Resources*, Addison-Wesley, Reading, Massachusetts, 1972.

6

From Institutional to Instructional Decisions

EDITH A. BUCHANAN

As teachers strive to provide good learning experiences for children, they are faced with ever-recurring situations demanding educational decisions. What learning opportunities should be provided? Which decisions should children make and which ones should teachers make? How much time and effort and what kinds of materials should be devoted to each area of the operational curriculum? Along with these somewhat general concerns come the more specific problems of planning instructional activities for a particular child with his unique set of abilities, achievements, and interests. Small wonder that so many teachers, schools, and districts have selected prescribed instructional recipes which remove all but the most routine decisions from the teachers' domain. Without reasonably consistent value positions, clear-cut allocation of responsibility, and provision for time and assistance with instructional tasks, rational curriculum decision making loses out by default.

But even if supportive conditions do exist, is it realistic to expect teachers to participate in, and contribute to, curriculum development? What are some of the difficulties to be encountered in such activity? Does involvement in the process increase teachers' understanding and commitment to educational goals? What outcomes might be expected, and will the value of these outcomes compensate for the time, energy, and resources spent in the process?

This chapter attempts to shed some light on these questions as they relate to the particular curriculum development undertaken in the Early Childhood Unit of the University Elementary School, University of California, Los Angeles. The process, the enlightenment and frustrations of the participants, and the products and outcomes are described, primarily as these relate to the formulation of institutional goals, the clarification of instructional requirements, and the emergence of new programs.

At the time the project was begun, the University Elementary School was organized into graded, self-contained classes from kindergarten through grade six with a nursery school for three- and four-year-olds. Prior to the early 1960's, the Early Childhood Unit consisted of three nursery and two kindergarten groups and was, in many ways, an exemplary child-centered school. As in most child development nursery schools, the major emphasis was on social and emotional development,[1] and although teachers were familiar with the work of Freud, Erikson, Gesell, and Montessori, among others, no one theory or philosophical position explicitly governed their work. Consistent with extant practice, children were grouped into age-segregated classes, all of which offered a similar array of materials commonly found in schools for young children. Paints, clay, and blocks were supplemented with tricycles, climbing apparatus, and sandboxes out of doors.

The apparent similarity of the room environments was deceptive, for at that time there was no formal coordination among classes. It was their desire to build consistency and continuity that led the teachers to schedule meetings for several hours each week to deal with immediate problems related to the conduct of educational programs for young children. They dealt with questions such as, "Should children have the option of choosing to spend the entire morning out of doors or should they be required to spend part of each day in the room? Should reading be taught to four- and five-year-olds? Which instructional group is most appropriate for a given child?" Knowledge of these particular children and of children in general was utilized in making decisions, but suggestions and solutions were of an intuitive nature rather than the result of any systematic process. Even though personal assumptions, values, and goals were, no doubt, inherent in the intuitive responses, they were not at a conscious level, and no conceptual or curricular framework provided explicit goals against which to validate decisions.

It was at this point that John Goodlad, the newly appointed director of the University Elementary School, and Louise Tyler, Professor of Education, joined the group as consultants, instructors, and guides. Primarily they served two basic functions. The first was to question and extend the teachers' assertions, suggestions, decisions, and solutions with an ever-recurring "Why?" Later they acquainted the group with Goodlad's conceptual framework and guided them in its use as the teachers struggled to build a framework within which to systematize curricular decisions.

Three major questions guided the conduct of the weekly meetings: "What is being done?" "Why is it important?" and "What evidence do you have as to the effectiveness of what is being done?" Questions such as "Why do you have a sandbox?" and "Why do you have guinea pigs, ducks, and other animals at school?" were provocative and evoked a variety of answers. For example, animals were seen as important because they help children learn to value life and living creatures or because children enjoy having something smaller than they are which they can control. These answers led to other questions: "How does having animals lead to valuing life?" or "Why is it important for children to control something?"

Many frustrating sessions were spent in such discussions focused on the *reasons behind* decisions which were being made, and many resulted in circular reasoning and justification. It soon became evident to the teachers and consultants that in many instances no clear rationale governed teachers' conduct of school and their selections of activities, materials, and procedures. The teachers frequently became defensive, rationalizing their actions with statements of faith, dogma, or accepted practice—"Everybody has a sandbox!" Occasionally their discomfort led to the suspicion that these experts surely knew the answers and were trying to elicit from them the "correct" responses. However, as teachers studied transcripts of recorded weekly sessions, they began to realize that the persistent questioning was designed to promote thinking about their implicit values, goals, and motives. Communication improved and the task of rational curriculum building began in earnest.

The most important source of data for the work of this group was the learners themselves, especially since the teachers were already deeply involved in observing and interacting with them daily. To facilitate their work, individual teachers took on specific assignments to be completed between meetings, and their findings were shared with the group. Teachers prepared detailed descriptions of the characteristics of the children in each group and researched current literature for further information which would be useful in establishing priorities for educational and developmental goals. One specific task was gathering detailed descriptions of those children in each group who appeared to be thriving in the school setting. By contrasting their characteristics, abilities, and behavior with children identified as experiencing some difficulty, several positive differentiating behaviors were revealed. From these the teachers made the following generalizations about successful functioning in school:

1. The child enters the school situation with minimal anxiety—he separates comfortably from his parents or other significant adults.
2. The child knows his own strengths and weaknesses; he knows those things he does well and those with which he has difficulty.
3. The child does many things for himself; he manages clothing, takes care of bathroom needs, etc.

4. The child controls impulses well enough to manage in a group situation. (This may be a very small group and only for a short period of time.)

5. The child expresses feelings and ideas spontaneously and in appropriate ways.

6. The child masters basic skills of moving and manipulation; he walks, runs, jumps, hops, and manipulates objects and instruments (e.g., crayons, paint brushes, puzzles).

7. The child listens to and follows simple directions; he speaks clearly enough to be understood.

These generalizations later were further refined into the following descriptive statements of behavior:

1. The child trusts himself and others.

2. The child is gaining a realistic concept of himself, his personal attributes, strengths, and limitations.

3. The child is gaining independence, self-reliance, and self-control.

4. The child is spontaneous in expressing his feelings and ideas.

5. The child interacts with his environment as he tests and defines reality.

If, indeed, these behaviors were indicators of successful school performance, they suggested new questions. The teachers wanted to know the extent to which the school could influence attainment of these behaviors, whether they could be measured, and whether early measurement would have predictive value. In other words, would it be possible to rate incoming children on these characteristics, and would these ratings prove useful in identifying children who were likely to profit from the school experience as now provided and children who could be expected to experience difficulty? The group set about formulating a behavioral observation and rating instrument for preliminary assessments. After many trials and modifications, an instrument (see pp. 169–175) was developed which proved useful in predicting school adjustment and identifying those children who would need special help in coping with school. The teachers assumed throughout that problems in coping might very well be because of problems inherent in the school environment rather than in the child.

The instrument was useful in other areas, too. For one thing, it helped teachers to focus their teaching on those specific behaviors which were viewed as indicators of a successful performance. It also provided them with baseline data against which to compare a child's later behavior. In the long run, however, the most important effect of the instrument was that, from it, four categories were identified which became the initial framework for improving the early childhood curriculum: Response to Self, Response to Adults, Response to Children, and Response to Materials and Ideas. A fifth category, Response to Group, was added later. These five major areas and their extension into programs are dealt with later in this chapter.

Even though the learners themselves were the most important data source, information from both society and subject matter also had an influence on these curricular decisions. The primary functions of the University Elementary School are innovation and experimentation in educational practices, and its accountability is to the director who is, in turn, responsible to the Graduate School of Education and the University. Even so, it was viewed as important for teachers to be aware of, and to give thoughtful consideration to, the concerns of parents regarding the education of their children. For example, parents frequently expressed the opinion that instruction in academic skills was important, especially early instruction in learning to read. It was up to the teachers to weigh the value of reading instruction against their other goals. They invited a reading specialist from the University to share his knowledge and opinions on the subject and also to suggest other resources which would further their knowledge of children's development in language and reading. As a result, several language and pre-reading goals were formulated and, ultimately, a self-selection reading plan was incorporated into the Early Childhood Unit.[2]

In addition, teachers became acquainted with other relevant subject matter literature and research into child development, especially the work of Jerome Bruner, Jean Piaget, and Lev Vygotsky. Each teacher selected a particular source of ideas to summarize for the group and all joined in attempting to relate the readings to curriculum building. Relating the theories and research of scholars to their own observations and knowledge of children was a difficult undertaking, and frequent lengthy discussions focused on attempting to apply various conceptual schemes to the formulation of instructional programs.

Among developmental tasks identified as critical in a child's early years is the structuring of an identity—a way of viewing self. The child development literature stresses that such factors as the child's perception of his role in the family, his sex, and his personal strengths and characteristics are of vital importance in the formation of an internalized concept of self. Whether an individual views himself as competent and acceptable affects his willingness to reach out to new experiences with relative security. In a circular fashion, those things he learns to do well support and enhance his feelings of competence. Working from such assumptions, the group identified the overarching goal for each learner in the Early Childhood Unit to be the development of a wholesome self-concept. Other objectives were to be included or excluded according to their relationship to this goal.

The next task was to identify attributes which appeared to support self-acceptance and feelings of worth. The following were selected: skill in physical movement—the child could run, jump, climb, paint, build, and draw; he could manage his own clothing and bathroom needs; he requested and accepted help from adults in a balance of dependence and independence; he sought out or accepted other children in his work and play; generally, he was accepting of his own feelings—not only happy "good" feelings but also anger, disappointment, and fear. The five categories of the rating instrument were viewed as supporting the self-concept goal and thus became the framework for organizing instructional objectives and providing a way of looking at children. The wording was changed from *response* (response to self, response to adults, etc.) to *relationship* (relationship to children, etc.) in an attempt to communicate an interaction—a dynamic process—rather than a static set of intended behaviors.

The next step was to delineate the major objectives for each of the five categories. The result was an outline of the Early Childhood Curriculum.

RELATIONSHIP TO SELF

Independence in personal tasks
  Dressing and undressing
  Toileting and handwashing
  Caring for personal property

Physical movement
  Basic movement skills—walking, running, hopping, skipping, climbing
  Manipulative skills—painting, drawing, building

Acceptance and expression of feelings
  Expresses positive and negative feelings in appropriate ways

Self-control
  Manages his behavior consistently enough to function in a group setting
  Persists in completing a task
  Makes choices from specified alternatives
  Attempts to solve situational problems

RELATIONSHIP TO ADULTS

Accepts and utilizes adults as sources of support, guidance, and control

RELATIONSHIP TO CHILDREN

Works and plays cooperatively

Contributes ideas and helps in work and play situations

Incorporates ideas and help from others in his work and play

Settles differences by talking it over

RELATIONSHIP TO GROUP

Cares for and shares group property

Observes school boundaries

Participates in group activities

RELATIONSHIP TO OBJECTS AND IDEAS

Selects and uses a variety of materials, objects, and apparatus

    Manipulable materials—paint brushes, crayons, scissors, etc.

    Malleable materials—clay, sand, play dough

    Construction materials—wood, blocks, etc.

    Interpretive materials—dramatic play, rhythm instruments

Formulates and expresses ideas and concepts related to experiences with materials and objects

In daily practice, these goals helped teachers to determine how well a child was doing, but they were of little use in determining en-route behavior for those learners who had not mastered the stipulated optimal level. Knowing that a child could not write his name did not necessarily indicate the instructional steps to be taken, for children who were unable to meet a given criterion were not all at the same level of achievement, nor did they have the same needs. One child might have the fine motor skill to control the writing instrument but not know which symbols make his name. Another might know all of the symbols but lack the control to write them. To remedy this gap, the teachers undertook extensive observation of children and analyses of criteria and thus were able to specify representative behavioral levels and to arrange them into hierarchies or continua. The levels were stated as a series of steps in which the last step was the final one toward which the planning and teaching were to be directed. Following are examples taken from each category:

RELATIONSHIP TO SELF

Caring for personal property.

    1.   Identifies personal belongings as his.

2. Is unable to locate own belongings when needed; asks others to put things in his locker for him.

3. Verbalizes way to care for property in response to teachers' questions; cries or otherwise expresses objections when others use his belongings which he has left around room or yard.

4. Usually puts sweaters, jackets, or shoes in locker; may leave personal toys around room.

5. Keeps personal belongings in locker unless in use by self or on loan to others.

RELATIONSHIP TO CHILDREN

Works and plays cooperatively.

1. Plays in solitary fashion (contact with peers limited to physical).

2. Plays on parallel level or watches on periphery of activity.

3. Plays on associative level with some verbal or nonverbal interaction. Initiates some verbal contact with peers.

4. Engages in play with one or more peers.
    a. Communicates ideas to one or more peers.
    b. Defends himself verbally and/or physically when attacked or limited by peer(s). (May become upset when his efforts for solutions fail.)

5. Plays on cooperative level. Able to maintain sequential play, incorporating others' ideas and help.
    a. Communicates agreements and disagreements, usually in a verbal fashion (settles differences with others by talking it over).
    b. From time to time refuses to participate in activity suggested by another child. (Is able to withstand pressure when he is involved in his own pursuits.)

RELATIONSHIP TO MATERIALS AND IDEAS

Selects and uses a variety of materials, objects, and apparatus.

1. Makes no observable reaction to materials.

2. Watches materials being used.
   a. Makes no overture toward or against materials.
   b. Uses materials only at teacher's request.
   c. Easily frustrated by failure or lack of skill.
3. Resists using materials by physically moving away or verbally refusing.
4. Chooses from a limited number of activities.
   a. Selects only from a narrow spectrum of materials but is involved with them.
   b. Uses many materials with surface involvement.
5. Makes choice of material independent of teacher suggestion.
   a. Works with involvement for at least ten minutes.
   b. Cleans up after task is completed.
   c. Chooses a variety of material and apparatus; may use in creative way.

RELATIONSHIP TO ADULTS

Utilizes adults as sources of support, guidance, and control.
1. Avoids contact with adults or demands excessive contact.
   a. Refuses to interact with teacher on verbal or nonverbal level.
   b. Ignores or rejects adult suggestions or offers of conversation.
   c. Insists on nearness to or help from adult. Demands teacher attention by repeated verbal or physical contact.
2. Complies positively to adult direction.
3. Sometimes resists adult help, guidance, or limitation (verbally or physically).
4. Makes contact with adults.
   a. Responds to verbal contact from adult.
   b. Initiates some conversation and physical nearness.
5. Seeks or accepts appropriate adult guidance, limitation, or comfort.

a. May request explanation for limitation or protest his dislike but complies when reasons are made clear to him.

b. Takes positive action in response to teacher directions.

c. Comfortable with adults; "gives and takes" easily with adults.

RELATIONSHIP TO GROUP

Cares for and shares group property.

1. Identifies materials, equipment, and space that are provided for the group.
2. Uses group materials without damaging or destroying them. May leave materials for others to put away.
3. Shares or takes turns with materials, equipment, and space that are provided for the group.
4. Puts group materials away when he is finished with them.
5. Assists at group cleanup beyond his own personal work place.

Obviously, not all readers will agree with the hierarchy selected by this group of teachers. For example, many teachers have questioned the placement of "complies positively to adult direction" at a level before "sometimes resists adult help." This placement reflects the bias of the teachers in the unit and their feeling that a child who has the strength (courage) to resist the adult is further along in his identity development than one who always complies positively without questioning or resisting.

These behavioral descriptors were taken to the classrooms where, through systematic observation, the teachers were able to locate the point on a continuum which described a child's characteristic level of functioning at any given time and then plan strategies for helping him move toward the stated objective. In addition to guiding instructional decisions, the continuum served as a criterion model for recording and evaluating a child's performance and progress.

As teachers worked with the objectives and continua, it became clear that evaluation was no longer a separate element but was embedded in the observation and instructional process. At any time it was possible to discern a child's achievement relative to specific objectives. This was true for en-route behaviors as they appeared on a continuum as well as for terminal behaviors. This information provided a profile on each child and was an invaluable resource in conferring with parents.

Although the curriculum-building work of the Early Childhood Unit is the major focus of this chapter, the unit's work did not occur in isolation but was related to the total curriculum efforts of the school. The other units, Lower Elementary (corresponding approximately to first, second, and third grades) and Upper Elementary (corresponding approximately to fourth, fifth, and sixth grades), also were engaged in examining and evaluating current practices and in formulating goals for their pupils. Occasionally, two or more groups arranged to combine meetings when their interests were the same or when they needed information about the characteristics and expectations of another level. The Early Childhood staff met most frequently with the Lower Elementary, often with only those teachers who would receive children next as they moved through the school. In addition, a "math task force," made up of representatives from each unit, worked on preparing a math curriculum for the entire school.

Besides working as units and task forces, the total faculty met on curriculum matters from time to time. Some of these meetings were devoted to discussion of curriculum theory and practice with Goodlad. Others dealt with problems common to all groups; relevant information was shared. Probably the most productive total faculty efforts were the off-campus, three-day retreats which were held once a year. These sessions afforded the participants an opportunity to meet both formally and informally without the pressures of school responsibility. The circulation of a predetermined agenda meant that individuals could read, or in other ways prepare in advance, in order to make the most of the conference time. Meeting days were organized into both large- and small-group work sessions, sometimes with outside consultants who offered information or inspiration. The composition of the work groups was determined by the agreed-upon task.

It was primarily at these retreats that goals for the school's three units were examined for intergroup consistency as well as congruence with institutional aims and values. Both institutional and instructional objectives were revised, refined, and extended through the interaction of the various groups. For the Early Childhood Unit, this work resulted in the following set of institutional objectives for children:

1. To relate to teachers as individuals and to accept teachers as sources of support, control, and guidance.

2. To develop the ability to communicate effectively.

3. To develop an attitude of inquiry about the world. To be persistent in learning and to search for meaning. To develop skills in ways of learning more about the world.

4. To utilize fundamental movement skills with control and mastery (running, jumping, walking, climbing, balancing, skipping, hopping); to develop eye-hand coordination in manipulation of small objects (pencils, crayons, beads, pegs, puzzles, blocks, scissors); to utilize fundamental skills of perception.

5. To use the essential processes of conceptualization (associate ideas, classify, generalize, draw logical conclusions).

6. To relate to peers as individuals; accept differences and similarities in children (needs, interests, skills, strengths). To recognize the effect of one's behavior on others and others' behavior on one's self.

7. To relate to one's self as an individual; to develop self-appraisal, self-reliance, and self-control.

8. To recognize and accept the limitations, privileges, and responsibilities of being a member of a group; to understand that these limitations, privileges, and responsibilities are flexible, according to the situation; to understand that group living creates a need for rules.

The above list represents generalized objectives extrapolated from the major objectives found in the five categories of the Early Childhood Curriculum. Each unit of the school contributed institutional objectives which were examined for consistency with institutional aims and values, evaluated as to feasibility and, in some cases, restated. These became elements of the curriculum guide to institutional curriculum planning (see Chapter 5).

This brief description does not do justice to either the curriculum as it was developed and conducted or to the time, thought, trial, and revision that occurred over a period of several years. Neither does it communicate the agonies and the ecstasies experienced by all the participants. This was a dynamic process of reaching out, stretching, consolidating, and internalizing. There were long, heated discussions aimed at clarifying and resolving differences. The excitement which accompanied the occasional "ah ha" phenomenon was equaled only by the despair felt when it seemed no amount of effort was enough to resolve an impasse. And what is there to show for the considerable investment of time and effort? Tangible products are few. Teachers are not noted for their inclination to record their knowledge and experiences in print. Still, some rather important things happened; the effects of the project spun off in a variety of ways over a period of time. To recount some of them may illustrate the benefits derived from this attempt to relate theory and practice, process and product.

The reader will recall that this chapter began with a brief description of the University Elementary School as it existed at the time this work began. To reiterate briefly, the school was organized into self-contained graded classes where an activity-oriented discovery approach to learning was the predominant mode. Consistent with this structure, in the Early Childhood Unit children were placed in one of the five classrooms on the basis of their age, and each of five teachers was responsible for her own group. No explicit goals or guidelines were in evidence.

Against this description, let us examine some of the changes emerging from the activities of the curriculum groups. One of the first innovations resulting from the curriculum work and careful observations of children was the early childhood self-selection reading program referred to earlier in this

chapter. As teachers began to look at children's development—academic, social, and personal—it became clear that
some children of four and five were ready and eager for
reading instruction. Because a move to the first grade might
not be appropriate at this time for other reasons, the teachers
designed an experimental summer project combining two
classrooms to accommodate twenty-six pupils from four to six
years of age. One room was designated as the "reading room"
while the rest of the environment remained unchanged.
Pupils could elect to go to the reading room where instruction
was tailored to their needs and interests, or they could choose
to stay in the more traditional environment. Twenty-three of
the twenty-six children asked for reading instruction, and
most showed marked gains in reading accomplishment over
the six-week session. The program was considered a success
and as a result, self-selection reading was included as part of
the kindergarten program in the fall and still remains a part
of the Early Childhood Curriculum.

Probably the most significant change in the school was the
replacement of the age-related classroom organization with
a multi-age nongraded organization where decisions were
made on the basis of individual needs rather than graded
expectations. This innovation started in the Early Childhood
Unit, where children were first permitted and then encouraged to "visit" groups older than their own.[3] As teachers
observed their own students and those from other classes
against the framework of emerging program criteria, they
noted the wide divergence of behaviors within a group and
the overlap and similarities between groups. Some four-year-
olds already had achieved most of the objectives designed
for children a year or more older, while others still had a
long way to go. Obviously, factors other than age must be
considered in determining the best program and placement
for a pupil.

Previously, when making placement decisions for those
children who had attained or were nearing their sixth birth-
day, there were only two alternatives available, both of them
first-grade classes. Now teachers recommended removing
grade labels and making placement decisions based on

specified identifiable needs and abilities. For example, some youngsters might need additional time in the Early Childhood Unit. They might be making satisfactory academic progress but perhaps needed time and guidance in achieving personal or social growth. Although some of them could already read and write, they had not mastered the relationship-to-self and the relationship-to-children goals which the Early Childhood Unit was uniquely designed to promote.

Whatever the placement, it now became the manifest responsibility of the teachers to provide for the individual needs of each pupil, not as a first-grader or a six-year-old, but as a unique person with identifiable competencies and needs. This change did not take place all at once, nor was it made without stress and uncertainty for both teachers and parents. However, within a few years the entire school was changed into nongraded, multi-age classrooms. At any given time, there were at least three possible placements within the school for any given child and the teachers who knew him best conferred to make the decision as to which of these was the most appropriate.

A more recent development growing out of the continuing process of curriculum development was the exploration of "movement" as an intervention procedure. This came about after a long period of attempting to clarify and refine affective or expressive behaviors described under Relation to Self (expresses feelings appropriately, etc.). Each year a number of children were identified as unable to express their feelings appropriately, leading teachers to look for some means of altering this aspect of their behavior. Such things as talk groups, dramatic play, and rhythmic expression were tried and discarded as ineffective. Finally, with the help of Professor Valerie Hunt, a program of "movement behavior" was designed as an intervention possibility. Although the theory and rationale behind the movement behavior program are not within the scope of this chapter, it can be summed up briefly as an attempt to reinforce a child's perception of his own incoming sensation and to legitimize his sensations through language. A film was made illustrating the movement curriculum in action, and two research studies were initiated to answer the question of effectiveness.[4,5,6] Movement continues as a prescription for certain children in the Early Childhood Unit and has been incorporated into other units of the school as well.[7]

One of several studies summarizes some of the results of these years of curriculum involvement as they affected the ultimate clients—the children. In 1970, Charles Ray Williams compared six- and seven-year-old children who had been in the University Elementary School two years or more to a group attending neighborhood schools who had applied for admission.[8] Since the five categories of objectives comprised the major emphasis of the Early Childhood Unit, they were included as primary variables to be measured. Included also were the stated objectives of the other schools, primarily reading readiness skills, handwriting, and mathematics. The results of this study showed the UES subjects scored significantly higher on all variables. Williams commented:

A major difference in the programs of the two institutions involves the specificity with which the goals and objectives of the University Elementary School program are stated contrasted with the very general, and often only implied, goals for the public school kindergarten. Interviews with the teachers in both programs seem to indicate that teachers in the kindergarten program do not see objectives as being as important as do teachers in the University Elementary School program. Teachers in the University Elementary School program can readily state the objectives of their program and classroom activities are planned around these objectives. Most teachers in the kindergarten program cannot state the objectives of their program and often express the opinion that objectives are not necessary for kindergarten children or that objectives already exist in the mind of the "good" teacher.

This chapter has described rather briefly the ongoing process of curriculum development as it occurred in the Early Childhood Unit of the University Elementary School, citing some of the outcomes directly attributable to that process. Instead of continuing the intuitive, trial-and-error, or recipe-book instruction, teachers learned to utilize curriculum theory, concepts, and processes in addressing the questions and problems which confronted them in their work. They developed a framework and objectives to guide them in making decisions and to serve as means for validating those decisions. Problems were not solved "once and for all," for that is not the nature of school or of life. Rather the resolution of one problem led to increased insight, knowledge, and commitment to be applied in dealing with each new problem. The time, effort, and involvement invested in the project paid dividends in the significant professional development of the teachers involved and the positive effects of their work on the training of new teachers and the schooling of each new wave of children. Succeeding pages provide the instrument developed by them and used to diagnose a child's school adaptation, provide special learning opportunities, and revise the School's program.

Pupil's Response to Adults

	Never	Rarely	Occas.	Usually
Brings ideas to teacher	0	1	2	3
Checks ideas with teacher	0	1	2	3
Requests information from teacher	0	1	2	3
Verbal interaction with teacher	0	1	2	3
Physical interaction with teacher	0	1	2	3
Attempts to control adults	3	2	−1	−3

Pupil's Response to Adults (cont.)

		Separation from mother	Separation from father	Separation from Significant Adults	Separation from teacher	Actions toward teacher	Feelings toward teacher				
Assertively	+1										
Cooperatively	+1										
Happily	+1										
Independently	+1										
Readily	+1										
Serenely	+1										
Anxiously	−1										
Fearfully	−1										
Hostilely	−1										
Indifferently	−1										
Placatively	−1										
Dependently	−1										
Resistently	−1										
Tentatively	−1										

Pupil's Response to Peers

	Never	Rarely	Occas.	Usually
Requests information from peers	0	1	2	3
Offers information to peers	0	1	2	3
Brings ideas to peers	0	1	2	3
Checks ideas with peers	0	1	2	3
Reacts to peers as persons	0	1	2	3
Interacts with peers	0	1	2	3
Leadership of peers	0	1	2	3
Accepts ideas of peers	−3	−1	3	−3
Reacts to peers as objects	3	2	−1	−3
Withdraws from peers	3	3	2	−3
Manipulates peers verbally	3	+1	−1	−3
Manipulates peers physically	3	+1	−1	−3
Dominates play group	3	2	−1	−3

Pupil's Response to Peers (cont.)

		Plays alone	Plays beside others	Plays with others			
Assertively	+1						
Cooperatively	+1						
Happily	+1						
Independently	+1						
Readily	+1						
Serenely	+1						
Anxiously	−1						
Fearfully	−1						
Hostilely	−1						
Indifferently	−1						
Placatively	−1						
Dependently	−1						
Resistantly	−1						
Tentatively	−1						

Pupil's Response to Environment

	Never	Rarely	Occas.	Usually
Active toward materials	0	1	2	3
Works with materials for concentrated period	0	1	2	3
Expresses feelings through use of materials	0	1	2	3
Asks complex questions about material	0	1	2	3
Relates information about materials	0	1	2	3
Gives explanation about phenomena	0	1	2	3
Asks questions about phenomena	0	1	2	3
Notes similarities & relations in phenomena	0	1	2	3
Active toward natural phenomena	0	1	2	3
Unaware of materials	3	2	−1	−3
Withdraws from materials	3	2	−1	−3
Ignores materials	3	2	−1	−3
Participates by watching peers	3	2	−1	−3
Watches until a material is suggested	3	2	−1	−3
Ignores natural phenomena	3	2	−1	−3
Withdraws from natural phenomena	3	2	−1	−3

Pupil's Response to Environments (cont.)

	Pleasure	Skill	Abandonment	Creatively	Tentatively	Aggressively
	+	+	+	+	−	−
Apparatus						
Books						
Blocks						
Clay						
Clothes						
Graphic						
Music (melody)						
Music (percussion)						
Paint (finger)						
Sand						
Water						
Woodworking						
Dough						

Pupil's Response to Self

	Never	Rarely	Occas.	Usually
Enjoys physical movement	0	1	2	3
Pleased with one's behavior	0	1	2	3
Accepts own skills	0	1	2	3
Relaxed about oneself	0	1	2	3
Confident in new situations	0	1	2	3
Independent in caring for self	0	1	2	3
Perceives oneself adequately	0	1	2	3
Accepts own feelings	0	1	2	3
Tolerance of small groups	0	1	2	3
Punishes oneself	3	2	−1	−3
Denies feelings	3	2	−1	−3
Denies skills	3	2	−1	−3

NOTES

1. For an analysis of nursery schools and their goals, see John I. Goodlad, M. Frances Klein, Jerrold M. Novotney, and Associates, *Early Schooling in the United States*, McGraw-Hill, New York, 1973.

2. Edith Appleton, "Kindergartners Pace Themselves in Reading," *Elementary School Journal*, vol. 64, no. 5, February 1964, pp. 248–252.

3. See the film, "This Is a Laboratory School," Educational Media Center, University of California, Los Angeles.

4. Edith Buchanan, "The Relationship of Affective Behavior to Movement Patterns, Body Image, and Visual Perception in Four- and Five-Year-Old Children," unpublished doctoral dissertation, University of California, Los Angeles, 1970.

5. Deanna Stirland Hanson, "The Effect of a Concentrated Movement Behavior Program on the Affective Behavior of Four-Year-Olds at the University Elementary School," unpublished doctoral dissertation, University of California, Los Angeles, 1970.

6. "A Time to Move," film distributed by Special Purpose Films, Malibu, California, 1970.

7. Edith Appleton Buchanan and Deanna Stirland Hanson, "Free Expression Through Movement," *National Elementary Principal*, vol. LII, no. 2, October 1972, pp. 46–51.

8. Charles Ray Williams, "A Comparison of Contrasting Programs in Early Childhood Education," unpublished doctoral dissertation, University of California, Los Angeles, 1970, p. 58.

7

Instructional
Decisions in
Curriculum

M. FRANCES KLEIN

INTRODUCTION

The preceding chapters have developed and illustrated the use of a conceptual system designed to reflect some of the reality of curricular decision making as well as to suggest decisions to be made. The papers have defined and illustrated levels of curricular decision making suggested by Goodlad.[1] One of these is the instructional level. Because it is so close to students, it is crucial. The teacher performs the transactional role between students and what society wants for them in schools.

Presumably, the planning which has occurred at the societal and institutional levels, including all the political and social transactions taking place between levels, gives considerable, if often confusing, guidance and direction to teachers regarding what to do in their classrooms. Certainly, if the ministry or board of education decides that valuing a plurality of cultures is to be one of the educational aims of schools, and that study of Spanish and black cultures should be included as part of the elementary school social studies curriculum, teachers must pay attention to these decisions. Aspects of the two cultures must be made available for study by the students, and thus teacher choices as to what to teach are defined. But these directives still need to be refined at the instructional level where teachers make decisions within (and sometimes in spite of) these constraints.

Criteria must be set to suggest what or how students think and feel when they understand and appreciate these cultures. Specific content with which students will be expected to deal must be selected. Then, organizing centers must be devised which allow the student to practice the behaviors and deal with the content of the cultures specified in the objectives. There must be instructional selections of the major elements of the curriculum. Materials appropriate to the students and to the subject must be chosen from what is available or perhaps created "from scratch." Finally, ways of assessing student progress toward attaining the objectives, as well as when assessment should occur, must be decided upon. The teacher still faces extremely important curricular decisions even though some significant decisions may have been made for him or her at preceding levels of decision making (see Chapters 1 and 2).

There are resources to assist the teacher—and other curriculum makers—in some of the decisions to be made. These resources are defined in the conceptual system developed by Goodlad[2] at the ideological or ideaistic level—a data source composed of the ideas, concepts, or products of scholars which could be used in making curricular decisions. The use of such a data source should make curriculum processes more thoughtful and thus increase the cumulative impact of the curriculum upon student learning. This chapter identifies some of the resources which may be extracted from the ideological data source and used in curriculum decision making at the instructional level. It describes how teachers utilized one product of such a data source, the now well-known *Taxonomy of Educational Objectives: Cognitive Domain.*[3] The *Taxonomy* is a useful tool in dealing with cognitive aspects of objectives in curriculum planning. Six broad categories of cognitive behavior are defined which, in turn, are broken down into 21 discrete behaviors. According to a commonly held view, objectives must state the type of behavior the student is expected to develop and specify the content or realm of human activity with which the student is to be engaged.[4] The *Taxonomy* can be used as a definition of cognitive behavior and utilized as a basis for the behavioral part of objectives specifying attainment of cognition.

SOME RESOURCES FOR INSTRUCTIONAL PLANNING

Other, similar resources are available from ideological sources. Also, taxonomies for the affective[5] and psychomotor[6] domains of human behavior exist and can be utilized in determining rather precisely what the student should be able to do in acquiring proficiency in these realms. Conceptualizations of human behaviors expressed as precise objectives are designed to give assistance to educators making decisions at the institutional and instructional levels of curriculum. All of this exists. Whether and how to use them is another matter.

Still other types of resources are available to educators working at the instructional level. To assist them in the selection of educational objectives, the Instructional Objectives Exchange (IOX) has been established.[7] IOX provides a comprehensive list of instructional objectives in several content areas. From these lists of objectives, a teacher is able to select those with which he is most concerned and plan an instructional program designed to achieve the selected objectives. Sets of test items are also available. These can be used as diagnostic devices to help determine where instruction should begin for a specific objective and as summative evaluative instruments to determine how well the students achieved.

The large array of instructional materials available today is another resource for educators involved in instructional planning. These materials are a rich storehouse to help implement a program. It appears obvious that materials have a significant impact upon what students learn from the curriculum. Not all learning aids have to be created by each teacher, school faculty, or school district for instructional use.

Materials now commercially available give educators an incredible array of choices for what to include in the curriculum. Some materials present traditional curricular areas such as reading and mathematics in new formats, through new media, and based on new concepts and processes. In addition, there are disciplines and topics not traditionally included in the elementary and secondary school curricula; anthropology, economics, human relationships, oceanography, global education, and many more. Although these learning materials and programs represent a tremendous resource for instruction, they also present complicated problems of making choices. Not only are there choices regarding which materials to include in the curriculum but, in addition, there are choices to be made among competing, comprehensive programs in subject fields. Unfortunately, not all learning materials and programs are planned and evaluated as carefully as they should be, but there are now promising efforts to improve the quality of these materials and, thus, the richness of this resource for educators.[8]

Various directories of available learning materials and curriculum projects exist, some of which analyze and evaluate programs according to selected criteria.[9] These directories are designed to alert teachers to programs prepared for specified objectives and can assist the teacher in selecting those which were developed according to some standards or to meet selected evaluative criteria. All of the preceding resources are representative of what Goodlad defines as the ideological or ideaistic data source for curriculum planning. They represent an invaluable storehouse of great potential benefit to the educator in curriculum planning at the instructional level.

USING AN IDEOLOGICAL DATA SOURCE FOR INSTRUCTIONAL DECISIONS

The existence of such sources, however, does not automatically result in improved decision making; these sources make a difference only when understood and used by teachers. Teachers do not always understand, and sometimes fall far short of using, these available resources.[10] Therefore, it appears that teachers should be assisted to use such resources more frequently and wisely. In the project reported here, assistance to teachers was provided in using the *Taxonomy* for curriculum decisions at the classroom level. The project sought to develop and use a test for primary school children based on the *Taxonomy*.[11] The *Taxonomy* had been developed by compiling and categorizing objectives drawn from the upper levels of schooling, but its potential usefulness at the lower levels had not been tested. A curriculum in the social studies was developed to help young students develop cognitive behaviors and a paper-and-pencil test was devised according to the *Taxonomy* in order to determine the success attained in seeking to elicit these behaviors in children of primary school age.

Prior to the initiation of this project, a small group of educators at the University Elementary School, UCLA, began to investigate extant student understanding of a few selected generalizations considered to be very important in the social studies program and the effectiveness of two teaching techniques—discussion and dramatic play—in helping students develop these generalizations. This exploration by a few teachers utilized the *Taxonomy* as a basis for defining the behavioral dimensions of instruction. They attempted to determine the level of cognitive behavior reached by students in their discussions and in dramatic play, instruction having been focused upon the selected generalizations. Simultaneously, the faculty as a whole was considering what the overall objectives of the school should be (see Chapter 5). The entire faculty also was studying the *Taxonomy* as a tool to help clarify school objectives. Thus, the classroom objectives being explored at the instructional level by a few teachers were derivatives of those being developed at the institutional level by the total staff.

Two outcomes of the exploratory activity led to a later, more structured project. First, even though one of the teachers was highly skilled at leading students in stimulating discussions (during which she *thought* she helped students develop some of the higher cognitive behaviors as defined by the *Taxonomy*), an analysis of tapes of these discussions showed that rarely did the teacher call for student behaviors at the application level or higher.[12] The class discussion usually moved on when at least the most vocal children appeared to have acquired basic information. Second, there had been prepared a very comprehensive content analysis of a social studies unit called "Boats and Harbors," which outlined specific content to be taught as well as statements of some of the major generalizations about the content of the unit. With these two outcomes in hand, a second project was undertaken.[13]

This subsequent project utilized the extensive content analysis of the social studies unit prepared previously, on the one hand, and the *Taxonomy* as the basis for determining the objectives for the classroom program, on the other. The content analysis of the pilot project about "Boats and Harbors" was supplemented with an analysis of the social living aspects of the social studies curriculum. The concern among the teachers about basic research methodology also was included.

During the semester prior to the implementation of this project, the two teachers who were to teach the curriculum met with this writer in a series of meetings designed to familiarize them with principles of curriculum decision making at the instructional level and the *Taxonomy*. These meetings focused at first on the setting of objectives at every level of cognitive behavior in the *Taxonomy*. Considerable time was spent on understanding the objectives, particularly the behavioral part, and then, finally, came the acceptance by the teachers of those objectives considered to be both important and applicable in their classrooms. The group also discussed ways in which the organizing centers could be set up so that students would have opportunities to deal with the content and to practice the behaviors specified in the objectives. They spent only a limited time on ways of arranging the organizing elements of the curriculum so as to maximize learning.[14]

The teachers were aware that the writer was constructing a test to determine if the behaviors specified in the objectives were, indeed, elicited through goal-directed instruction in the social studies program, but the actual test items were not discussed with the teachers. The teachers knew that the test was to be administered at the end of the instructional unit and that each of the items was designed to elicit a certain behavior selected from the *Taxonomy* in accord with the teachers' objectives. Test items were developed for every objective previously determined by the teachers (with the help of the *Taxonomy*) for the social studies program. After these discussion sessions, extending over a semester, the teachers embarked upon the instructional implementation of the planned curriculum in a team-taught, nongraded group of forty-eight primary school pupils. The writer provided a modicum of guidance and supervision.

At the conclusion of the semester, the test was administered to the pupils. Meanwhile, the writer had established acceptable levels of validity and reliability for the instrument. Although not all of the specific behaviors sought were elicited among these children, the results were encouraging enough to suggest that the *Taxonomy* can be a very useful tool to assist with curriculum decisions at the institutional and instructional levels for primary schooling. For the most part, behavioral levels were determined to be discrete and internally consistent. Admittedly, most of the behaviors elicited were at the lower levels of cognition—that is, the acquiring and understanding of knowledge—but some of the behaviors were also elicited at the upper levels.

An aside regarding the *Taxonomy* itself is in order. The subcategories under the major six held up very well, seemingly discrete from each other and, with an exception or two, each properly arranged according to its designated classification. It is a data source worth using *for the purposes for which it was intended.*

From the point of view of usefulness, it should be noted that more children reached higher levels of cognitive performance than had been the case before introduction to, and initiation in, its use and that the class group spread out over a wider array of categories than before. However, these results were attained at considerable expense of time and effort by the teachers. And they had the help throughout of a person with some considerable understanding of the *Taxonomy*. It is doubtful that many teachers go into such enterprises with similar advantages and equivalent preparation—and yet the difficulties were considerable. Perhaps all this provides at least one explanation for teachers' continuing to use relatively simplistic instructional resources such as textbooks and why publishers enter the multimedia field, for example, with caution. We should have relatively little fear at this time of instructional curriculum planning becoming an overly rational process involving systematic analysis and utilization of well-developed ideological or ideaistic resources.

PROBLEMS AND ISSUES AT THE INSTRUCTIONAL LEVEL OF CURRICULUM DECISIONS

The preceding pages describe a process by which an instructional curriculum was planned, implemented, and evaluated. The problems and successes experienced by the teachers involved and the resources available from the ideological data source used suggest a number of problems and issues which need explicit identification. If the planned curriculum—the set of intended learnings[15]—is to be implemented or operationalized in the classroom, a critical factor becomes the understanding of and acceptance by the teacher of other preceding decisions about the curriculum (see Chapter 3). The teacher can resist, modify, or even openly reject preceding decisions—in which case the curriculum planned at societal and institutional levels may never have a chance of being implemented. But even if the teacher accepts and thinks he understands the curriculum planned at preceding levels, there are likely to be difficulties in translating these formal plans into an operational curriculum in the classroom. A variety of factors affects this translation, assuming that there have been societal and institutional decisions. Among them are the skills, knowledge, and attitudes which the teacher possesses; the materials available for use in refining and implementing the curriculum; the operational definition of significant elements in the subject matter; the role of the student in the process; formative and summative evaluation procedures and instruments; the organizing centers provided to students; and many more.

Even though the legislature may decree (at the societal level) that the values of society should be taught in the schools, and even though the school faculty at the institutional level decides that this should be done through a social studies program embracing objectives dealing with intergroup relations, such goals and substance may never be implemented if the classroom teacher does not know about, or fails to understand, these expectations. An insecure teacher dealing with a vocal group of parents may back away from dealing with issues of prejudice and discrimination in the classroom. A teacher prejudiced against the rights of others will subvert goals seeking tolerance and acceptance of all cultures, all people. An ill-prepared teacher will not know about the available resources from which to draw. Thus, the skills, knowledge, and attitudes of the teacher are a key in the final determination of what is taught and how.

Another factor affecting curriculum planning at the instructional level is the availability of materials on planned topics. With the advent of an open-door policy on China, let us suppose a new curriculum topic on China has been approved at the societal and institutional levels, and now the classroom teacher confronts the need to teach it. A search for materials yields little on China at the appropriate maturity levels. This hampers the teacher both in setting objectives and in operationalizing a daily program for children. The actual development of curriculum materials for this new topic is probably an unrealistic expectation to hold for the classroom teacher; an array of learning materials from which to choose would enormously facilitate planning for teaching. Low-level cognitive objectives for children such as recalling information from the teacher's lectures or general readings on China provided by the teacher might be possible, but the provision of much more than this would be unrealistic. And to change children's affective behaviors would require considerable involvement in Chinese studies, with a variety of approaches over a period of time. It is well and good to talk about leaving teachers free to choose, but freedom becomes academic when the choices are limited.

The teacher—or other persons planning the curriculum at the instructional level—is faced also with the dilemma of identifying the significant organizing elements around which to arrange specific topics. Preceding levels of planning usually do not provide enough detail for such a task. There will be from such planning suggested topics for each subject, perhaps broad behaviors desired and value positions to be incorporated into classroom programs. Presumably, teachers are now to translate these into instruction by emphasizing those most important central concepts, skills, and values contained in such expectations. They must select a little from much to accomplish a great deal. It is to be expected that their choices will be random and perhaps even whimsical, except perhaps in those countries where what is to be taught is specified day-by-day and even hour-by-hour from on high, leaving little choice for teachers. Just how much specificity in societal and institutional planning is helpful and how much is restricting to the point of being harmful to teacher creativity in instructional planning is one of the most critical theoretical and practical issues in the field of curriculum. Some of the issues involved are enjoined by Griffin in Chapter 3.

Another question confronting curriculum planners at all levels, but especially at the classroom level, is the role of the student (see Chapter 8). There are very few, if any, schools which grant the student total freedom to plan his curriculum. Guidelines, criteria, and decisions established elsewhere and by others usually are present to act as constraints upon the student and to determine the curriculum he actually experiences. The identical question raised above for teachers is at issue. To what extent should a student's curriculum be planned for him? What should be his participation in this planning? What kind of data should the student contribute to curriculum planning? Is he only to experience the curriculum and not help plan it? There are many points and ways for students to become involved. They might select appropriate organizing centers based on their own interests for achieving predetermined goals. They might determine some goals of their own, an alternative which is seldom open to them, especially at precollegiate levels of schooling. Or, more conservatively, students might help build alternative activities from which to make choices in working toward groups of objectives. It is the belief of this writer that much more meaningful ways of involving the student in curriculum decisions must be identified and used.[16] We are at a primitive stage in the much-lauded quest for student self-guidance in learning.

A very practical problem which the classroom teacher must face is to identify ways of evaluating student progress toward the objectives of the curriculum. Curriculum planning conducted remote from classrooms may propose that students be assisted in developing a meaningful philosophy of life. At the instructional level of planning, the teacher becomes concerned not only with how to operationalize this lofty goal in a classroom program but also with ways of evaluating student progress toward such an end. Adequate evaluation procedures and instruments for some new trends and topics in the curriculum simply do not exist. When curricula involve values, creativity or empathy, for example, evaluating student progress may be quite difficult, if not impossible, at this time. It may be impossible for teachers to determine the impact of the curriculum in seeking to help students achieve some of the most significant objectives. The expectation that they make such evaluations can only be frustrating to teachers.

This chapter suggests that planning appropriate organizing centers at the instructional level is exceedingly complex and difficult to do. For example, in the pilot project reported earlier, the teacher skilled in leading discussions found that she was not developing the higher cognitive behaviors she thought she was. The organizing center—in this case discussion of a topic by an entire class—apparently was not providing the necessary stimulus and sustained practice. The preponderance of low-level telling and questioning exhibited by teachers observed in another study[17] suggests that teaching for higher cognitive behaviors is not often practiced by teachers. One of the persistent problems identified by this writer in her analysis of curriculum materials is the absence of organizing centers designed specifically to help students attain one set of objectives rather than another (or any!). Too often, the student is led to a preordained set of conclusions by the author of the materials, or reading and discussion elicit only recall when the stated objectives of the materials specify development of higher cognitive abilities. The planning of appropriate organizing centers designed specifically for clearly differentiated objectives could be of assistance in an area where teachers need considerable help. The improvement of instructional decisions requires, in addition to other things, vast improvement in the quality of societal and instructional decisions.

In summary, this chapter has identified some resources available from ideological curriculum planning which are relevant to instructional planning, described an example of curricular decision making at the instructional level using such a resource, and identified some problems and issues associated with implementing curriculum plans at the instructional level. The instructional level of making curricular decisions is one to be guided by more than teacher intuition if any systematic implementation of society's expectations for schooling is to occur. Decisions may be made by default through letting the textbook become the curriculum or by thoughtless acts of commission. But decision making through omission or commission cannot be considered adequate for helping students build the kinds of skills, attitudes, and knowledge they need now and in the future. The Goodlad conceptual system suggests a model for decision making which should help lay people, educators, and students assess current practices and, perhaps, replace considerable chaos in curriculum planning with at least a little more order.

NOTES

1. John I. Goodlad (with Maurice N. Richter, Jr.), *The Development of a Conceptual System for Dealing with Problems of Curriculum and*

Instruction, Cooperative Research Program USOE, Project No. 454, University of California, Los Angeles, 1966.

2. Ibid.

3. Benjamin S. Bloom (ed.), *Taxonomy of Educational Objectives: Cognitive Domain* (referred to hereafter simply as *Taxonomy*), Longmans, Green and Co., New York, 1956.

4. This position is outlined in a basic primer of curriculum: Ralph W. Tyler, *Basic Principles of Curriculum and Instruction,* University of Chicago Press, Chicago, 1950. There is currently much discussion, however, over how best to state educational objectives and whether behaviorally stated objectives function as a help or hindrance in the educative process. This controversy has been discussed and a possible resolution suggested by Louise L. Tyler and M. Frances Klein in "Not-Either-Or," a paper delivered at the American Educational Research Association Conference, held in New Orleans, Louisiana, February, 1973. Although there are other positions in the literature, the stating of educational objectives in behavioral terms appears to be the most popular as well as controversial extant position.

5. David R. Krathwohl, Benjamin S. Bloom, and Bertram B. Masia, *Taxonomy of Educational Objectives: Affective Domain,* David McKay Co., New York, 1964.

6. Elizabeth Jane Simpson, "The Classification of Educational Objectives, Psychomotor Domain," *Illinois Teacher of Home Economics,* vol. 10, Winter 1966–67, pp. 110–144.

7. W. James Popham, *Instructional Objectives Exchange Rationale Statement,* P.O. Box 24095, Los Angeles, California 90024, 1970.

8. See, for example, the following articles: Louise L. Tyler and M. Frances Klein, "Caveat Emptor: Let the Educational Buyer Beware," *Educational Technology,* April 1973, pp. 52–54; M. Frances Klein and Louise L. Tyler, "Curriculum, Bone or Bane?" *Elementary School Journal,* February 1972, pp. 225–229; Frances Castan, "The Great Instructional Materials Game," *Scholastic Teacher,* February 1973, pp. 10–16.

9. See, for example, (a) *ALERT,* A Sourcebook of Elementary Curricula Progress and Projects, Far West Regional Laboratory for Educational Research and Development, San Francisco, California, Superintendent of Documents, U.S. Government Printing Office, Washington, D.C., 1972; (b) *CAS Curriculum Advisory Service Quarterly,* published by Curriculum Advisory Service, Chicago, Illinois, 1973; (c) *Product Development Reports No. 1-20,* American Institute for Research in Behavioral Sciences, U.S. Department of Health, Education, and Welfare Office of Education, Office of Program Planning and Evaluation, Palo Alto, California, March 1972; (d) *Seventh Report of the International Clearinghouse on Science and Mathematics Curricular Developments,* 1970. A Joint Project of the American Association for the Advancement of Science and the Science Teaching Center, University of Maryland; (e) *Social Studies Curriculum Materials Data Book,* Social Science Education Consortium, Inc., Boulder, Colorado, 1973.

10. See, for example, the following references which suggest that teachers do not always understand or adequately use the concept of behavioral objectives: Eva L. Baker, "Effects on Student Achievement of Behavioral and Nonbehavioral Objectives," *Journal of Experimental Education*, vol. 37, Summer 1969, pp. 5–8; Stanley L. Deno and Joseph R. Jenkins, "On the 'Behaviorality' of Behavioral Objectives," *Psychology in the Schools*, vol. 6, 1969, pp. 18–24.

The following references suggest that *The Taxonomy*, specifically, is not adequately utilized: Mary Lee Marksberry, Mayme McCarter, and Ruth Noyce, "Relation Between Cognitive Objectives from Selected Texts and from Recommendations of National Committees," *Journal of Educational Research*, vol. 62, May–June 1969, pp. 422–429; Robert W. McFall, "The Development and Validation of an Achievement Test for Measuring Higher Level Cognitive Processes in General Science," *Journal of Experimental Education*, vol. 33, Fall 1964, pp. 103–106; Isobel Pfeiffer and O. L. Davis, Jr. "Teacher-Made Examinations—What Kind of Thinking Do They Demand?" *Bulletin of the National Association of Secondary School Principals*, vol. 49, September 1965, pp. 1–10.

11. A more extensive report on the development of the test instrument can be found in M. Frances Klein, "Use of Taxonomy of Educational Objectives (Cognitive Domain) in Constructing Tests for Primary School Pupils," *Journal of Experimental Education*, vol. 40, Spring 1972, pp. 38–50.

12. Other evidence which reports a similar finding can be found in Drew C. Tinsley, Elizabeth P. Watson, and Jon C. Marshall, "Cognitive Objectives in 'Process-Oriented' and 'Content-Oriented' Secondary Social Studies Programs," *Educational Leadership*, vol. 30, December 1972, pp. 245–248.

13. The pilot project and a discussion of organizing centers in curriculum planning has been reported by John I. Goodlad, "The Organizing Center in Curriculum Theory and Practice," *Theory Into Practice*, vol. I, October 1962, pp. 215–221.

14. The major topics of discussion were those discussed by Ralph W. Tyler, *op. cit.*

15. Goodlad's definition, *op. cit.*, p. 12.

16. This view is supported by other writers in the curriculum field. See, for example, Tyler and Klein, op. cit.; Ralph H. Ojeman, "Who Selects the Objectives of Learning—and Why?" *Elementary School Journal*, vol. 71, February 1971, pp. 262–273; Ole Sand, "Curriculum Change," *The Curriculum: Retrospect and Prospect*, 70th Yearbook, National Society for the Study of Education, University of Chicago Press, Chicago, 1971; James B. McDonald, Bernice J. Wolfson, and Esther Zaret, *Reschooling Society: A Conceptual Model*, A.S.C.D., Washington, D.C., 1973.

17. John I. Goodlad, M. Frances Klein, and Associates, *Behind the Classroom Door* (rev. 1974, retitled, *Looking Behind the Classroom Door*), Charles A. Jones Publishing Co., Worthington, Ohio, 1970.

8

The Personal Domain: Curricular Meaning

LOUISE L. TYLER and
JOHN I. GOODLAD

TOWARD GREATER EMPHASIS ON THE HUMAN ELEMENT

Enlightened statements of educational aims, from Aristotle to Whitehead and Dewey, always have attempted to recognize equally both personal and societal well-being.[1] The ideal, to be attained through *paideia,* is a broad, enlightened, mature outlook harmoniously combined with maximum cultural development. The entire culture educates. One form of this concept in modern dress is Skinner's *Beyond Freedom and Dignity,* in which the contingencies reinforce behavior which is presumed to be simultaneously good for both the individual and the community or society in which one lives.[2]

With the fully educative society not yet attained, it became necessary, even in Athens, to provide gentle tutoring to attain the ideal in some individuals. In more recent times, all nations have created schools to do what the surrounding society does not naturally do. And there has emerged the art and science of pedagogy (or paedagogy) by means of which, presumably, what is to be done will be achieved effectively.

What is to be done by schools and pedagogy emerges from a continuing sociopolitical process through which certain present conditions are deemed unsatisfactory and others posed as more satisfactory or desirable. The gap between these two sets of conditions provides goals or purposes as well as tasks. There are ends to be accomplished and means for their attainment.

What begins to emerge in the above is the familiar Western rational model for getting things done—from fighting wars to producing automobiles and running schools. It assumes that progress occurs by setting goals to be accomplished; means are subsumed under, and are instrumental to, the goals. "Rational" is virtually equated with "efficient." Accomplishing goals more efficiently is improvement and, therefore, progress.

Such a view tends to make the person or the individual virtually instrumental to societal goals. Not surprisingly, the traditional balance between individual and societal well-being in educational aims is skewed to favor society in statements of goals for schools. Through the nineteenth century in this country, the emphasis for schooling was on responsibility—a degree of education that would enable one to perform all social, domestic, civic, and moral duties.[3] Even today, when the individual is mentioned in goals for schooling, preparation for economic, social, political, and national participation is stressed. Such goals as enhancing personal powers of knowing, building individual autonomy and initiative, developing self-awareness and understanding, and nurturing diverse interests and talents tend to appear at the end of lists. At best, such goals can be described as only emerging in popular acceptance.

The dominant view, at least among a nation's political, industrial, and educational leaders and policy makers, is that individuals must be educated to make that country more powerful and more productive. Most nations, even relatively affluent ones, tend to regard emphasis on the person—on development of the individual for his or her own sake—as a luxury they cannot afford. Only a minority of the people believe that what is good education for the person is best also for the well-being of the nation.

And yet, the thinkers who produced the great ideas of the Western world addressed themselves almost exclusively to the person, to the human being, when they discussed the character of education. They believed that development of a broad, mature outlook in individuals assured societal well-being. What they quarreled over was the emphasis to be given to the cultivation of intelligence or reason in contrast to the spiritual dimension of man.

Interestingly, the content of rational humanistic educational writing speaks scarcely at all about preparation for vocational specialty, profession, or business. The purpose of education is to produce a sensitive person who performs whatever he and she does with justice, compassion, and thoughtful competence. And yet, such a purpose is almost an afterthought in most statements of the goals of schooling in Western nations.[4]

A *descriptive* conceptualization of curriculum development does not go far afield from extant practice when it depicts the process as moving in direct, linear fashion from delineation of ends and means at the societal level to refinement and implementation at the instructional level, with little or no modification in-between. Perhaps this is why many readers simply failed to see the arrows going in both directions between levels in the initial presentation of the conceptual system used in this volume. It simply is assumed that this is the way the socio-political process works. The closer and more direct the link between the societal level and the instructional, the less the interference and distortion along the way. An intermediate set of interpretations and transactions at the institutional level would be disruptive, interfering with rationality defined as efficiency. Perhaps this is why Griffin found the institutional to be the least active in decision making. Indeed, the more that societal-level decision makers specify precisely the what and why of instruction, the less the degree of slippage from societal intent to instructional implementation. This probably is why Hill had no difficulty in identifying long lists of legislative decisions dealing directly with instructional matters.

However, a *prescriptive* conceptualization of curriculum decision making with two-way arrows between levels opens up possibilities for theories of curriculum development other than the Western linear one that has dominated. For example, one position referred to in Chapter 2 argues that the school as a cultural or societal system interacting with its community should become the initiating point for curriculum development and change, with the rest of the educational system, including state agencies, becoming a supportive infrastructure providing services, materials, and the like. Goodlad has developed this responsive model, as he terms it, elsewhere.[5] Many citizens are speaking out for such an approach, preferring to join the principal and teachers in making decisions about their school instead of having so many decisions made more remotely.[6]

Still another beginning point in curriculum development assigns much more authority and responsibility to professionals, as is now the case in higher education. Although this alternative is not popular with citizens, it is receiving a hearing in collective bargaining with increasing inclusion of matters pertaining to what and how to teach.

A third conceptual and theoretical alternative focuses on and begins with learners. The rhetoric so often employed by major participants in the continuing struggle to place one set of interests over another refers frequently to the welfare of children and youth. So far, however, students have been used primarily as a rather impersonal data source for determining ends and means within the framework of the conventional linear model. Chapter 2 included the experiential curriculum in a five-stage research design for studying student reactions to curricula planned for them. Most of the balance of this chapter probes more deeply into this personal domain of curriculum.

None of these alternatives necessitates, presumably, a reformulation of the conceptual system summarized in Chapters 1 and 2 and employed throughout this volume. Whether one begins with schools, teachers, or students, there is still a societal context to be reckoned with. But a prescriptive formulation from the societal to the instructional, with one-way arrows to depict translations and transactions, simply will not serve assumptions and beliefs other than those embedded in the linear paradigm. When we begin with the personal or experiential level, for example, the flow of interpretations and transactions changes markedly and can be accommodated only by a conceptualization within which this flow is depicted by two-way arrows.

Stressing the personal domain also facilitates deviation from the standard mental set of defining rationality as formulating purposes before engaging in activities. This is, after all, only one way to view the world. But is it not the quality of the experience that is fundamentally important? And yet, current approaches to evaluation almost invariably focus on whether or not a rather narrow range of goals is being achieved, and rarely on the meanings students take from the curriculum or the personal traits being formulated. Clearly, beginning with the personal or experiential opens up avenues for theoretical formulations and research that differ markedly from the linear approaches which have dominated the social sciences, particularly experimental psychology, and curriculum development.

How one perceives the personal domain depends on one's theory of the person and humankind. Indeed, this theory will even determine the kind of weight to place on this domain in any theory or conceptualization of curriculum. If the individual is regarded as a relatively passive or at least, a relatively easily managed, recipient of inputs, then delivery mechanisms become of paramount importance. But if the individual is a choosing, self-selecting, reflective organism, forming his or her own meanings in spite of, as well as because of, stimuli provided, then the way the individual is involved in the curriculum-planning process becomes crucial. He or she is not just the end of the line in a carefully planned and structured delivery system.

The orientation of the writers of this chapter is toward the latter position or theory. They could not do justice to the former. Consequently, subsequent development of the personal or experiential domain must be regarded as only one view—the personal view of the authors. Further, since a large part of what follows was written by Tyler, it reflects her further personal orientation to understanding and interpreting the personal domain. She conceptualizes the personal around the idea of meaning.

When one works with and from a particular theoretical position and then further refines the lens, certain other things follow. First, one set of assumptions and not another is put forward or then runs implicitly through the discourse. Second, these assumptions and not others guide the translation of theory into practice. Third, certain kinds of inquiry and not other kinds are used to study practice and test the usefulness and validity of the theory.

The perspective, the assumptions, and suggested method of inquiry for the personal domain that follow are derived from psychoanalysis. Other perspectives (disciplines) have significant contributions to make and could have been used with productive results. Psychoanalysis is particularly useful because of its concern for, and investigations of, personal meaning. It is a theory of personality development, a method of therapy, a technique of investigation, and a philosophy. Psychoanalysis is viewed here as a semantic theory, dealing with reasons, not causes. It is concerned with the motives and behavior of a self who experiences and shapes his environment.

The mode of investigation is humanistic, usually involving rather exhaustive analysis of a few cases. In Chapter 2, a study for getting some insights into students' perceptions of and reactions to school and classroom life was described briefly. Such an approach is useful for the re-examination of policies and practices. But more sustained kinds of inquiry are needed in seeking to determine the meaning of particular aspects of schooling for specific individuals.

THE PERSONAL DOMAIN

Because of our concern and commitment to persons, it is most important that we conceptualize curricular questions in the most generative way possible. The central question becomes, "What does the curriculum mean to the learner?

Does it make sense?" Or, expressed in another way, "Is the curriculum meaningful?" Consequently, we will conceptualize the personal domain in relation to the idea of *meaning*.

Preoccupation with the theme of meaning is quite apparent if one perceives the titles of some of the significant volumes in various areas of knowledge which have appeared in the last fifty years: *Symbolism and Truth*;[7] *The Logical Syntax of Language*;[8] *Meaning and Change of Meaning*;[9] *Tractatus Logico-Philosophicus*;[10] *Symbolism: Its Meaning and Effects*;[11] *Interpretation of Dreams*;[12] and *The Voice of the Symbol*.[13] Education has had a few scholars who have attended to the concept of meaning. One of the most systematically thought-through volumes is that of Philip Phenix, *Realms of Meaning*.[14]

Rather than defining the term *meaning*, we hope the reader will note the way the term is used and the way the reader understands the term. We believe that it is not merely words that have meaning but that they are given meaning by the writer (speaker) or reader (listener). A few illustrations might be of some value in clarifying our "sense-giving" of the term *meaning*.

First, a passage from Helen Keller's autobiography:

> She brought me my hat, and I knew I was going out into the warm sunshine. This thought, if a wordless sensation may be called a thought, made me hop and skip with pleasure.
>
> We walked down the path to the well-house, attracted by the fragrance of the honeysuckle with which it was covered. Someone was drawing water and my teacher placed my hand under the spout. As the cool stream gushed over my hand she spelled into the other the word *water*, first slowly, then rapidly. I stood still, my whole attention fixed upon the motion of her fingers. Suddenly I felt a misty consciousness as of something forgotten—a thrill of returning thought; and somehow the mystery of language was revealed to me. I knew then that w-a-t-e-r meant the wonderful cool something that was flowing over my hand. That living word awakened my soul, gave it light, hope, joy, set it free! There were barriers still, it is true, but barriers that in time could be swept away.
>
> I left the well-house eager to learn. Everything had a name, and each name gave birth to a new thought. As we returned to the house every object which I touched seemed to quiver with life. That was because I saw everything with the strange, new sight that had come to me.[15]

A second illustration can be drawn from a well-known and often-quoted dream:

> Joseph had a dream, which he told his brothers, and it made them hate him worse than ever. He said to them, "Do listen to this dream I have had. Methought, as we were binding sheaves in the field, my sheaf stood up, while your sheaves all around did homage to it!" His brothers answered, "And are you to be king over us? You to lord it over us!" They hated him worse than ever, for what he dreamed and what he said. He had another dream which he told his brothers. "Listen," he said, "I have had another dream! The sun, the moon, and the eleven stars were doing homage to me!" When he told this to his father and his brothers, his father reproved him, saying, "What is this dream of yours? Am I and your mother and your brothers actually to bow before you to the earth?" His brothers bore him malice, but his father kept mind of what he said.[16]

A third illustration related to meaning is from Polanyi.[17] He describes a person using a stick to feel his way in the dark for the first time. Polanyi says (and we can all supplement his account by our own experience in somewhat similar situations) that the person will first feel the impact against his palm or fingers when an object is hit. But as he learns to use the stick effectively, the user of the stick no longer attends to the jerks in his hand but attends, rather, to their meaning at the far end of the stick.

A final illustration pertains to the unconscious meaning conveyed by the traditional cowboy story. According to Grotjahn,[18] the cowboy is independent, asexual, self-reliant, trusting, resourceful, and, perhaps, attractively innocent. The cowboy does not rebel and remains guiltless through all adventures. Conflicts are avoided, disguised, sidestepped, or saved by wish fulfillment. Cowboys have no mother, but only their horse to rely on. The television performance or movie is enjoyed, not suffered, by the viewer.

If these illustrations are insufficient to convey the significance and complexity of the sense-giving involved in deriving meaning, try the following:

1. Think through what a scar on a face signifies.
2. What does the ringing of a bell mean?

3.   Walk around your home in the dark and find your way from one room to another by touch.

4.   Carry on a conversation with a friend with a minimum of eye-to-eye contact.

5.   Attempt to account for why you consistently view a particular program on television or why you responded with such intensity to a particular play or film.

In order to facilitate dialogue, a series of assumptions which underlie the conceptualization of the personal domain will be sketched, some briefly, others more extensively. The first assumption—that persons are always creating and obtaining meaning in life—is so fundamental that no further elaboration is required. A second assumption is that persons are choosing and self-assertive. As people make decisions and act upon them, they become what is inherently possible. Bettelheim's volume, *The Informed Heart*, deals with his concentration camp experience in Germany and gives a very moving description of a young woman's behavior, which sheds light on this second assumption. She was in a group of naked prisoners about to enter a gas chamber. When the commanding SS officer learned that one of the women prisoners was a dancer, he ordered her to dance for him. She did, and as she approached him in her dance, she seized his gun and shot him. She, too, was then immediately shot. Bettelheim comments:

> Exercising the last freedom that not even the concentration camp could take away—to decide how one wishes to think and feel about the conditions of one's life—this dancer threw off her real prison. This she could do because she was willing to risk her life to achieve autonomy once more. If we can do that, then if we cannot live, at least we die as men.[19]

"The unexamined life is not worth living" is a third assumption. This assumption suggests that to reflect upon life and its meaning, about the wisdom of our decisions, and about the good and evil of our behavior is essential if existence is to be worthwhile. Aristotle states, "For reason more than anything else is man." That reason is an essential aspect of man's being is unquestionable. Decisions and the meaning of decisions are shaped in large part by a person's reasoning.

Still another assumption, closely related to the preceding one, presents a more comprehensive conception of reasoning than is usually encountered. Reasoning is both logical and intuitive. Ornstein explains that the cerebral cortex of the brain is divided into two hemispheres. The structure and fucntion of these two hemispheres influence the two modes of consciousness. The left hemisphere is predominantly involved with analytic thinking (linear and sequential), whereas the right hemisphere, which appears to be responsible for—among other things—our orientation in space and artistic qualities, processes information diffusely while it simultaneously integrates material.[20]

Freud said, "The voice of the intellect is a soft one, but it does not rest until it has gained a hearing." This statement, frequently encountered in the psychoanalytic literature, usually comes as a surprise to individuals not familiar with the totality of Freud's writing. Because psychoanalysts write much about love and hate and about feelings which occur within and between persons, readers have not perceived the concern that psychoanalysts have about the use of intelligence in making decisions. However, although rationality is essential, it is not sufficient. On this point, Bettelheim says:

> ... heart and reason can no longer be kept in their separate places. Work and art, family and society, can no longer develop in isolation from each other. The daring heart must invade reason with its own living warmth, even if the symmetry of reason must give way to admit love and the pulsation of life.[21]

An assumption pertaining to learning has been discussed by Bettelheim somewhat as follows: Individuals learn because of an inner conviction that learning has *personal* value for them and not to please parents or teachers or a vaguely concerned society.[22] Undoubtedly, much learning has occurred temporarily which was to please parents, teachers, and friends, but it usually is quickly forgotten. All of us have had the experience of passing courses with excellent grades and then attempting to remember what we had learned. We could remember very little about the content, much more about the teacher or professor or classmates. Possibly what we learned or reaffirmed was the desire to please others. Hardly, in one sense, an outcome worthy of our person, our energy, our time!

Polanyi, in his many writings, has stimulated the formulation of another assumption which has to do with knowing. He has elaborated in a number of essays the notion of tacit knowing: We can know more than we can tell.[23] His example to explain what this means is that we can recognize a person's face among thousands, indeed, even among millions. But we usually are not able to put most of this knowledge into words. We recognize the moods of the human face without being able to tell—except quite vaguely. Further, Polanyi observes that great efforts are made at universities to teach students to identify cases of disease and specimens of rocks, plants, and animals—but that we can only do so by relying on the students' intelligent cooperation for catching the meaning, and that any definition of an external thing must ultimately rely on pointing at such a thing. We leave something behind that we could not tell and its reception by the individual relies on the person addressed discovering what we have not been able to communicate.

Polanyi states that the basic structure of tacit knowing has two components, which he refers to as the two terms of tacit knowing. He cites the work of Lazarus and McCleary, who presented a person with a large number of nonsense syllables and, after showing several of the syllables, administered an electric shock.[24] Soon the person showed symptoms of anticipating the shock at the sight of the syllables; yet, on subsequent questioning, he could not identify them. Eriksen and Keuthe exposed a person to a shock whenever he uttered associations to certain words.[25] The person learned to forestall the shock by avoiding the utterance of the associations but did not know he was doing this. In these experiments, the syllables and shock associations are the first element (term) and the electric shock which followed is the second one (term).

According to Polanyi, we know the shock (second term) by

attending to it and know the shock syllables and shock associations only by our awareness of them while attending to the electric shock, not separately. Hence, our knowledge of them remains tacit. In addition, when the sight of certain syllables or the saying of certain associations makes us expect an electric shock, it can be said that they signify the approach of a shock and that is their meaning to us. This then is learning without awareness, and certainly without any awareness of a goal.

So long as you look *at* X, you are *not* attending *from* X to something else which would be its meaning. In order to attend *from* X to its meaning, you must cease to look *at* X, and *the moment you look at X you cease to see its meaning.* ... We shall presently see that to attend *from* a thing to its meaning is to *interiorize* it, and that to look instead *at* the thing is to *exteriorize* or *alienate* it. We shall then say *that we endow a thing with meaning by interiorizing it and destroy its meaning by alienating it.*[26]

Another assumption underlying the personal domain of curriculum is that education is an art based upon science. Art, in this sense, works with nature and, by so doing, facilitates the results which occur. To elaborate with an illustration from Socrates: "It is the mother who labors and gives birth, so it is the student who is primarily active in learning. ..." The teacher, like the midwife, merely assists in a natural process which might be more painful and might possibly fail without such help. Science, the base for the art of education, is the intellectual manipulation of carefully verified observations which result in knowledge about particular phenomena. Education is based upon knowledge from other fields, such as psychology, sociology, and economics, which has been derived as a consequence of inquiry. Curriculum development, too, is an art based upon science.

Next is a set of assumptions pertaining to knowledge. The work of Phenix is particularly useful. He has conceptualized the kinds of patterns of meaning that scholars have created and discovered. Phenix's conception, somewhat abbreviated, is that the disciplines can be divided on the basis of logical structure. Every cognitive meaning has two logical aspects:

quantity and quality. There are three degrees of quantity: singular, general, and comprehensive; or, in other words, knowledge is of one thing, or of a selected plurality, or of a totality. The qualities of meaning can be designated as fact, form, and norm; that is, meanings may refer to what actually exists, or to imagined possibilities of what exists, or to what ought to be. In all, he conceptualized six fundamental patterns of meaning: Symbolics (ordinary language, mathematics, nondiscussive symbolic forms), Empirics (physical and life sciences, social sciences), Esthetics (music, visual arts, literature), Syndetics (philosophy, psychology, religion); Ethics (special areas of moral and ethical concern), and Synoptics (history, religion, and philosophy).[27]

The last assumption derives especially from some of Buber's writings. One of his fundamental terms is I-Thou.[28] I-Thou is not easy to put into words—if at all possible. I-Thou has to do with a subjective relationship in which "one stands, addresses, and responds," and it is the I-Thou relationship that establishes the world of relation. The I-It term gives stability. I assume that the I-Thou relationship is basic to the teaching-learning situation which should more correctly be termed the educational relationship. It is characterized by words such as helping, serving, caring for. The teacher communicates trust and courage and helps a student to be responsible for a dialogue with life.

To summarize the import of these assumptions: persons discover, create, and express meanings; they are choosing and self-assertive, using logic and intuition in reflecting on life and its meaning. Heart and reason are interwoven. Individuals learn what has personal meaning for them, and their knowledge is an active creation. Institutions (schooling) are to be developed and organized so that the growth of personal meaning emerges. The experiential domain of the school curriculum is of utmost importance.

The emphasis here is on the person—in this instance, the student. But the student is not alone in the curriculum. There are others—significant others. It is impossible to talk or think about the person as student and his thoughts, feelings, and

reactions without implicitly thinking about the others—
whether fellow students, teacher(s), teaching aides, or principals.

IMPLICATIONS FOR PRACTICE AND ITS STUDY

The preceding assumptions have certain implications for
the learning environment provided by institutions such as
schools, for the study of that environment, and for inquiry
into the meanings students derive from it and in it. First,
students should be actively engaged in creating and recreat-
ing this environment. Setting one's own purposes, suggesting
and choosing among alternatives, and evaluating the worth
of time spent are not merely optional approaches; they
constitute learning itself. Studies show that students do very
little of this.[29] On a scale of little to considerable freedom to
plan and choose, most classrooms would rank toward the
"limited" end of the scale. But other kinds of studies are
needed to determine the meanings students derive from
being drawn into or not having a say in determining the ends
and means of their daily learning.

Second, all aspects of the school environment should
encourage continuous reflection on its meaning. This means,
in part, a questioning of the significance of schooling and the
activities it promotes. Do teachers encourage this? Do they
regard it as a form of disrespect or even rebellion? What is
the meaning to students of being supported or rebuffed in
seeking to lead lives of self-examination in school?

Third, in addition to studies involving logical, ordered
processes of reasoning, students are given opportunities to
use their intuitive abilities. They are encouraged to explore
various interpretations and not to stop with an answer believed to be right or wrong. What orientation to knowledge
and truth do students acquire in environments stressing
"correct" responses?

Fourth, teachers are simply older, more experienced, more
knowledgeable companions and helpers. They open doors,
assist, encourage, ask questions, listen. Relationships be-

tween student and teacher would be of an I-Thou kind. The prevailing concern is one of helping students to become "caring-for" persons. One anticipates a model of a caring-for teacher in a supportive environment. Is this characteristic of schools? What meanings are students deriving from their relationships with teachers? With the principal? "Relationship educates, provided it is genuine educational relationship."[30]

Fifth, students experience an array of approaches to deriving meaning, such as symbolics, empirics, and ethics, as identified by Phenix. The curriculum is necessarily broad; the basics are much more than reading, writing, and arithmetic. And the approaches to learning are varied and diverse; telling and questioning are not enough. Are these the characteristics of most classrooms? Do students employ several perspectives and approaches in seeking to acquire understanding and meaning?

The foregoing probably provides enough illustrations of what emphasis on the personal domain implies for practice, the study of practice, and inquiry into what students derive from educational settings. Needless to say, gaining insight into personal meaning is not easy, requiring techniques going far beyond observing and recording student behavior.

Sometimes the necessary inquiry involves detailed analysis of both the medium or stimulus for learning and what the learner appears to be getting from it. Bettelheim has contributed significantly to an understanding of literature as stimulus of meaning. His work on the underlying themes of fairy tales as they relate to the intellectual and emotional characteristics of children is seminal.[31] Psychoanalytic concepts provide useful insights into, for example, what children and youth emphasize or omit in retelling the stories they have read.

For decades, the importance of using knowledge about children and youth in planning curricula has been part of educators' conventional wisdom. Likewise, teachers have been urged to adapt their instruction to the characteristics and needs of those students with whom they work. But we have given little more than lip-service to these ideas. How many institutional curricula have been influenced by student reactions to and perceptions of the programs they are experiencing? How many teachers redesign their instruction as a result of eliciting from their students data on how these students feel about and otherwise react to what goes on in the classroom? In seeking to appraise pupil effects of schooling, we simply do not gather such information.

Inquiry at the level of the personal domain in curriculum opens up exceedingly fertile ground. The possibilities for studies are virtually limitless. Hardly any classroom practices have been examined at the level of personal meaning—for both teachers and students.[32,33] More insight is needed into the transactional process which is a basic part of classroom life.[34] We need to know about the impact and meaning of the various subjects as experienced by students at successive developmental levels. Analysis of children's writings tells us a great deal about what is happening to them as they progress. What does school mean to the child? What do students fear in the school setting? What function is played by jokes and humor? What is the meaning of play?

The study of curriculum practice is markedly deficient if it stops short of analysis of the personal or experiential domain. By giving the personal a meaningful place in any descriptive or prescriptive conceptualization of the field, attention is focused on its importance. Such inclusion carries with it the implication that students are not simply the receptacles for or recipients of a process that ends with instruction—that how they think and feel and react is of fundamental importance.

But recognition of this importance will come slowly. As stated at the outset of this chapter, for nearly three centuries the goals of American education stressed religion, family, civic and vocational responsibility, saying virtually nothing about development of the self. All of the major political and governmental ideologies of the world are similarly oriented. Their educational goals, too, stress civic and national responsibility. For the past several decades, the socio-political goals of state and local school districts in this country have included at least one (of perhaps a dozen statements) wherein self-development, individuality, and the person are predominant. For the most part, however, the commitment is hesitant and rhetorical. We remain somewhat fearful and uncertain about the potentialities of the free self.

It is unlikely that the personal domain will receive the attention it deserves in curricular practice until the societal commitment is more sure and confident. But perhaps this commitment can be accelerated by increased focus on and knowledge about the personal side of what young people derive from their schooling.

NOTES

1. For an analysis, see Val D. Rust, "Humanistic Roots of Alternatives in Education," *The Conventional and the Alternative in Education*, by John I. Goodlad et al., McCutchan Publishing Corporation, Berkeley, California, 1975, chap. 4.

2. B. F. Skinner, *Beyond Freedom and Dignity*, Random House, New York, 1971.

3. John I. Goodlad, "An Emphasis on Change," *American Education*, vol. 11, January–February, 1975, pp. 16–21, 24–25, 28.

4. John I. Goodlad, "On the Cultivation and Corruption of Education," *The Educational Forum*, XLII, March 1978, pp. 267–278.

5. John I. Goodlad, *The Dynamics of Educational Change: Toward Responsive Schools*, McGraw-Hill, New York, 1975.

6. This observation is suggested by some preliminary data from A Study of Schooling in the United States, administered by the Institute for Development of Educational Activities, Inc. (| I | D | E | A |), an affiliate of the Charles F. Kettering Foundation. Financial support has been provided by an array of private and public agencies.

7. Ralph Munroe Eaton, *Symbolism and Truth*, Harvard University Press, Cambridge, Massachusetts, 1925.

8. Rudolf Carnap, *The Logical Syntax of Language*, K. Paul, Trench, Trubner & Co., London, 1935.

9. Gustav Stern, *Meaning and Change of Meaning*, Indiana University Press, Bloomington, Indiana, 1931.

10. Ludwig Wittgenstein, *Tractatus Logico-Philosophicus*, K. Paul, Trench, Trubner & Co., London, 1922.

11. A. N. Whitehead, *Symbolism: Its Meaning and Effects.* Macmillan, New York, 1927.

12. S. Freud, "The Interpretation of Dreams," vols. IV and V, *The Complete Psychological Works of Sigmund Freud*, Hogarth Press, London, 1962.

13. Martin Grotjahn, *The Voice of the Symbol,* Mara Books, Inc., Los Angeles, California, 1971.

14. Philip Phenix, *Realms of Meaning,* McGraw-Hill, New York, 1964.

15. Helen Keller, *The Story of My Life,* Doubleday, Doran & Co., Garden City, New York, 1936, pp. 23–24.

16. *The Bible, A New Translation* by James Moffat, Concordance Edition, Harper, New York and London, 1954, Genesis, chap. 37.

17. Michael Polanyi, *The Tacit Dimension,* Anchor Books, Doubleday, Garden City, New York, 1967.

18. Grotjahn, op. cit., pp. 11–15.

19. Bruno Bettelheim, *The Informed Heart,* Free Press, Glencoe, Illinois, 1960, p. 265.

20. Robert E. Ornstein, "Right and Left Thinking," *Psychology Today,* May 1973, p. 86.

21. Bettelheim, op. cit., p. viii.

22. Bruno Bettelheim, "Decision to Fail," *The School Review,* vol. 69, no. 4, Winter 1961, pp. 377–412.

23. Polanyi, op. cit., p. 4.

24. Ibid., p. 7.

25. Ibid., p. 8.

26. Michael Polanyi, *Knowing and Being, Essays,* Marjorie Grene (ed.), The University of Chicago Press, Chicago, 1969, p. 146.

27. Philip Phenix, op. cit., pp. 3–14.

28. Martin Buber, *Between Man and Man,* Macmillan, New York, 1965.

29. For a summary of some of these, see John I. Goodlad, "What Goes on in our Schools?" *Educational Researcher,* vol. 6, no. 3, March 1977, pp. 3–6.

30. Martin Buber, *A Believing Humanism,* Simon and Schuster, New York, 1967, p. 98.

31. Bruno Bettelheim, *The Uses of Enchantment,* Alfred A. Knopf, New York, 1976.

32. Louise L. Tyler, "Materials in Persons," *Theory Into Practice,* vol. 16, no. 4, October 1977, pp. 231–237.

33. Louise L. Tyler, "Evaluation and Persons," *Educational Leadership,* vol. 35, no. 4, January 1978, pp. 275–279.

34. Louise L. Tyler, "The Utilization of Psychoanalytic Concepts for Processing Classroom Transaction," *The Journal of Educational Research,* vol. 60, no. 6, February 1967, pp. 260–266.

9

Designing Institutional Curricula
A Case Study of
Curriculum Practice

ELIZABETH C. WILSON

The first chapter of this book summarized a system or framework for conceptualizing the field of curriculum initially developed by Goodlad and several associates at the University of Chicago during the late 1950s. Before the results of that work appeared in print (1966), Goodlad entered into what came to be a long-term consulting relationship with a large school district committed to more rational curriculum development processes. The work that ensued may very well be the most concerted effort ever made to employ this conceptual system as a guide to large-scale, comprehensive curriculum development. This chapter is a case study, a retrospective summary and analysis of that work. All of the substantive, political-social and technical-professional domains encompassed by that system are seen in dynamic interplay.

Goodlad was brought into the process initially to give a series of lectures to administrators, supervisors, and instructional leaders on curriculum planning. These contributed to shaping the plan of work that emerged. Later, he participated in various small group sessions and workshops.

Since nothing regarding the ongoing conceptual work at the University of Chicago had at that time been published, transcripts of addresses and informal presentations served as source materials for those involved. There is little doubt that these two sets of activities—one abstract or theoretical and the other concrete or practical—influenced and modified each other to a considerable degree.

THE DISTRICT AND THE SCHOOL SYSTEM

The district is a large (approximately five hundred square miles) county unit on the East Coast, with a relatively high per capita income. There are more children enrolled in school here than in each of the dozen or so smallest states. Some large governmental agencies and an array of research and development firms are located within its borders.

A large proportion of county residents are professional, scientific, and managerial people who demand a high level of academic performance from themselves, from their children, and from the schools. As might be expected, the school population is skewed toward the academically talented. This fact, however, can be misleading, since the student body contains in sizable numbers a full range of educational interests, aptitudes, and parental backgrounds. Indeed, there are pockets of poverty, inhabited by both blacks and whites, as economically and culturally desperate as sections of Appalachia, or portions of New York City and the District of Columbia. Increasingly, fingers of real urbanization are reaching out along main transportation corridors and threaten to envelop whole sections of what was middle class suburbia.

This county is a fascinating example of a community that has experienced rapid social and economic change. Only a few decades ago it was essentially a rural area, characterized by large farm holdings dating back to grants from the English

Crown. A landed gentry from these estates and a conservative elite from comfortable suburbs made up a recognized social and political leadership group. In a relatively short time, this traditional stability was shattered by the influx of large numbers of "foreigners" from all over the nation. The infiltration of "outsiders" began in the thirties; the population doubled in the forties and again in the fifties. Growth only began to taper off as the seventies began.

The county is part of the megalopolis stretching from Richmond to Boston along the East Coast. The population is mobile and frenetic, with little feeling of community in the old sense of that word. The pendulum of political and educational opinion tends to swing from one pole to the other. Political power structures do not conform to traditional patterns. Communication between the diverse groups which make up the county is difficult. Pressure groups, articulate and noisy, abound. The county has been known both for its progressive leadership and as a bellwether. Many dedicated and informed citizens have for years given tirelessly of their time and effort to promote and support a drive for better education. But the schools have also been the target for explosive, sometimes irrational, controversies. The school system has a reputation of being above average in quality and service but its citizens are not satisfied.

The school system quite naturally has many of the same problems and tensions that the county does. For what was in the forties and early fifties a loosely structured series of schools, intimately and personally related to the community and to the central authority vested in the Superintendent of Schools and the Board of Education, became in the sixties a large and complicated organization. The school system is now inevitably involved in big business, bureaucratic procedures, and mass education.

In the late fifties, a dynamic Board of Education and professional staff started to rebuild old organizational patterns into an institution better equipped to deal with size and complexity. It was a huge undertaking. Understandably, the energies of the leadership group concentrated first upon the development of orderly plans and procedures to cope with a continuing demand for more buildings and more staff to accommodate a constant stream of new students. Recruiting and personnel practices were streamlined and systematized.

Administrative reorganization was another matter which demanded attention, for with growth came the necessity for greater specialization and differentiation of function. New offices appeared in rapid succession as part of the central office structure. First on the horizon were an office of research and an office of staff development, to be followed quickly by such offices as curriculum development, pupil services, instructional materials, supervisory services, and testing. As these staff functions were becoming operative, administrative lines were undergoing change. Geographical administrative districts appeared, each headed by an administrative "line" officer known as an area director. Schools and offices were urged to keep pace with the times, to incorporate innovation, and to take part in a variety of formal and informal in-service activities and research projects.

During the late fifties and early sixties an air of excitement and change pervaded the county school system. But the innovations and reorganization had a price. With growth, communication became increasingly difficult. It continues to be a major unsolved problem both within and without the school system.

In the fall of 1962, internal and external dissensions erupted when four of the seven board members came up for reelection and were decisively defeated. The new board members were pledged to cut school costs, to wipe out "frills" and "experimentation," and to promote "basic" education. The rhetoric sounded very much like the rhetoric of reform characterizing much of the 1970s.

During intervening years, the balance of ideologies represented on the board has swung back and forth. Rising taxes, no marked improvement in student achievement regardless of the dominant ideology, increasing teacher militancy and growing problems of violence in and around schools have made the educational problems no less critical.

Curriculum Development—1957–1962

Throughout the late fifties and early sixties, there was considerable unrest nationwide on the curriculum front. Responding, as did many schools throughout the nation, to Sputnik and its aftermath, the Board of Education took cognizance of pressures to reform the mathematics and foreign language offerings. In both cases they were besieged by well-organized, dedicated, and articulate citizen groups. (Note here the reaction to what Goodlad calls the ideological level of decision making when its products begin to move into the political-social arena.) In relatively short order an experimental "new" mathematics program replaced the traditional mathematics courses in Grades 7 and 8. French, using the aural-oral approach, also became a standard offering throughout the junior high school, making possible a six-year sequence for those students who elected it in the seventh grade.

At the same time, the Board of Education (the sanctioning body at the societal level of decision making for this public school system) officially adopted a set of goals of education in the school system. These goals were developed by a representative staff committee and reviewed by every school faculty in the county. Interestingly, a major revision of these goals in 1970 and 1971 included substantial numbers of students and citizens as well as teachers. The 1958 goals, however, represented the first systematic attempt of the Board of Education to select, articulate, and officially sanction general values and purposes for the school system.

Despite these responses, citizen groups in the late fifties continued to clamor for a voice in curriculum planning. Accordingly, in June, 1960, the Board of Education authorized a cooperative and comprehensive curriculum survey involving a large number of influential citizens. That Curriculum Study Committee, with the help of seventeen study groups, worked intensively for a year and a half and published its finding in August, 1961. The major report contained 132 separate recommendations, covering the curriculum in all subjects from kindergarten through junior college; curriculum design for elementary education, secondary education, and education beyond the high school; new ideas for experimentation and research; needed studies for the future; and school-community relationships. When the chairman of the Curriculum Study Committee presented the final reports to the Board of Education, he remarked, "If you put all of our recommendations into effect, you will need to quadruple the budget and extend the school day to seventy-two hours!"

During these years and those immediately following, the school system not only made extensive studies of the curriculum reports resulting from the study but also made a systematic survey of existing classroom practices. In addition, it organized a representative sanctioning body of professionals to consider policy and procedures for curriculum development, to review instructional innovations of all kinds, and to make continuous evaluations of the county program. By early 1962, the county had managed to do considerable stocktaking of its curriculum and to organize or streamline some machinery for communication concerning the curriculum within the burgeoning school system. But the nagging questions remained. In what direction should the county move? Who should decide? On the basis of what criteria could the school system make choices among the large number of well-intentioned recommendations for curriculum improvement before it?

CURRICULUM DESIGN: PEOPLE, PROCESSES, PRODUCTS

A Consultant and A Conceptual Scheme

For a long time, the professional leadership group had been concerned about building curriculum design. Indeed, an attempt had been made by a group of supervisors in 1955–56 and was resurrected in the spring and summer of 1961. Some design elements were identified, such as the nature of values and goals, the nature of the learner and the learning process, and the nature of knowledge and the cultural heritage—our language for Goodlad's "data sources." But the conceptual scheme used to pull the elements together was vague. Furthermore, our backs were to the wall. The need for an operational design was urgent. So also was the need for sustained expert help.

John Goodlad appeared in the county for the first time in late 1960 to talk about the nongraded school. At that time, his substantial work and interest in curriculum design was uncovered. Later that year the county was able to persuade him to accept a sustained consultancy in the county, a consultancy which continued through 1964.

Goodlad was asked to present an address, "Curriculum Design." He outlined ideas on levels of decision making—societal, institutional, and instructional—stressing the need for clearer operational definition of these functions in school systems across the nation. Most of his work, however, was with groups of teachers, supervisors, and curriculum specialists in workshops. For example, in July, 1962, he spent two days with a curriculum design workshop. He described and illustrated a way of dealing with the concepts, generalizations, and methods of inquiry in fields of knowledge. He also defined the kinds of cognitive, psychomotor, and affective behavior to be specified in a design at an institutional level and urged us to use the work of Bloom[1] and Krathwohl[2] as tools and texts. Taking examples from the local work he had observed, Goodlad showed how to juxtapose large concepts or generalizations from a discipline against a desired behavior and thus create objectives containing both the desired behavior and the substance for developing it. These objectives in turn defined and gave direction to "organizing centers," or the series of concrete, everyday occurrences in classrooms which make up the curriculum which is actually taught and learned. These two-dimensional charts, known locally as "Goodlad Grids," became the direction finders for the struggle toward institutional designs in all the subjects, K-12, in the county curriculum.

Again in June of 1964, at a workshop on design, Goodlad listened to progress reports from various groups, in particular to the science people who by this time had developed a working institutional model; he reacted to the model, used it to review elements of design with the supervisory and curriculum staff, and made suggestions about how to deal with problems of language and differing levels of abstraction in building an overarching design containing all the subjects.

Meanwhile, some of the subject groups that had refined their designs were struggling with specific problems which required expert help. An intensive all-day session with the science supervisors and teacher leaders provided the catalytic spark needed to touch off their final push toward a full-fledged design for science, K-12. Through formal lectures, planning sessions, reporting and reacting to meetings, and give-and-take working seminars, Goodlad provided us with a conceptual scheme for curriculum planning. He served as idea man, as catalyst, and as sympathetic critic.

Societal-Level Decision Making: Attempts at Operational Definition

An important committee, which was part of the first large summer workshop on curriculum design in 1962, was created to study and clarify problems relating to levels of decision making, in particular to decisions to be made by the Board of Education and by the central office staff. In its study that summer, the committee addressed itself to the following questions:

1. Which curriculum decisions should be made at the following levels? (a) societal (community and board of education); (b) overall institutional (the superintendent and central office staff); (c) institutional and instructional (schools and teachers).

2. Is there a central purpose (responsibility) of the school that differentiates it from other societal agencies in the total educational process? What criteria should be used to define what should and should not be included in the curriculum?

3. Should there be a common core of basic content for all students?

4. In what ways should the curriculum be constructed so that it meets the particular needs and abilities of each individual?

5. What should be our position toward recent studies of

the structure and nature of knowledge? Toward large-scale national studies in the subject areas?

6. What changes, if any, are needed in current evaluative procedures?

7. What should our position be toward the teaching of controversial issues?

This summer work generated considerable interest in problems of decision making and other basic issues on the part of the central office staff. As a consequence, the Council on Instruction spent two days before the opening of school in September, 1962, listening to the tapes of presentations made by Goodlad at the summer workshop and reviewing the position papers prepared by members of the committee on basic issues.

During the following academic year, one of the resource teachers assigned to the curriculum office, assisted by the directors and an editor, put a great deal of time and energy into the drafting of a statement of curriculum policy for the county's public schools. This statement used as a base the recommendations of the summer committee on basic issues and the discussion of these issues by the Council on Instruction. The proposed policy statement elaborated in formal language the following prologue:

WHEREAS the Board of Education is a corporate arm of the State of Maryland entrusted by the State and the citizens with the authority and responsibility for the maintenance and supervision of an effective system of public education and for the development of educational policy relating to curriculum; and

WHEREAS the Superintendent of Schools, supported by such staff as he deems necessary, is recognized by the law as executive officer and professional leader of the public school system and thus also is charged with authority and responsibility for the development of curriculum policy and practice; and

WHEREAS the Board of Education and the Superintendent of Schools affirm their belief that centrally important to improved curriculum and instructional practice are the authority and responsibility of the principals with the faculty of each school; and

WHEREAS the sound development and evaluation of curriculum and instructional practice are continuous and complex processes requiring initiative, cooperation, and assistance of all spheres of operation within the school system; and

WHEREAS the improvement and development of curriculum and instructional practice within the total school operation require unity of purpose, clarity of function, and the delegation of authority with commensurate responsibility;

NOW THEREFORE BE IT RESOLVED THAT within the framework of State Law, the Board of Education, the Superintendent and his staff, and the principal and faculty of each school shall have recognized spheres of authority and responsibility for curriculum development and instructional practice; and within the policy established by the Board, the several bodies herein named are empowered to make decisions regarding curricular objectives, content, organization, and evaluation appropriate to their spheres of authority and responsibility.

1. The Board of Education, upon the recommendation of the Superintendent of Schools, shall formulate general curriculum policy.

2. The Superintendent of Schools shall establish such curriculum plans, programs, and procedures which will ensure effective implementation of Board policies.

3. The principal and faculty of each school, operating within the framework of Board policy and such curricular plans, programs, and procedures as are set forth by the Superintendent, shall adapt the county curriculum to the needs of the community and students served by the school.

After the prologue, the specific curricular duties and responsibilities of the Board of Education, the Superintendent of Schools and his central office staff, and the principal and faculties of each school were detailed in further policy statements. For example, the proposal suggested that the Board of Education shall

. . . assume, as a major responsibility, the establishment of central goals and functions of the school system; and formulate and evaluate long-range curriculum policies based on

(a) the best data about trends and forces at local, state, national, and international levels; and

(b) study of the educational needs and desires of the County; and

(c) definition of the population that the public schools shall serve; and

(d) selection of those values and areas of man's accumulated knowledge which shall be incorporated into a balanced and organized curriculum; and

(e) consideration of the needs of society and the needs of individuals

. . .

For each level, the draft assumed that a process of continuous appraisal and evaluation was going on, and that answers to three basic questions—Why are we teaching? Whom are we teaching? What are we teaching?—are the concern of each level of school operation. It further assumed that curricular decisions made in answer to these questions differ, in degree of specificity, at different levels; that is, that those studies and decisions made by the teacher are the most specific; those made by the Board of Education, the most general. The document suggested that specific decisions must be reasonably consistent with, and supportive of, the general ones. It proposed that patterns for organizing the classroom, the school, the central office, the Board of Education, together with the machinery for communication, operation, and evaluation grow out of answers to the value questions the document posed.

This draft of a curriculum policy also included some procedures to be used by the Board of Education in the execution of its duties and responsibilities. Procedures for the use of the central office staff and the principal and teachers were never finished. Indeed, the proposed policy did not progress far beyond the confines of the curriculum office. For, just as the statement was to receive serious study, the makeup of the Board of Education changed radically. The temper of the times did not lend itself to the kind of study and action required by a document of this nature.

Building Curriculum Designs at the System-wide Level

1. *Data Sources and First Attempts at Model Building.* Building curriculum designs for the county as a whole was a long process. The document called *Curriculum Design— Institutional Level,* which sets forth designs in ten subjects, generally on a K-12 basis, was not formally published until five years after initial work began.[3] But the progress reports, working papers, and projections for the future in all subjects which appeared in the interim formed the base on which all new curriculum materials and related instructional guides were built for the next ten years.

The basic work from 1962–1964 involved representatives from all professional staff members in the school system including area directors, elementary and secondary supervisors, elementary and secondary teachers, and school psychologists. The starting point was the set of "Goals of Education for the County" formally adopted in 1958. These goals, mentioned earlier, survived many different Boards of Education with a wide range of educational philosophies, and defined in at least global fashion the county instructional program. They were:

1. Competence in the fundamental skills of listening, observing, speaking, reading, writing, spelling, mathematics, and the arts;
2. Recognition of and respect for the worth of each individual;
3. Appreciation for and power in logical, critical, and creative thinking;
4. Understanding and acceptance of the responsibilities and appreciation of the privileges inherent in the American way of life;
5. Understanding and evaluations of the cultures and contributions of other peoples;
6. Understanding of scientific truths of the universe and man's relationship to them;
7. Effective human relationships for democratic living as they apply to the individual in the family, in the school and community, in the country, and in the world;
8. Wise use of human, natural, and material resources;
9. Competence in choosing and pursuing a vocation;
10. Respect for and pride in good workmanship;
11. Values in aesthetic appreciation and creative expression;
12. Ethical behavior based on moral and spiritual values.

These goals were soon reformulated in behavioral terms as the product of mixed groups set up to compose statements behaviorally descriptive of how the well-educated graduate might demonstrate his progress toward the achievement of each of the county's twelve overall goals of education.

In addition, subject matter groups reconsidered the twelve county goals in terms of what general and special contributions each subject area could make to the development of the well-educated graduate. Another exercise in which that early workshop engaged was an examination of which goals are most central and appropriate for the school as an educational agency and which are shared with other educational agencies in the community.

Primary data sources for the development of curriculum designs were the value statements endorsed and sanctioned by the Board. Another data source was the learner—a source examined by a workshop group organized to bring together agreements from learning theory and from social and clinical psychology. The resulting pamphlet entitled, *A Report on the Learner and the Learning Process*, provided the institutional design builders with a review of major recent resource findings from psychology and sociology.

A third data source which required an extraordinary amount of work and controversy was what was called the nature of the discipline or subject field. An attempt was made by each subject group to examine the subject and to identify the method of inquiry of the field, if possible; the syntax, or structure, or major concepts of the field; and the generalizations about the field which could serve as organizing threads. These three elements, if they could be identified, were seen as the ideas and processes that should form the skeleton of the curriculum in each subject, K-12, and be visited and revisited in more and more complex forms through the longitudinal sequence of each subject.[4]

The subject matter groups were asked also to articulate major objectives for each subject, translate them into behaviors and classify them as cognitive, psychomotor, or affective. Again, translation and classification were difficult and controversial.

Curriculum design continued to be a major focus of attention during the summer of 1963. Again, the working groups included teachers, principals, supervisors, and pupil services personnel representing all subjects in the curriculum and both elementary and secondary levels of instruction. Small design groups in each subject were coordinated by a steering committee and assisted in their work by persons working on the learner and the learning process. Each subject matter group was requested to:

1. Identify the "organizing elements" of each field.
2. Describe the end behaviors sought in cognitive, psychomotor, and affective terms and related to the overall goals of the county.
3. Analyze the behaviors sought according to levels of difficulty consistent with a K-12 spiral curriculum and related to the developmental patterns of child growth described in the papers on the learner and the learning process.
4. Develop, if possible, sample illustrative units or organizing centers at appropriate levels of difficulty in each field.

The group assigned to the learner and the learning process was to refine further the papers already prepared in this area, and the steering committee was to work on balance, scope, and sequence for the whole, as well as to consider problems of internal consistency. These were large assignments, and they were by no means completed by the end of the workshop. But, although the glue to hold the framework together was still lacking, pieces of designs were beginning to appear with greater precision and clarity.

2. Design for Science. The design for science deserves special comment since it was the first palpable and systematic design product and, as such, influenced the progress of all others. During the month of March, 1964, the staff completed a physical model of a design for science (K-12). This model defined the large elements of process and content which should permeate the total curriculum in science and form the skeleton upon which specific teaching units could be built and evaluated. On one axis of the model were listed five major kinds of behavior thought to be important for inducting the student into the process of scientific inquiry. These were:

1. Observing events and using symbolic forms.
2. Relating and developing event meanings.

3. Investigating meaning and relationship.
4. Restructuring events.
5. Acquiring attitudes and values.

On the other axis were broad categories of content, namely:

1. The nature of matter.
2. The nature of energy.
3. Physical interactions.
4. Biological processes and interdependencies.
5. Cultural, social, and technological implications of science as a field.

This skeleton was elaborated and further defined in four levels of schooling—for the primary grades, for the upper elementary years, for the junior high school, and for the senior high school. When a color spectrum was added to the working model, the resulting "atomic pile" was a first approximation of a series of operational criteria for judging and reorganizing existing science curricula, for the examination of units developed by the various national studies, and for the building of new materials and content, whether such development would take place locally or in science curriculum centers elsewhere. In brief, the science design attempted to organize desired behaviors according to what is known about growth patterns of children and according to ascending levels of cognition. It also dissected the field of science logically from simple to complex generalizations. It tried to bring together the learner and the concepts and attitudes to be learned—the process and the content, the psychological and the logical. The model also permitted, indeed encouraged, a diversity of topics to be selected and studied. No content was sacred per se. Content in depth was to be sought, not as an end in itself, but rather as a vehicle for enhancing the scientific conceptual development and commitment of the learner.[5]

This institutional model of K-12 science curriculum was influenced not only by John Goodlad, but also by the aims and objectives of most of the "new" science curricula. These courses and materials were carefully examined and studied. The model, like the curriculum reforms in science, attempted to "stress the importance of understanding the structure of the discipline, the purposes and methods of the field, and the part that creative men and women played in developing the field."[6] It also emphasized the importance of making discoveries and developing some of the tools of scientific inquiry. The work of Benjamin Bloom and his associates in the dissection of educational objectives into cognitive, psychomotor, and affective domains also affected the building of this design. Extensive use was made of the taxonomy of educational objectives in the cognitive realm. Such experts in psychology as Piaget, Bruner, Havighurst, and Guilford, as well as child development authorities like Prescott, were consulted. The model also took cognizance of the writing of authorities in science education such as Schwab, Hurd, Blough, Blackwood, and Watson, as well as other attempts at science design like that of the National Science Teachers Association. Indeed, it is impossible to give credit where credit is due. The ideas certainly have their roots in the writings of Ralph Tyler, John Dewey, and Alfred North Whitehead.

3. *A Model for System-wide Institutional Design and Some Illustrations.* There were produced curriculum designs for each of ten subjects in the curriculum, similar to, yet different from, the science design. Each related itself to the twelve goals of education for the district. Each provided a framework for local school curriculum in the subject and each identified three major design elements; namely, behavioral elements, substantive elements, and temporal elements. Indeed, the introduction to the county design bulletin described the background and rationale for the ensuing ten designs as follows:

No reputable builder would start construction of a school without a series of detailed architectural drawings which blueprints all the stages and steps necessary to produce the finished structure. And no teacher worth his salt would begin instruction without a goal in mind and a series of learning activities designed to reach that goal. But, until very recently, curriculum building has proceeded without a systematic plan.

Historically, both educators and the public have been more or less content simply to add new subjects and approaches to the curriculum. This gradual modification has occurred over the years in response to the demand of changing societal needs, to greater insights into the learning process, to new ideas and knowledge about humankind and the world we live in, and to the greater numbers and varieties of students populating the schools. By and large, however, overall curriculum planning and building have been rule-of-thumb operations. Dissatisfaction with this state of affairs has mounted within the last decade. Now, the increasingly rapid rate of the accumulation of knowledge makes it not only difficult but impossible to change the curriculum only by adding to traditional offerings.

For the past five years, the curriculum workers of the County's public schools have been attempting to develop and to make operational some of the conceptual systems or theoretical frameworks outlined by researchers in education. During this period, local builders of design have borrowed heavily from John I. Goodlad of the University of California, Los Angeles, who has been a continuing consultant for the schools.

The subject designs which make up the content of this booklet need to be understood as part of a developing Goodlad-County conceptual system described more fully elsewhere. For instance, the curriculum designs for each subject are the result of what we call "institutional decision making." According to Goodlad, decision making also occurs in school systems at "societal" and "instructional" levels. Decision making at the *societal level* is performed largely by a board of education through powers delegated to it by state legislature. The curricular decisions made at this level are primarily related to goals of education, to matters of broad policy, and to budget judgments. The *institutional* level is comprised of the administrative and supervisory staff, headed by the superintendent, and the principals and teachers, when they are looking at a whole school system. Their curricular decisions relate largely to design, a term which will be defined shortly. The schools and the classrooms within them make up the *instructional level*. True curriculum decisions are made only at this level. Here the administrators, teachers, and students decide on the actual experiences which will go on in the classroom.* . . .

The designs in this document are intended to be a translation of general societal goals into teachable and learnable objectives for each subject in the curriculum. . . . Each design identifies the *content* of the subject or discipline under consideration—the knowledge to be gained and the skills

---

*Note: As will be seen from Chapters 1 and 2, this is not a completely accurate interpretation of the Goodlad Conceptual System. In his system, the school is at the institutional level and teachers alone or teachers and students, but not administrators, make instructional decisions.

to be taught. It also identifies the developmental *behaviors* to be practiced by students as they encounter the content. Finally, it defines the climate for learning which will be most propitious for accomplishment of goals and for the achievement of mental health.

The Goodlad-County conceptual scheme calls the content and the behaviors the *organizing elements* of a design. In many designs, these are depicted graphically on charts with the *behavioral elements* written along a vertical axis and the *substantive* (content) *elements* along the horizontal as can be seen in [Figure 9.1].

The points of intersection of behavioral and substantive elements on the graphical representation of a subject design are another important element of the curriculum theory. The points at which behaviors and content meet represent the *learning objectives.* They identify blocks or segments of the total design which are capable of being organized into specific teaching and learning strategies. The point at which learning objectives are identified is also the point at which another important curricular concept begins. These objectives, combined with lists of resources and teaching strategies, constitute an *organizing center.* In many ways, the *organizing center* resembles the older idea of the *teaching unit,* which in its more sophisticated forms included not only segments of subject matter but also represented a union of experience with facts and big ideas.

Within the chart itself, the intersections of the axes provide space for showing the generalizations which the learner derives from experiencing a given behavior with respect to specified content. Thus the curricular design shows visually how the learner approximates the experience of the scholar in a discipline, how he encounters big ideas (substantive elements) and derives generalizations from that experience which will lead him on to further learning.

In a sense the points of intersection of behavior and content mark off not

	Substantive Element A	Substantive Element B	Substantive Element C	
Behavioral Element III				
Behavioral Element II		▨▨▨	←————	Learning Objectives
Behavioral Element I				

Figure 9.1. The Concepts of Design and Learning Objectives, Progenitors of Organizing Centers.

only the learning objectives but also the point at which institutional design leaves off and the instructional level of decision making begins. In the Goodlad-County theory, this is also the meeting point of the institutional specialist and the classroom teacher.

The curriculum designs in this bulletin differ as the designers and the raw material of each subject differ. They represent more than three years of work and countless revisions. Even so, they must be examined as a prospective builder looks at an architect's first rough sketches for a new house—knowing that all will be modified by the topography of the land, the demands of the householder, and the art and workmanship of the builder and architect.

Unlike an architect's drawing, however, these first approximations of design will never be really finished. They should change as our knowledge of the learner, our understanding of society's demands and values, and our concepts of the structure of knowledge change. At the same time, these tentative thrusts toward the future hold within them high hopes for an improved educational fare for the students of our public schools.[7]

As indicated in the introduction, there are major differences between the designs just as there are between the subjects they organize for instructional purposes (see Figure 9.2, Design for Art, K-12).

Each section of the summary chart is detailed in the full description of the design. As an illustration, note the following partial description of the element called *Space*, as it is to be understood through the arts:

Space encompasses all things, and all things exist in space. It is both relative and actual.

Space is unique because the artist cannot choose to work without it, and it remains unchanged until one or more of the elements of art is introduced and becomes visually apparent only when defined by these elements.[8]

The curriculum design for *English/Language Arts* serves as another design model (see Figure 9.3, Design for English/Language Arts). That design also carefully depicted its substantive elements, this time describing the *nature, function,* and *structure* of language and then listing such behavioral outcomes as:

Uses multi-sensory observation to gain information.
Distinguishes significant sounds.
Recognizes sounds in meaningful combinations.

BEHAVIORAL ELEMENTS + CONCEPTUAL CONTENT ELEMENTS through ART MEDIA to BEHAVIORAL GOALS

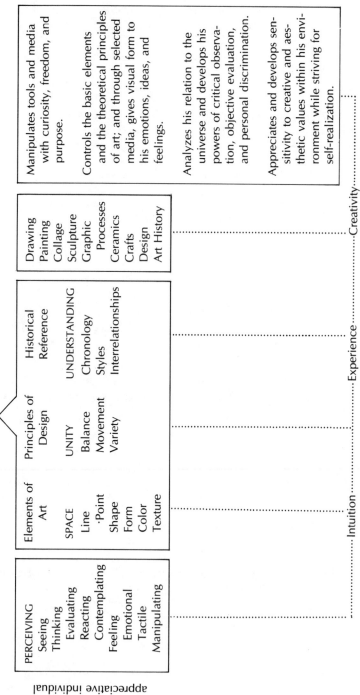

| PERCEIVING | Elements of Art | Principles of Design | Historical Reference | Drawing Painting Collage Sculpture Graphic Processes Ceramics Crafts Design Art History | Manipulates tools and media with curiosity, freedom, and purpose. |

Seeing
Thinking
Evaluating
Reacting
Contemplating
Feeling
Emotional
Tactile
Manipulating

SPACE
Line
·Point
Shape
Form
Color
Texture

UNITY
Balance
Movement
Variety

UNDERSTANDING
Chronology
Styles
Interrelationships

Controls the basic elements and the theoretical principles of art; and through selected media, gives visual form to his emotions, ideas, and feelings.

Analyzes his relation to the universe and develops his powers of critical observation, objective evaluation, and personal discrimination.

Appreciates and develops sensitivity to creative and aesthetic values within his environment while striving for self-realization.

The potentially creative and appreciative individual

Intuition·······Experience·······Creativity

Figure 9.2. Design for Art, K-12

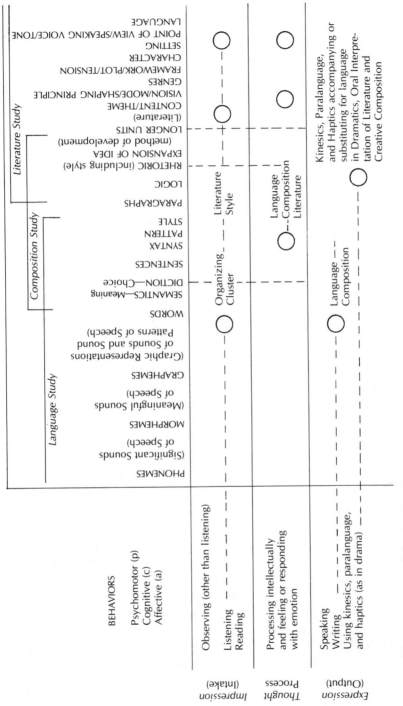

Figure 9.3. Design for English/Language Arts

Recognizes literal and metaphorical use of words.
Uses language to inform, persuade, question, command.[9]

These samples from selected designs reflect both the likenesses and differences among them. The designs served as guides to curriculum development activity for several years. They probably would serve well today, despite the fact that both the patterns and the specifics within the patterns might change substantially.

4. An Overall Institutional Curriculum Design and A Conceptual System for Planning and Managing the Instructional Program.

Logically preceding curriculum designs in each subject and certainly preceding the development of a system for planning and managing a large instructional program is the building of an overall instructional curriculum design. In fact, according to our own definition,

The overall curriculum design should perform for the instructional program as a whole the tasks which a curriculum design performs for each subject field: define its scope, provide the basis for sequence and integration, and suggest the focus of instruction.[10]

Many groups worked on this task. There exist many unfinished and abortive efforts. For example, in June, 1964, the matter was attacked by all subject supervisors serving during the period as generalists. Here an attempt was made to establish a common vocabulary and to tease out behavioral and substantive elements common to all subjects. Massive bits and pieces of the whole are on file. The dimensions of the task have been clarified. Vocabulary and levels of abstraction are more streamlined and consistent than they were. There was much talk about values and large areas of knowledge. Various patterns have been suggested to pull everything together. We never were satisfied, however, with any of the suggested patterns of simplifying the diversity before us nor of serving as the transactional links between the adopted "societal" goals of education for the school system and a professional "institutional" design for the whole curriculum, K-12. In short, the development of an overall curriculum design proved to be the most difficult of the curriculum planning tasks we tackled.

Also difficult, but more yielding to continued assault, was the task of developing a conceptual system for planning and managing the instructional program for the school system. A research assistant in the Curriculum Department reviewed the work of the school system since 1960 in "the development of components of the new instructional program, in administrative invention, and in conceptualization . . . ."[11] She used the history of county efforts at general instructional improvement as well as the curricular ideas of Ralph Tyler and John I. Goodlad. These ideas, adapted and refined by the curriculum developers of the county school system, and further elaborated in the light of systems analysis, formed the foundation for a paper by Baldwin which describes and develops a conceptual system for planning and managing the instructional program of a public school system. This paper is an excellent summary of the county program and of administrative improvement from 1960–1966, of the Tyler-Goodlad conceptual framework, of the "Goodlad Grid," and of the county institutional model of curriculum design.

The county needed an orderly and articulate statement both to explain its actions and to orient the continuous stream of new personnel who move into instructional leadership positions. The document therefore has had several printings. But more important than the well-organized description of activities on the curriculum and instructional front is Baldwin's process model and articulation of system components for that model.

In this model, Baldwin telescopes Tyler's four classical curriculum questions into three categories: *ends, means,* and *evaluation*. She then adds Goodlad's three categories of decision making—*societal, institutional,* and *instructional*—and presents each level with a vertical feedback system derived from experience in the county. This process she calls the *translational process* and suggests that it occurs along a *formulation-revision continuum*. All three decision-making areas are connected, after Goodlad, in a *transactional process* which occurs along a *generality-specificity continuum* (see Chapter 1, Figure 1.1).

The full model is shown as Figure 9.4. It is further described in the words of its inventor whose work clearly relates to the conceptual model described by Goodlad in Chapter 1:

The model demonstrates that planning and managing the instructional program of a public school system involve two processes (a translational process and a transactional process), both of which occur along continua and operate on four categories of components (ends, means, evaluation, and decision-making agents). Within the transactional process, decisions are made on three categories of issues. The decisions differ along a generality-specificity continuum according to the area of responsibility in which the decision-making agents operate. Within the translational process, decision-making agents formulate ends, means to achieve them, and methods of evaluating the efficiency of the means in achieving the ends. Decision-making agents make such revisions as are necessary.

The systems approach has two effects on the model. The first is to establish the boundaries which are essential to analysis, within which the process of planning and managing the instructional program of a public school organization operates as a system. Boundaries are difficult to define for any system. They are notoriously difficult in this case. . . . Nonetheless, boundaries are essential; and when logic fails in defining them, intuition succeeds, though its definition is often arbitrary. The boundaries of the process of planning and managing the instructional program of a public school system are those of "the school system." Ultimate responsibility for its operation resides in the citizenry operating through the political process; and requirements are laid on its operation by state law. But when the process of planning and managing the instructional program is analyzed as a system, its boundaries may be defined for our purposes as the area of responsibility of the Board of Education.

The second effect of the systems approach is to require that decisions relating to particular elements be made in terms of the other elements in the system. This effect, with reference to the operation of the translational and the transactional processes, is as follows: The model demonstrates a precise relationship between the categories within each area of responsibility and also between each category in the three areas of responsibility. These relationships require that decisions made in any area of responsibility with respect to any category must reflect decisions previously made and must permit the making of subsequent decisions. There is thus a precise integration of decisions.[12]

5. *Other Institutional Level Tasks.* During the period of intensive work on societal and institutional curriculum design, there was parallel work on the preparation of teacher's guides, courses of study, and evaluative instruments for use

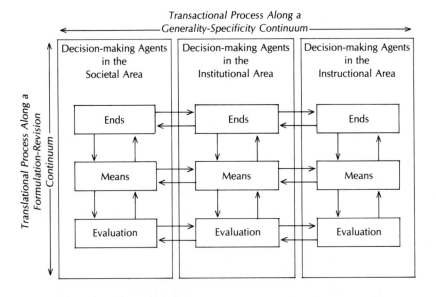

Figure 9.4. A theoretical model of the process of planning and managing the instructional program of a public school system.

in the classrooms of the county. In the majority of cases, the materials for teacher use in the classrooms were heavily influenced by the continuing work on institutional design in all subjects. Concepts from the field and behaviors to be practiced were more clearly defined than before, and there was an attempt to plan the learning sequences on a K-12 continuum rather than in isolated sections. In English/Language Arts, for example, these years saw the production of a series of teaching guides on composition—elementary, junior high, and senior high; and a teacher's guide to literature, K-12, organized around the basic themes and forms which undergird the field of literature, with illustrative examples at several levels of maturity.

The mathematics program, highly sequenced, K-12, boasted sets of well-developed behavioral objectives which are not only backed up by guides and materials created in the county, but increasingly with nationally developed alternative programs for local schools. Tests and test banks were developed for county and school evaluative purposes. Also prepared (early in the 1970s) was a set of highly sequenced performance objectives, K-8, honed and sharpened after the pattern established by the intersection of behavioral and substantive elements demanded by the Goodlad Grid. The mathematics design, K-12, was reproduced in each teacher's guide or mathematics bulletin.

The science and social studies programs, although traditionally organized, were built on institutional curriculum designs. Science, in particular, had well-developed behavioral objectives and, in many instances, a variety of choices for local schools. Social studies throughout had the most difficulty in articulating its design and in building or finding a series of alternative "topics, problem units, events, or focal points, designed to stimulate appropriate behavior on the part of the students."[13]

Also growing out of the institutional curriculum designs were two volumes called *Evaluative Criteria,* one for the elementary and one for the secondary schools. These documents were developed by curriculum and test specialists with the help of selected principals and school faculties. In both instances, goals of instruction were identified; a point of view presented; and teaching procedures, learning activities, methods of evaluation, and anticipated outcomes were discussed.

The Instructional Level of Decision Making

Despite the amount of productive work accomplished and the number of instructional tools built as a result of use of the Goodlad curricular conceptual scheme, there remained in the county a tremendous task ahead if the discrepancy between the demands of the institutional curriculum designs and the realities of classroom practice was to be lessened. After time-honored methods of closing this gap had been tried and found wanting, the Supervision and Curriculum Department decided to shift its emphasis from institutional level curriculum development to the design of another set of models—this time relating to new supervisory techniques. In effect, we endeavored to put major developmental energies into designing, field-testing, and operating techniques to enhance the transactional processes between the institutional and instructional level of decision making.

During the ensuing era of work, our continuing consultant was Bruce Joyce, then of Teachers College, Columbia University. With his help, we concentrated on four major areas: communication, systematic support for curricular and instructional decision making by local schools, enhanced program management, and the development and testing of alternative curricular patterns and units. Concentration on communication included the establishment and nurturing of contact with field leadership and greater efforts toward design and operation of well-developed staff development programs.

Systematic support for local schools included developing support teams of experts to enhance local initiative; field-testing self-regulating supervisory systems such as micro-teaching; piloting of "mini-courses" coming out of the Far Western Educational Laboratory in Berkeley; working with Joyce's *Models of Teaching*[14] through analyses of videotaped teaching; and experimenting with the operation of mobile teacher laboratories designed to bring to teachers the latest curriculum units and packages and new self-supervisory and teaching strategies.

Enhancement of program management included in-service programs for all administrative and supervisory personnel in managerial techniques like PERT (Program Evaluation and Review Technique) and systems analysis; increasing data storage and retrieval capability for the school system; a beginning PPBS (Planning-Programming-Budgeting System) project; and the development of management intervention teams to respond quickly and decisively when schools get into serious trouble.

The design, development, and testing of alternative curricular patterns and modules mean that schools may have many curricular and instructional options out of which to tailor their own programs. Considerable work on the design of a curriculum bank of alternatives is an essential feature of this focus, a formidable task in and of itself.

These are all pieces of what Joyce calls "multiple-route"

management systems. They were designed in the hope that they could not only provide support and options to local schools and individual teachers and children, but also form an attack on the "glassy homogeneity" of the American school. In other words, the aim was to encourage unique local-unit curriculum options and teacher initiative and creativity.

The approach described above assumed that the school as a social and educational unit does not now have within it the technical skill and material support it needs to ensure the quality of instructional decision making demanded by the Goodlad conceptual scheme. Goodlad's later work on change, however, demonstrates the power of the local school as the key unit for curricular improvement when it *does* receive the encouragement and technical help of a supportive infrastructure.[15]

CONCLUDING REFLECTIONS

Progress in this rational planning of curriculum and instruction has been slow and uneven during recent years. It often has been necessary to retreat and retrace steps through what we thought was well-mapped territory. At other times we put a great deal of effort into following will-o'-the-wisp ideas and procedures which succeeded only in getting us lost again. The problems involved in the development of a common language for communication often seemed insurmountable. Recent demands for more local autonomy, on the one hand, and more demands for accountability and quality schooling, on the other, have added even more complexity to the enterprise.

There have been and continue to be political and practical problems as well as conceptual ones. Any large school system consists of hierarchies of power and prestige and differing beliefs about the nature of the educative process. Some groups complained that most of the undertaking was ivory tower dreaming. Others were nervous about organization and structure in any form and subtly managed to resist planning. The struggles toward intellectual clarity and rigor were often seen as threats to creativity and to perceptions of and commitments to the tenets of the child development movement. In recent years, school systems seem more concerned about managerial control and about issues relating to internal power, efficiency, and territoriality than about instruction or rational planning of any kind.

It should be remembered that most of the people involved in what has been described had full-time assignments other than the development of curriculum designs. This had its advantages as well as disadvantages. In particular, the undertaking had constant feedback from teachers, administrators, and supervisors. Consequently, it had a vitality which would be difficult, if not impossible, to achieve were it not firmly planted in ongoing school processes. There often seemed to be renewed staff creativity after periods of concentration on other tasks.

Of great assistance throughout was the existence in the county of an exceptionally able staff of administrative and subject supervisors and of master teachers ready, indeed hungry, for ideas. They tackled the work with intellectual excitement and a sense of adventure. During struggles toward operational clarity, they succeeded in stimulating each other and their associates in other settings. They persisted through periods of bleak discouragement and returned to the task with renewed dedication.

In retrospect, it is clear that Goodlad's conceptualization of the domains of curriculum and their accompanying transactional and interpretive processes provided the needed glue for programmatic planning at the county (district) level. The problem of setting some overall direction and providing both a guiding framework and degrees of freedom in employing that framework is a classic one in the field. Had local initiative and individual creativity not been valued, we could have used the conceptual system with one-way arrows only in linear fashion and had no further thoughts as to the consequences. But in the design all the arrows between levels of decision making go both ways (again see Chapter 1, Figure 1.1). This is how curricular practice proceeds and must continue to proceed in this kind of community.

There is no doubt now in my mind that the school system delayed too long in seeking to provide adequately for local school and individual teacher involvement. Unusual circumstances exacerbated the problem we were endeavoring to solve at the outset—that is, to provide some kind of order in an otherwise badly segmented process of educational improvement. The expansion in student enrollment was explosive; new schools and new staffs were being created overnight, it seemed. The system paid little or no attention to readying these settings for, and assisting them in, the necessary processes of institutional and instructional planning, sometimes because the game within the central office and area leadership was power, not instruction, and sometimes because we failed to convince some important administrators and principals of the usefulness of the conceptual scheme and of the curriculum guides which were built on it. Simply representing school sites in the district enterprise was far from sufficient. We didn't know then what we know now about educational change.

Further, the ideas were new and difficult for all of us who were endeavoring to get our minds around them. We were challenged, exhilarated, and frustrated, often simultaneously. The added tasks of decentralizing greater responsibility to the local school and creating the necessary supporting infrastructure would have appeared overwhelming, even if we had been alert to them at the outset. Perhaps we should have spent less time actually building curricula at the county level and more time in both immersing ourselves thoroughly in the ideas and seeing to it that uniform attention was given to all levels of decision making.

There is, however, no question in my mind about the relevance and usefulness of the conceptual system. It describes what goes on somewhat abortively and haphazardly in most curriculum-planning efforts. But it also identifies what elements require careful attention if these processes are to reach an adequate level of orderly productivity. Studying the deliberate and deliberative processes of curriculum development in a sociopolitical context is an important kind of curriculum praxiology which has much to offer improved curriculum practice.

NOTES

1. Benjamin S. Bloom (ed.), *Taxonomy of Educational Objectives; Handbook I: The Cognitive Domain*, Longmans, Green, New York, 1956.

2. David R. Krathwohl, Benjamin S. Bloom, and Bertram B. Masia, *Taxonomy of Educational Objectives: Handbook II: Affective Domain*, David McKay, New York, 1964.

3. *Curriculum Design: Institutional Level*, Department of Supervision and Curriculum Development, Montgomery County Public Schools, Rockville, Maryland, 1967.

4. Jerome S. Bruner, *The Process of Education*, Harvard University Press, Cambridge, Massachusetts, 1960.

5. Edmund Hoffmaster, James Latham, Jr., and Elizabeth Wilson, "Design for Science," *Science Teacher*, vol. 31, no. 7, November 1964, pp. 15–17.

6. John I. Goodlad, *School Curriculum Reform in the United States*, Fund for the Advancement of Education, New York, 1964, p. 54.

7. *Curriculum Design: Institutional Level*, loc. cit.

8. Ibid.

9. Ibid.

10. Harriet B. Baldwin, *A Conceptual System for Planning and Managing the Instructional Program of the Montgomery County Public Schools*, Department of Supervision and Curriculum Development, Montgomery County Public Schools, Rockville, Maryland, 1966.

11. Ibid.

12. Ibid.

13. Goodlad, op. cit., p. 53.

14. Bruce Joyce and Marsha Weil, *Models of Teaching*, Prentice-Hall, Englewood Cliffs, New Jersey, 1972.

15. John I. Goodlad, *The Dynamics of Educational Change*, McGraw-Hill, New York, 1975.

10

The Role of the Curriculum Maker in Cross-Cultural Perspective

ALICJA IWAŃSKA

Such jobs as that of a dietitian, public relations person, or curriculum maker are new and in many countries do not yet exist. They are ignored as a possible field of specialization by the majority of young men and women even in the United States. Such jobs are among the newest and most luxurious cross-breedings in the large garden of specialization of labor characteristic of, and unique to, a rich, highly industrialized, and highly literate civilization.

Indeed, only in the countries which have these character-istics would a restaurant owner be conscious of the need for anyone else besides a cook, dishwashers, waiters, and some-times a manager for a large restaurant or cafeteria. A dietitian is neither housekeeper nor cook. She probably knows at least as much about certain aspects of cooking as does the cook, but does not do the actual cooking herself. And, like the housekeeper, she has to plan a great deal. Her planning, however, is restricted to a much narrower area than that of the housekeeper. She plans the food from the point of view of its healthfulness, costs, and appropriateness to the gourmet tastes of her employers. She has been trained as an expert in the nourishing qualities of food and as an administrator, a planner of meals adapted to the needs of those who will consume these meals.

Like a dietitian, a public relations person, and many other occupants of newly created jobs, the curriculum maker is trained as well in at least two ways. On the one hand, he has to know something about some more or less concrete subject matter; on the other hand, he has to know a great deal about planning, administration, organization, and such matters. In fact, the newer the job, the more indefinite the area of "such matters" in which the job holder gets involved, whether he was trained for his job or not. The best curriculum makers often are troubled with the necessity of dealing with things they were not trained for. Let us hope that they will experience some feeling of comfort in learning that this happens in the case of all holders of new jobs, and that to cope with things one was not trained for is the common fate of all occupational pioneers.

Only during recent decades have problems of curriculum become a part of the formal training of any teacher in the major academic schools and departments of education in the United States. In some of these schools, quite a few courses in curriculum are offered, and in a few places a student of education is allowed to specialize in "the science of curriculum" and thus to become a certified M.A. or Ph.D. curriculum maker. But before the field of curriculum became an academic field of higher specialization, curriculum making was practiced "innocently" (though not necessarily badly) by people who were not certified curriculum makers and, in fact, it is still practiced this way in most of the schools in this country, as well as in other countries. Self-appointed or forced-into-the-job curriculum makers have been emerging in different parts of the world out of various occupations (that of the mayor, teacher, priest, rich patron of the school, tribal chief, librarian, even policeman). Most of them do not know about the possibilities of training in curriculum making. They are not aware of the fancy name for the activity they perform, nor of the influence which their informal and unnamed curriculum activities may have on a new science in the making, the science of curriculum.

It may be helpful for students of curriculum, as well as for various curriculum makers, both duly labeled and self-conscious ones and those who remain untitled and unaware of their role, to analyze the role of a curriculum maker into its specific components, as one analyzes an unknown substance in a laboratory.

But the only substitute laboratory available to a student of human society is a society different from his own, and preferably a smaller and technologically simpler one. He is able to see such a society in a more detached manner than he could see his own society to which he is strongly attached by various economic, political, and emotional ties. And in such a society he is sometimes able to identify the individuals who have social roles similar to his own and who are faced with at least some similar problems. By suggesting such an imaginary excursion into "the laboratory of the social sciences," we assume, of course, that conscious action based on more rather than less knowledge is somehow better (though it may also be slower) than social action which is quick but blind.

We may define the educator as a person specialized in the more or less systematic transmission of a certain portion of a selected cultural heritage from one segment of a population to another and sanctioned in this capacity by at least one group within the society on behalf of which he performs his role. The teacher in an adult education program will be called an "educator" according to this definition, along with the teacher in the kindergarten, public school, barber college, or an African initiation school.

Though the nature of the selected cultural heritage and of the sanctioning group varies greatly from one case to another, the process of transmitting (though, of course, not the techniques of transmission) remains the same. In all cases, this is a conscious and more or less systematic transmission. Some minimum planning of how to transmit a given portion of the cultural heritage is demanded of every educator. Every educator is thus at least to some extent a sort of curriculum maker, if by curriculum making we understand the "how" of such transmitting. But do we really understand by "curriculum making" only the "how" of such transmitting?

In order to answer this question, we should turn to the definition of the role of curriculum maker in the society where this role was born and is most elaborated, the contemporary U.S.A. We could, for instance, study the formal documents: all sorts of books on how to make curriculum. We would not learn much, however, from such programmatic studies about the actual social role of curriculum maker, just as we would not learn much from reading the American Constitution about the role, say, of the labor lobbyist. We may learn far more about the role of the curriculum maker in the U.S.A. if we look at a "sample" of individuals involved in educational planning. Here, we will notice very soon that the planning of the "how" of educational processes is not the only activity of the educational planner. Practically everybody involved in educational planning is concerned not only with the "how" of transmitting a selected cultural heritage, but also with the numerous "what's" and "why's" and "to whom's" of that transmission. Labeled or unlabeled curriculum makers in the contemporary U.S.A. are thus involved not only in the planning of how to transmit a given cultural heritage to a selected social group, but also in making numerous decisions as to what part of cultural heritage is to be transmitted and why it should be transmitted to this group rather than to another, which group is to receive such and such a portion of cultural heritage first and which one later, which groups should be given how much, and even which groups should be prevented from accepting certain portions of the cultural heritage.

These curriculum makers not only transmit to a selected group whatever was selected to be transmitted by a sanctioning group of their society, but they also sometimes belong to that sanctioning group themselves, and, as members of that group, thus decide what is to be transmitted to whom and why. Such decisions are usually called "political decisions," and sanctioning groups are "political groups" in the large sense of this word. They must have some possibility of enforcing their decisions; that is, they must have some power. The contemporary American curriculum maker is thus either an educator specialized in educational planning (i.e., an expert on curriculum making) sanctioned by some power group; or he is a member of this sanctioning group himself, unconcerned with the details of educational planning but highly concerned with the problem of when and why a given portion of the cultural heritage should be transmitted to one group rather than to another; or often he is a sort of hybrid between an educator and a member of a sanctioning group— an originator of orders or "advice," and the supervisor of their execution (i.e., administrator), as well as their executor—a position as interesting and uncomfortable as the position of any in-between cultural hybrid may be.

Having in mind these three types of American curriculum makers, let us try now to see whether we will be able to find their counterparts in a few technologically simple, "primitive" societies for which roughly comparable data are available. In each case, we will try first of all to see whether we can identify approximations of at least one of the three types of curriculum makers in the society in question. Then we will try to identify the sanctioning group behind the primitive "curriculum maker," the content of the cultural heritage which is to be transmitted by primitive "educators," the groups to which it is to be transmitted, and, finally, the very process of transmission, the "how's" of the educator.

In the anthropological literature, we often find education in our sense of this word: conscious, and more or less planned transmission of certain parts of the cultural heritage from one segment of a population to another, sanctioned by at least one group of the given society. This involves, in the simplest case, so-called spontaneous social education, which has a great degree of visibility and emotional appeal to anthropologists. We have in mind all sorts of education by extended family and community such, for instance, as among the Zuni Indians where not only all the relatives cooperate to see that the child behaves well, but even other unrelated adult members of the community try to correct a misbehaving child.[1] Similarly, among the Hopi Indians, a great deal of such spontaneous social education of children takes place around a communal bowl, in the kiva, where stories, dreams, adventures, and actual experiences, such as a journey away from the reservation, are told and retold.[2]

Among Melanesians in the Bismarck Archipelago, children are supposed to learn how to tell folktales and myths, and here, unlike among Zuni and Hopi, we may already see a more structured educational situation. During a period of three to four weeks, adult males and females tell the children tales at night around the fire. Etiquette, taboos, and customs, as well as the punishments for those who break them, are all illustrated in these narratives.[3]

In these three societies, we are able to identify the educational content (among the Zuni, chiefly education in good manners; among Hopi and Melanesians, the teaching of the world view and ethos of the society) and also the educational process (among the Zuni, teaching children by constant correction by adults; among the Hopi and Melanesian people of Lesu, the teaching of children through instruction in listening and repetition). We are also able to identify both the sanctioning group (in all cases the whole society whose tradition is being transmitted) and the segment of the population (in all cases all the children of the given community) to whom the cultural heritage is being transmitted. When we ask, however, to what extent the transmitters of the selected cultural heritage were conscious of their job, and to what extent they were systematic (as even the rudimentary curriculum maker should be), we see that it is rather hard to identify any conscious planning in their educational activities. In the case of the Zuni Indians, the self-appointed casual adults were the transmitters of the cultural heritage to children casually met; in the case of the Hopi, the elders of the community were the spontaneous educators; in the case of the people of Lesu, the educators were the adult males and females. No one of those transmitters was even to the smallest degree a self-conscious specialist in educational planning. They all performed important roles in the socialization of children in their respective societies, but we would be greatly mistaken if we tried to search in those activities for any manifestations of even the simplest curriculum making.

This sort of spontaneous social education does not disappear, however, with the appearance of educational planning. Even in the country of the most specialized occupational roles—the U.S.A.—where curriculum making is already taught at the universities, the spontaneous social education of children by the family and relatives, by neighbors and peer groups, plays an extremely important role.

There is no point in searching for the elements of curriculum making in any type of spontaneous social education. We have a far better chance of finding it when we look into two different types of education encountered among technologically simple "primitive" people—education which is transmitted on the occasion of so-called crises of life such as puberty or marriage, and education which is transmitted on the occasion of training for specialized social roles such as that of medicine man, priest, or social leader.

Some degree of systematization of the educational processes which occur on occasion of the so-called crises of life is a common phenomenon among practically all "primitive people." In Africa, however, and particularly among the Bantu peoples of South and East Africa, it became one of the major social institutions.

In the Venda tribe of Northern Transvaal and Southern Rhodesia,[4] the *thondo,* an initiation school for boys, was a permanent and strong institution with an elaborate "administration" and great political significance. The *thondos* had functioned for a long time as military schools, providing the tribe with always ready, well-trained warriors. Later, when the wars among chiefs stopped, the *thondos* lost their military significance, but without having changed their administrative structure and their ritual. They became then, as it is reported, the places from which free labor was obtained by a chief, but they still functioned as compulsory schools for all boys of the tribe. During this period, the boys who did not want to attend *thondos* were allowed to commute their services for money payments.

Every eight- or nine-year-old boy out of each of the eighteen districts into which the Europeans had divided the country after the Anglo-Boer war had to enter the *thondo* and remain in it until he reached puberty. After graduation from *thondo,* which ended with an elaborate initiation ceremony, boys were released from the school and were attached to age sets which were something like tribal regiments. During the war, all the members of the same age set fought together and, during peace time, they remained in close contact with one another. At any time after the "graduation," for as long as they wished, and during all public feasts, boys and men sat together with their age sets. Their solidarity was somehow similar (though no doubt stronger and more formalized) to the solidarity encountered in fraternities or masonic lodges.

After this brief description of the place of the *thondo* in Bavenda society, let us see what was the sanctioning group or groups behind this institution, from what segment of society and to what segment the cultural heritage of the tribe was transmitted through this school, what was the content of the cultural heritage transmitted, and what was the "curriculum" of the *thondo.*

Originally, apparently, the *thondo* was a school only for the aristocracy, but we do not have any exact data available from that period. At later times, all Venda boys, regardless of their origin, had to attend the *thondo* until puberty. We may compare the *thondo* system with the system of public schools in the U.S.A. in that the *thondo* schools were also free and compulsory for all boys of a certain age. The differences between the *thondo* schools and American public schools are, however, much greater than are the similarities. Unlike the public schools in the United States, *thondo* schools were not coeducational. The atmosphere of *thondos* was enveloped in great secrecy, and the schools, in spite of being compulsory for all boys, had a certain elite flavor, so absent from most American public schools.[5]

The sanctioning group behind the *thondo* was the government of Bavenda itself. The chief of the Bavenda was the supreme head of all *thondo* schools and inspected them personally from time to time. The teachers were the elders of the tribe headed by the *Negota,* the head counselor, whose main job was to administer punishment, consisting of severe beating with a stick, to boys who did not obey the *thondo* rules. And obedience to the *thondo* rules (which were a version of tribal rules) was definitely part of the "curriculum," like some sort of civic education is a part of the curriculum in American public schools. The rules taught in *thondos* consisted, on the one hand, of an introduction to the rules connected with boys' future responsibilities as citizens of the tribe; on the other hand, *thondo* students were persistently drilled in tribal etiquette, trained to perform tribal dances, etc. This was more or less the content of *thondo* "general education," permeated, like all general education in all historical periods and in all parts of the world, with strong "do's" and "don't's" of the sanctioning group. But besides this "general education" a great deal of the time of *thondo* boys was devoted to military training, since being a soldier was to be the main task of every Bavenda man. Here again, instruction in such military arts as night attack, spying, etc., went side by side with "character training" in all sorts of physical hardships, obedience, punctuality, and so on.

Since it is possible to identify the "curriculum" of the *thondo* school, it must also be possible to identify some approximation of the curriculum maker. This job, it seems, was in large part performed by the Bavenda chief who not only inspected the school but also adapted its goals to the changing goals of the tribe. This he did, as we know, by transferring the school's military goals to labor-recruiting goals. This he did, also, by allowing boys to pay him certain dues in order to be exempted from the school. But the head counselor, whose main duty in *thondo* was the punishment of boys, probably also to a certain degree performed the work of an educational planner, planning the administration of social sanctions, and very likely changing them according to the changing objective of the *thondos.* We do not know to what extent the teaching elders were only *thondo* instructors and to what extent, side by side with the tribal chief and head counselor, they participated in some educational planning. If they did the latter, we would consider them to be also primitive curriculum makers.

Lasting usually a much shorter time (a few months only) but usually administratively more complex than *thondo* were all sorts of circumcision schools, common in Africa and particularly among the Bantu, but disappearing rapidly during the last few decades. The education received in those schools, or rather "workshops" or "camps," was always less specialized than in the *thondo*[6] and far more ritualistic, secret, and concerned with "character education" than the *thondo* and, of course, more preoccupied with the problem of sexual maturity of the boys and their preparation for marriage. In some tribes as, for example, the Bavenda, where initiation into manhood was the important part of the *thondo* "curriculum," there was also a special coeducational school, the *domba*, where Bavenda boys and girls received general preparation for marriage. We see clearly how different those *domba* classes were from American marriage or "facts-of-life" lectures, when we learn that all instruction was enveloped in an intricate ceremonial which, by means of symbols and metaphors, taught boys and girls the significance of marriage and childbirth and various pitfalls and dangers they would be likely to encounter during the course of their lives.[7]

In spite of the fact that the *thondo* "curriculum" was mainly concerned with the training of soldiers, this type of school cannot be called a prototype of vocational school since to be a soldier was not a specialized occupation but the common fate of all adult men in Bavenda.

In order to see how the training for specialized roles looks in technologically simple, "primitive" societies, we must turn elsewhere, to different types of learning situations. Though formalized learning is not always a necessary preparation for a successful performance of some of the highly specialized and important roles in a society (note, for instance, the lack of any formal training for such important roles as, for example, President of the United States), some formal prerequisites (often including a certain period of schooling) are often required for the performance of some important social roles, such as those of priest and doctor.

Among the Creek Indians of the U.S.A., the great majority of doctors and priests belonged to a class of learned men who received a special training considered necessary or at least highly desirable for the performance of their professional duties.[8] The medical training of Creek Indians was usually privately initiated by one to four students-to-be, who often had to go to town in search of a well-trained Indian medicine man who would agree to be engaged by them as instructor. There were very few potential teachers because not many Indian medicine men passed the full medicine course. Once the qualified teacher was found, the small "class" had to find some isolated place, preferably in a densely wooded creek bottom where they were not likely to be observed. The whole period of schooling usually lasted about two months and was given in several successive four-day sessions followed later by an eight-day session and finally by a twelve-day session which completed the training. The periods of instruction were unusually intensive; they required fasting, drinking great quantities of special medicine, and isolation from all noises and disturbances because nothing was written and everything had to become deeply imprinted on the mind. But between the sessions, students would return home, where they were to do their "homework," which, like their studies with the instructor, consisted of endless repetition of how to cure various diseases through specially prepared medicines and magical formulas.

As we see from the description, this was specialized vocational or professional instruction, in which the tribal ethos (how to be a good Creek Indian) can hardly be detected. No doubt, a careful examination of such "curricula" may show more elements of Creek ethos than we suspect at first, but in the same way, a careful examination of the curricula of British, French, or American medical schools may reveal the presence of unsuspected elements of national ethos or current ideology "between the lines" of purely medical instruction.[9] The sanctioning group behind the "medical schools" of Creek

Indians was the tribe itself. The students were self-selected; the teachers were selected by students on the basis of their qualifications. The portion of the tribal heritage which was here transmitted from teachers to students was largely determined by the tribal tradition, interpreted very likely by the teachers themselves. Were Creek medicine teachers at least to some extent curriculum makers? The answer is "yes"—they were involved in the curricular decisions at least in one way and very likely in two ways. As independent teachers, they certainly planned how to make students memorize the secular formulas involved in preparation of medicines as well as the magical formulas which have to accompany their making and administration. Further, they decided such things as whether a given site was isolated enough for successful teaching, whether the students' fasting was sufficient, whether a given student learned enough to "graduate," etc. Besides, if they were indeed interpreting the tribal tradition of "medical science," like any interpreters, they had considerable influence upon the "curricula" by dismissing some portions of that tradition and emphasizing others.

A very different type of training for a specialized role (that of a leader) in a technologically simple, "primitive" society may be observed among the Arapesh-speaking people of New Guinea.[10] In this highly cooperative society of confident, easy-going people, to be a leader is considered not a privilege but an unpleasant duty. No one, it is assumed, really wants to be a leader, a "big man." "Big men" have to plan, initiate changes, strut and swagger and talk in loud voices; they have to boast of what they have done in the past and are going to do in the future. All of this the Arapesh regard as most uncongenial, difficult behavior, the kind of behavior in which no normal man would indulge if he could possibly avoid it.[11] But, at the same time, it is recognized that leadership is necessary (mainly in order to organize, once every few years, a really exciting ceremonial) and therefore some men should assume this responsibility.

When boys are in their teens, their elders try to classify them into three categories:

1. Those whose ears are open and whose throats are open.
2. Those whose ears are open but whose throats are shut.
3. Those whose ears and throats are both shut.

The candidates for future "big men" (i.e., leaders) are selected from this first group of most attentive, wise, and articulate people, and they undergo a special training for leadership. This is done by assigning every selected boy in early adolescence a *buanyin,* an exchange partner, from among young men of the clan in which one of his elder male relatives has a *buanyin.* The exchange in which a candidate for a leader is to be involved from then on is an important Arapesh institution that develops aggressiveness and encourages the rare competitive spirit. The young candidate for leadership receives his training through participation in this institution, consisting chiefly of a reciprocal feast-giving relationship between him and his exchange partner. It is a duty of exchange partners to insult, embarrass, and shame each other whenever they meet, and this sort of behavior is supposed to go on, under harsh control from the elders as well as the other *buanyins* themselves, until a big initiation ceremony which establishes the candidate as a "big man" whose duty is to assume leadership whenever necessary. All through the duration of his "terms," a "big man" is obliged to continue to insult his exchange partner whenever he meets him and is pressured even into searching for opportunities for such exchanges. Only when his eldest son reaches puberty is a "big man" allowed to retire and assume the quiet life so highly cherished by the Arapesh.

Unlike the students of medicine among Creek Indians, the students here are not self-selected. They are carefully chosen by their elders, who are later to be their teachers, and they are forced to undergo the required training. The sanctioning group behind this type of schooling is the group of tribal elders representing the tribe itself. The elders are both tribal administrators and teachers. They are, no doubt, involved in all sorts of curricular decisions, such as how much aggression should be learned by a candidate to make him eligible for "graduation" as a "big man," and they are also involved in a constant supervision of their students and in passing judgment on their performance. The interesting thing among the Arapesh is that the selected cultural heritage which is to be transmitted through leadership training to the future "big man" is foreign and uncongenial to Arapesh cultural heritage since to be aggressive, initiating, and assertive is so atypical of the Arapesh people. But, at the same time, since the Arapesh consider leadership necessary for the very existence of their tribe, they support, cultivate, and enforce it among the selected few. In a similar way, we may say, some peace-loving modern societies do not hesitate to give money and moral support for the maintenance of the armies which they consider an unpleasant necessity. In a similar way, some people decide to teach in their schools the language of their hated enemies if they believe it to be instrumental for the well-being of their country.

A real problem occurs not when an uncongenial social institution, custom, or character trait is cultivated in a given society by the choice of the people themselves, but when two or more cultural systems within one society overlap. Technologically simple societies are often presented by anthropologists in such a manner that they look to us more isolated and homogeneous than they are in fact. A more careful look either at anthropological accounts or at the societies themselves provides us, however, with a more complex picture. Practically all technologically simple "primitive" societies are today in some (not always desired) contact with technologically complex, modern, urban civilizations. In all of them, practically, there is some conflict between two or more overlapping sociocultural systems. We learn, for instance, that Hopi children have often been transported, against their own will and that of their parents, to government schools from which many of them have tried to escape back to the Reservation.[12] Similar attempts at escape—often successful—used to occur in Africa, where the boys from European Mission Schools sometimes escaped to their tribal initiation or circumcision schools.[13]

How does the modern schoolteacher, curriculum maker, or curriculum-making administrator confront such conflicts? And how does his "primitive" counterpart in the native school do so? How do such changes influence their curricular decisions? These are *the* questions. But since we are unable to answer them without adequate data, let us turn again to the ideal type of technologically simple, isolated, "primitive" societies and see what we may learn from the analysis of the roles played in them by the tribal curriculum makers.

From such data, we learn, first of all, that whatever the problems of the curriculum maker in the modern complex society, and whatever his complaints about the limitation of his freedom by the group in power, he is certainly far more free than is his tribal counterpart. We have seen that the tribal curriculum maker is himself either a member of the sanctioning group—and then the problem of freedom does not enter into the picture—or he is completely subordinated to the sanctioning group, the only—or more—powerful embodiment of tribal tradition. In such situations, he cannot experiment with his new ideas (he usually does not get the chance to have any, in fact) as does the curriculum maker in a complex, modern society where dependence on many often conflicting power groups, though highly disturbing, provides him with numerous stimuli for innovation and allows him, at least to some extent, to choose between sanctioning groups. It is true that in every society an attempt to introduce new ways in the area of religion, education, social control, etc., is likely to be resisted by some strata of the population. The more homogeneous a given society, the stronger as a rule is such resistance. We cannot imagine, for instance, an experimental progressive school in any homogeneous "primitive" society. The greater the complexity of societies, and the greater the variety of subcultures, ideologies, and pressure groups, the more likely such an experimental school is to be found in them. Modern totalitarian societies, upon which oppressive homogeneity is artificially imposed, do not, of course, allow the curriculum maker any freedom of choice between sanctioning groups, simply because they do not allow such multiple groups to exist. There, a curriculum maker is greatly limited in his freedom to think and choose and sometimes painfully aware of these limitations.

When we ask ourselves what the significant similarities and differences between "primitive" and modern societies are in regard to the content of cultural heritage transmitted through education we notice, not without surprise, that the combination of instruction in intellectual or vocational subject matters with normative, moralistic education occurs both in technologically simple, primitive societies and in modern, complex societies. We thus learn that some selected aspects of the national or tribal world view always—and probably everywhere—find a place in the curriculum. Any schooling, formal or not, involves the teaching of some conceptions of the good life either explicitly, as in most primitive societies and on the elementary level in modern societies, or implicitly as in even the most scientifically oriented universities and academies known to our civilization. Perhaps an insight into the universality of such a pattern, which seemed at first to be restricted only to some societies, and many other insights of a similar sort, may release a disturbed curriculum maker from some unnecessary guilt feelings which make his hard job even harder.

NOTES

1. Li An-che, "Some Observations and Queries," *American Anthropologist*, Vol. XXXIX, 1937, pp. 62–76, cited in M. J. Herskovits, *Man and His Works: The Science of Cultural Anthropology*, Alfred A. Knopf, New York, 1960, p. 314.

2. Dorothy Eggan, "Instruction and Affect in Hopi Cultural Continuity," *Southwestern Journal of Anthropology*, vol. 12, no. 4, Winter 1965.

3. Hortense Powdermaker, *Life in Lesu: The Study of a Melanesian Society in New Ireland*, W. W. Norton & Co., Inc., New York, 1933, p. 93.

4. H. A. Stayt, *The Bavenda*, Published for the International Institute of African Languages and Cultures by Oxford University Press, London, 1931.

5. Margaret Mead, *The School in American Culture*. Harvard University Press, Cambridge, 1951.

6. See, for instance, Ngoma—a very interesting circumcision school in the Thonga tribe at the eastern coast of South Africa, described by H. A. Junod in *The Life of a South African Tribe,* University Books, New Hyde Park, New York, 1962.

7. H. A. Stayt, *The Bavenda,* cited in M. J. Herskovits, op. cit., pp. 101 ff.

8. J. R. Swanton, "Religious Beliefs and Medical Practices of the Creek Indians," *Annual Report of the Bureau of American Ethnology,* vol. 42, 1924–1925, pp. 473–672, cited in J. S. Slotkin, *Social Anthropology: The Science of Human Society and Culture,* Macmillan, New York, 1950, p. 529.

9. For instance, in the School of Medicine in Brussels, shortly before World War II, all students were required to take an examination on the history of ethics which was taught in the Department of Philosophy. The assumption was, no doubt, that every educated Belgian had to know this subject. The same was true of French schools for army officers, where philosophy was taught—a subject hardly connected with actual military training.

10. Margaret Mead, *Sex and Temperament,* W. Morrow & Co., New York, 1935.

11. Mead, op. cit., pp. 30–31.

12. Eggan, op cit., p. 352.

13. Junod, op. cit., p. 94.

11

Curriculum Development in Cross-National Perspective

M. FRANCES KLEIN and
JOHN I. GOODLAD

In Chapter 10 we saw that some form of curriculum work for educational activities goes on even in cultures described as simple or primitive. One purpose is to assure in the society the continuing presence of individuals with skills and abilities (for example, in leadership or folk medicine) not normally or naturally developed through daily life in family or tribe. As life becomes increasingly complex, less of what is needed for economic and social sufficiency is taught in the family. More and more is required of schools; the demand for curriculum work and workers increases.

The need for continuous, systematic curriculum planning has been legitimated relatively recently in many countries through the creation of curriculum development centers,

NOTE: The survey and related work reported in this chapter were made possible by a grant from the National Academy of Education which supported M. Frances Klein as an Academy Associate.

most of them charged with some degree of national responsibility. Even today, relatively little is known about their functioning. We thought it would be useful to find out what curriculum tasks they seek to perform and, through them, perhaps learn something about the present status of curriculum development in countries other than our own. Such an inquiry provided a unique opportunity to employ the conceptual system discussed in this volume in national settings other than the United States. A major question in our minds was whether or not it would prove useful for our purposes.

This chapter reports a survey of curriculum centers in eighteen countries. These centers were located in developing as well as developed countries, some with centralized and some with decentralized systems of schooling. Our attention was directed to the kinds of curricular questions dealt with, the data sources employed in making decisions, and the problems and issues confronted—not to the products, such as textbooks or other instructional materials, and not to the impact of curricula on students. We hoped to be able to make some cross-national comparisons as well as to be able to formulate some conclusions about the usefulness of the conceptual system for such a purpose.

BRIEF HISTORICAL BACKGROUND

In January, 1968, UNESCO sponsored a meeting in Moscow which focused on the curriculum of general education. Thirty-three representatives from twenty-two countries attended the sessions. Among the recommendations growing out of the deliberations of this group were:

1. That member states of UNESCO be assisted in the formation of national centers for curriculum development and research. This assistance was to be in the form of financial support, consultants, training opportunities, and the dissemination of information.
2. That national teams concerned with curriculum development and research be brought together for a training session of a month or more which would be followed by other meetings at regular intervals.

Acting upon these recommendations, UNESCO invited Professor Benjamin S. Bloom of the University of Chicago to submit a proposal for a six- to nine-week training program which would be in partial fulfillment of these recommendations. The training program developed by Professor Bloom ultimately was approved by the UNESCO General Council, and the International Association for the Evaluation of Educational Achievement (IEA) was invited to take full responsibility for developing and conducting such a program to be held during the summer of 1971 at Gränna, Sweden. Twenty-three countries from South America, Africa, Asia, and Europe sent teams of from four to six persons who had responsibility for curriculum development to participate in the Gränna seminar.[1] The United States did not send a team; it has no comparable center or, indeed, national entity for curriculum development. But several Americans, including Benjamin S. Bloom, John I. Goodlad, and Ralph W. Tyler, served on the faculty.

At the end of the conference, a group came together under Tyler's chairmanship to recommend follow-up activities. The major recommendation was for the creation of a small international curriculum organization through which curriculum concerns common to participants could be explored, international assistance in the education of personnel in curriculum development and evaluation could be obtained, approaches to common problems among nations in curriculum planning and development could be reported, and a network for dissemination and exchange could be developed.

As a beginning effort in setting up this new international group, a planning session for the formation of an International Curriculum Organization (ICO) was held at the International Institute for Educational Planning in Paris from November 30 to December 2, 1972. This meeting brought together representatives from several of the countries that had been particularly active and interested since the Gränna seminar. It was decided there that from twelve to fifteen countries with curriculum centers should comprise the membership of the proposed ICO.

Goodlad had been from the beginning a member of the planning group selected at the Gränna seminar in the summer of 1971; Klein's attendance was made possible by a grant from the National Academy of Education (USA) and her accompanying selection by that group as an Academy Associate. In using Goodlad's conceptual system,[2] we were interested in studying the functioning of curriculum centers in the participating countries. Specifically, we hoped to secure the cooperation of conference participants in surveying, through the curriculum centers, curriculum decision making at societal, institutional, instructional, and personal or experiential levels. We planned to identify the extent to which each nation's curriculum center was involved in the kinds of curricular activities identified by Tyler: formulating goals and objectives, planning and selecting learning opportunities, organizing learning activities, and evaluating students' progress.[3]

Participants in the Paris conference were agreed that the proposed study would contribute significantly to the all-too-meager body of knowledge about curriculum planning as it occurs in various nations. They agreed, further, to critique the initial draft of a questionnaire and, subsequently, to respond to it. A copy of the questionnaire, in its final form, appears as an Appendix at the end of this chapter. Data were obtained from curriculum centers in the following countries: Chile, Ethiopia, Finland, Ghana, Hungary, India, Iran, Israel, Japan, Kenya, Korea, Malaysia, New Zealand, Norway, Spain, Sweden, Thailand and Venezuela. Information obtained from the questionnaires was, in many instances, supplemented by various official documents and reports.

During the conduct of the survey, which extended over an unexpectedly long period of time, it became apparent to us that a mail survey is an unsatisfactory way to accomplish our goals. For several rather obvious reasons, especially the opportunity to probe more deeply into otherwise rather superficial responses, face-to-face conversations are virtually essential to understanding curriculum development activities in countries other than our own. Limited time and money prevented the implied arrangements.

Some of our terms, even though accepted by collaborators during pilot testing, simply were not understood by all respondents. Second, respondents tended to be constrained by the questions and did not exercise the suggested liberty in adapting their responses to local circumstances. Third, we sensed a reluctance on the part of some participants to identify "problems." Perhaps even to admit to having problems is, in some cultures, a sign of weakness or even failure. Finally, securing the return of questionnaires, even under the favorable circumstance of our knowing a large proportion of the respondents, proved to be exceedingly difficult. The questionnaire was exceedingly long, requiring the expenditure of time taken away from more pressing things; distances between respondents and us were great, effectively removing the pressure to comply. Through great persistence over a relatively long period of time, we were successful in securing information from centers in all eighteen countries.*

ORGANIZATION AND WORK OF THE CENTERS

It should be remembered that we entered into the survey with very little knowledge of these so-called curriculum centers. We could not even begin with a precise definition because we did not know the range in varieties of centers likely to be uncovered. Goodlad's experience at Gränna had taught him that some of the participating countries (e.g., India and Israel) had relatively well-developed institutions that had been created for curriculum research, development, diffusion, and improvement. Others were in the process of creating such centers; some sent persons who customarily did some kind of curriculum work in the ministry of education, universities, or schools. Our questionnaire went to persons connected with entities charged with curriculum development responsibility. The questions asked ranged over pur-

---

*It should be noted that funds for general support of the ICO were not forthcoming; the formal consortium of curriculum centers and an adequate supporting secretariat never emerged. Seminars in all major regions of the world had been anticipated but only an African one materialized. The Organization was disbanded some three years after its creation. It would be interesting to determine what residue remains and whether the ICO had any lasting impact on curriculum development around the world during its all-too-brief history.

poses, governance, structure, sources of influence, activities, involvement, evaluation, impact or use of work done, need for assistance, problems and issues, and so on.

All but one of the curriculum centers surveyed served as arms, or under the direct influence, of the Ministry of Education or Ministry of Science and Higher Education. All but two reported that these ministries were the most powerful source of influence in determining their functions. All other groups of potential influence clearly played a secondary role. Our data reveal a close relationship of the centers to official branches of government, with employed educators and scholars having a major say in the work to be conducted. Reports from the field, including local needs assessments of schools and, somewhat surprisingly, even the reports of commissions and review bodies, were mentioned by a small minority of respondents but, clearly, direction is set by governmental authority. Students and parents were never mentioned as groups having input into determining the functions of the centers.

Not surprisingly, given the locus of control, all but one of the centers were funded almost exclusively from government sources. Only a handful received some limited support from other agencies (including international ones) or the sale of materials and reports. The professional staffs employed appear to us to be pitifully small in relation to the magnitude of the responsibilities, the modal range being from 17 to 45. One employed only 7 professionals. One employed 145, but this center is in a very large country and is charged with a full range of responsibilities from research to in-service training of teachers. Several of the centers were augmented in the field by having the inspectors of schools tied closely into their work. Indeed, in some instances we had difficulty in determining whether the inspectors were actually the field staff of the curriculum centers.

The overall functions, listed consistently, were, at the time of our survey, curriculum development, research, and evaluation for the primary and secondary levels of schooling. However, this responsibility was only rarely relegated exclusively to these centers; all but two reported that other groups in the country also were engaged in curriculum development work. The work listed in fulfillment of the functions included such activities as conducting educational needs assessments for the nation, identifying curriculum goals, reviewing and assessing current curricula, planning new curricula to be implemented in the future, defining and improving content for new curricula, developing teacher's guides and syllabuses, improving teaching methods to be used in the implementation of new curricula, and developing media and print materials to accompany curricular plans. Activities mentioned as curriculum research and evaluation included assessing student outcomes and school achievement. In addition, the conduct of in-service programs for teachers, educational planning and management, dissemination of information about curricula, and maintaining a liaison with teachers' in-service centers were other activities for which the curriculum centers were responsible.

A major part of the time of the staff in fourteen of the centers went into refining (sometimes into behavioral terms) the educational goals set by the Ministry, planning units of work related to these objectives, preparing teacher's guides to the use of materials, and training teachers who assist in various tryout stages as well as in later dissemination activities. Other activities reported by a dozen or more respondents were supervising the implementation of new curricula in pilot schools, maintaining a resource library of materials, conducting educational research, and providing in-service training for members of the center staff. Half of the centers reported time spent in training staffs for specific curriculum projects, maintaining a clearinghouse function for the dissemination of curricular information, supervising the implementation of new curricula in schools generally, training teachers for the use of revised curricula, conducting or monitoring needs assessments in local schools, and preparing student examinations.

There was nothing in the data to suggest some sort of finite character to the work of the centers. At any given time, what they had done was undergoing review, or they were about to embark on a subject field not tackled before, or something done previously was being readied for revision. We were unable to come to any conclusions as to why or when new work or revision was scheduled; seldom was any regular schedule reported for reviewing and updating. The reasons for updating a piece of the curriculum ranged from teachers' views of need and committee reports to decisions simply made by the Ministry. Most centers reported reasonably regular, systematic efforts to secure teachers' and scholars' reactions to curricula. Five reported that a review to determine what required updating took place automatically every ten to twenty years.

Most of the centers reported some kind of built-in processes for follow-up of curriculum work after a cycle of development. These included securing reactions from teachers (fifteen centers), advice from scholars and administrators (twelve), studying critiques and reviews in professional and other publications (eleven), studying achievement test data (ten), and securing student reactions (nine). Most of the available data came from professional adults; very little from parents and lay school councils. We learned little about what, specifically, is done with the data in revising old or developing new curricula.

We got the impression that the ongoing work done at the center or for it (as with subprojects) is given top priority; what happens after products go out into the field is a secondary consideration. Only nine centers reported preparing materials and regulations directed to implementing at the classroom level work done in the centers. Seven reported holding in-service seminars to help teachers use center products; five used supervisors and inspectors as disseminating agents; four used experimental or demonstration models in the field. Teacher education at the universities and the use of other divisions (e.g., teacher education) of the Ministry only occasionally were employed. We were unable to determine the comprehensiveness of the printed information or the duration and intensity of the teachers' seminars employed for dissemination purposes. It is of interest to note that *all* of the participants (representing 20 countries) in Goodlad's section of the seminar at Gränna agreed that the limited ability of teachers to use effectively new curriculum products and processes constituted the major block to school improvement in their countries.

While the respondents to our questionnaire identified teacher education as an area of need in curriculum improvement, their range of vision regarding problem areas did not extend far beyond home base. The training of their own personnel ranked high as an area requiring attention. They saw a need for center staff to get special training in evaluation (thirteen), research (twelve), curriculum as a specialized field (twelve), subject matter (eight), and teacher education (six). By contrast, no area of in-service need on the part of teachers was mentioned by more than five centers.

There was no consistency in the responses regarding immediate or long-range problems, except as related to the staff personnel training need identified above. But there were patterns, nonetheless. One was an extension of the training need to include the problem of attracting and holding people well qualified to do the work of the centers. A second had to do with dilemmas—some of them ideological in nature— arising out of the centers' functions and work: the apparent slow pace of production in relation to overwhelming growth and need of the educational system; how to secure a defensible and productive balance between central control and local autonomy; how to evaluate the curriculum of a nation; how to effect change through the infusion of new curricula; how to secure and use a base of data drawn from long-term studies; how to handle conflict and jurisdictional disputes among agencies concerned with curriculum development; how to evaluate the work of a center; and how to keep it in a leadership rather than reacting role. These are not problems likely to be resolved through increased financial and logistical support. Such problems, together with the implicit one of a shortage of well-qualified curriculum workers, could be predicted, given the relatively recent appearance of this new institution on the educational scene.

The self-image of success on the part of center respondents pertained primarily to the curriculum planning and development processes but not much beyond. Only one cited implementation and two evaluation as success areas. Three saw their centers as successful in the area of in-service education of teachers to use the results of curriculum development. The criteria used in determining success areas were predominantly the subject evaluations of "experts." Subjective judgments regarding growth in the interests of students and teachers and in the willingness of teachers to use the programs also were given as evidence. But student achievement was reported only once as a criterion of success. It appears that the allocation of funds and personnel and psychological support and acceptance of the work of the centers may depend more heavily on the opinions of Ministry officials, scholars, and curriculum experts (including those staffing the centers) than on some "proof" of student success in curricula. As with other areas of the educational system, the centers apparently were not clear as to what kinds of evidence would be most indicative of success—and, consequently, did not choose to gather, consistently and thoroughly, one kind of datum rather than another. Perhaps the directors of centers believe that the futures of their centers are more tied to the vagaries of political life than to any cumulative body of data regarding their accomplishments.

LEVELS OF DECISION MAKING

It is clear from the foregoing that a major role of almost all of the centers surveyed was, at the time of our investigation, the operationalizing of rather broad functions assigned to them by the Ministries. Following Tyler's four curricular questions or tasks, it becomes apparent that a major task for the centers is the translation of educational goals (usually those stated for the nation) into more specific objectives and the revision or development of curricular units and topics intended to meet these objectives. From another section of our questionnaire, we learned that these units and topics were organized within the traditional disciplines of mathematics, history, the physical and biological sciences, etc., in most of the centers (sixteen). Eight centers reported some attempt to combine or integrate the subject disciplines and four reported experimental efforts to organize learning opportunities around concepts, processes, or issues cutting across subjects. Evaluation, either of curricular products developed or of the centers' efforts to fulfill functions, was receiving relatively little attention and was identified by several centers as an unfulfilled need.

Our conclusion from the centers' reports of their work is that most of them are busily endeavoring to set a single curricular framework for their nations' schools. The task is sufficiently overwhelming to virtually negate the development of clear alternatives—and many of the nations reporting are so hard-pressed for money and trained talent that developing one comprehensive plan, with accompanying materials, teacher's guides, and implementation strategies is a luxury not yet realized.

In seeking to fulfill the assigned functions, the Ministry of Education or Education and Science is the dominant influence. Into the operationalizing decisions of the centers goes a considerable amount of advice from university professors, school inspectors, teachers connected with center work, professional educator and religious groups, teacher unions, and various panels of experts. Our sources reported very little significant influence from students or parents. Actual curriculum construction is almost exclusively in the hands of professional people.

Generalizing from all of this, we see in perhaps seventeen of the eighteen centers surveyed a charge from their respective Ministries to develop at the societal level a curriculum for the primary and secondary schools of the nation. Nowhere in our data is there any serious questioning of this charge, even though our questionnaire was designed to be open-ended and provided ample opportunity for raising issues and problems. (Needless to say, if this is the charge effectively internalized by center personnel, it is unlikely that any of our respondents would use our survey as an opportunity to express doubt as to its desirability or feasibility.) There was, however, in response to the question pertaining to long-range problems, a hint of recognition of the centralization-decentralization issue.

It is difficult to determine specifically in most countries the sources of the programs schools provide for their students. Partly from their own experience as students, partly from their education for teaching, partly from courses of study and textbooks, and partly from the supporting educational infrastructure, teachers develop an image of what and how they are to teach. Just how much this orientation to teaching is changed by new curriculum products and directives from a centralized, semipolitical or politically legitimated curriculum development source is difficult to determine. Such an influence probably is slow in taking hold and very much diluted or distorted by the teachers' present orientations— and probably would be considerably greater if a revision to follow the present revision were not anticipated by the teachers.

Our respondents reported that virtually all elementary schools and a large proportion of secondary schools used the center's work. They reported that curriculum activities also took place at the level of the local school: learning activities in addition to or other than those planned in the center were selected for students; curricular policies set by the Ministry were revised to fit local conditions; selections were made from alternatives prepared elsewhere; new units were planned locally; and procedures and instruments of evaluation sometimes were developed locally. But a substantial number of respondents also reported no local school planning at the level of course revision except in a few selected areas such as art, physical education, and, occasionally, the social sciences. For most schools, it appears from the reports sent to us that the work done at these centers provides the major curriculum plan. Less than a third of our respondents reported creative work on curriculum, including adaptations to local circumstances, at the institutional level. The societal plan is, in effect and according to our sources of information, in many places virtually the institutional plan.

The data suggest some acceleration in curriculum activity

at the instructional level. Teachers engaged in some determination of learning activities for their students (reported by twelve center respondents), refined Ministry policy to fit classroom needs (seven), determined objectives for students (six), planned and implemented their own units and courses (six), selected from among courses approved by the Ministry (four) and organized elements of the curriculum to suit their own views (four). One could hardly conclude all of this to be vigorous teacher-directed curriculum work; most of it appears to be implementation of plans and directives developed at the societal level.

Most of our respondents (ten) reported that students have no say in the decisions determining curricula. Six reported that students assist in evaluating their own progress and four reported a degree of involvement in determining their own learning activities. As reported elsewhere in this chapter, the curriculum centers gathered some data on student achievement in center-produced curricula, but we have no knowledge regarding use, if any, of such information in curriculum revision.

A modification of Goodlad's conceptual system for curriculum as depicted in Chapter 1 (Figure 1.1), based on the data from our survey, would produce a strongly linear model. The arrows from societal to institutional to instructional to experiential would be very heavy and strong; arrows in the reverse direction would be exceedingly weak and perhaps depicted best by a dotted line. Such reverse flow (e.g., instructional to societal) as occurs is more in the nature of feedback about center-produced curricula than fresh curricular formulations deemed more appropriate to school or classroom realities. It must be noted, also, that much of this feedback is from individuals and groups, almost exclusively professional, very similar to those staffing the centers. A truly countervailing perspective is not to be expected.

Likewise, as suggested earlier, one would not expect the respondents to raise serious questions about the flow of curriculum products and activities from their centers to the field. After all, to produce what is used, to provide teachers with what is only minimally changed, to have a visible impact, are the reasons for maintaining the centers. It is to be expected that the respondents would want to report themselves in the best possible light and that, therefore, their value position would be oriented toward center dominance in the nation's curriculum work. Almost uniformly, they expressed a positive view of the work of the centers and of how the centers were conducted, whether they saw themselves as a direct arm of the Ministry or with considerable powers of self-determination.

SUMMARY AND IMPLICATIONS

Our sample presents an interesting mixture of developing and relatively developed countries. It should be noted, however, that almost all have relatively centralized educational systems with a great deal of power and responsibility vested in the respective Ministries of Education (or Education and Science). All but one of the curriculum centers surveyed were directly responsible to the Ministry and were essentially "national" entities.

No comparable institution exists in the United States. The USA was not able to have a member center in the proposed International Curriculum Organization because no appropriate institution could be identified. A constitutional arrangement provided only for individuals from this country to serve on the Council. Our closest parallel would be the curriculum division or unit of a state department of education, but, clearly, such an entity is in no way national. And no such unit ever has taken on the kind of responsibility for curriculum development implied in most of the responses to our questionnaire. Our state departments of education play more of a screening role in determining which among several series of textbooks and other materials will be approved and, therefore, may be purchased with state funds. Local school districts then exercise their options in choosing from these alternatives or adding and supporting from their own funds still other alternatives. In most school districts, individual schools make further choices, most often in the realm of so-called supplementary materials—charts, maps, globes, reference books, fiction, etc. And individual teachers make choices among these—and sometimes have some resources for purchasing materials not on any state or local list.

Part of this curricular diversity stems from the governmental structure by means of which responsibility for education is divided, part from the way in which the development of materials emerged to a considerable degree as private enterprise, part from the emergence of a rather fully developed public educational system, and part from affluence. While all of these conditions exist elsewhere, they do not exist often in this particular combination, the most unusual and least paralleled characteristic being the division of federal, state, and municipal responsibility and authority.

It is important to remember that each of the countries represented in our sample differs from the United States in at least one of these ways—sometimes all of them—and that each has some unique structural and contextual characteristic of its own. Japan, for example, shares several of these characteristics but clearly differs in its centralization of authority in the Ministry. New Zealand is similar in many respects but the enormous difference in size alone accounts for many differences in the way curriculum work operates and influences.

According to our respondents, in most of the countries surveyed, curriculum activity at the societal level heavily overshadows the relatively little that transpires at institutional and instructional levels. The federal government, through its appropriate Ministry, is the greatest source of influence on the curriculum centers, all but one of which are essentially arms of the Ministry. A descriptive conceptualization of what transpires is necessarily linear, from the curriculum center outward or downward, with relatively weak feedback loops. Schools and teachers implement, presumably imposing their own interpretations. Our data give us no leads as to how what is disseminated fares in translation. In all probability, a good deal is lost or changed—and this is not necessarily bad from an ideological point of view but is likely to be regarded as inefficient by any central group seeking curricular uniformity.

The controlling agency is the Ministry. How well it represents the people, the sanctioning body in the rhetoric of most governments, probably varies widely in our sample, partly as a factor of the size of the country. At any rate, overall educational goals are enunciated by this controlling agency. After that, our data suggest, professional individuals and groups—academics, educators, and curriculum "experts"— appear to have an inordinate amount of influence over the translation of goals into objectives and the selection of what is to be taught. A relatively large number of groups appears to have potential influence but these are not very diverse in their membership. Schools as units, teachers, students, and parents have relatively little to say about curricular content and organization.

If the major purpose in maintaining the centers is to have an identifiable place and group responsible for producing a rather common societal-level elementary and secondary curriculum sanctioned by the Ministry, it would appear that the purpose is met. It would also appear, however, that the resources put into these centers simply are inadequate for the production phase and especially inadequate if implementation at institutional and instructional levels is an expectation. The process of curriculum change, defined as changes in content and method in the classroom, drops off rapidly after development occurs in the centers. We do not know whether this is because of inadequate funds and a paucity of well-prepared personnel (probably major factors in many instances) or some uncertainty as to how best to do the job. We picked up no data from the respondents as to their dissatisfaction with, or uncertainty about, the approach represented by their centers.

Studies on site would be required to determine whether there exists at the level of schools and classrooms any considerable degree of dissatisfaction with the apparently dominant role of curriculum centers in providing the framework and much of the substance for teaching and learning. Or whether teachers would like to reduce or even reverse the flow of curricular influence so that what goes on in the centers is largely reflective of their perceptions of what is required. Or whether they regard the centers as hindrances, perhaps drawing off funds they would like to see spent elsewhere and differently. Studies of this kind would provide some interesting cross-national comparisons of what teachers desire their role to be in curriculum development.

It appears from our data that schools represent a rather inactive level of curriculum development. It will be recalled that Griffin's study (Chapter 3) revealed a similar relative condition at the institutional level in the schools of his sample. In recent years in the United States, it is at this level that many parents want to be involved; parental pressure frequently has forced needs assessments, the setting of long-term goals and plans, and additions to or deletions from schools' curricular offerings. Our experience has been paralleled in some other countries. Is this kind of involvement to be anticipated in other countries as their educational systems become more fully developed? Why is it that educators have not taken the lead in assuring dynamic curricular activity at the level of the local school?

The work of the curriculum centers studied is focused heavily on the production of paper products for teachers and students. Most of what goes on at the instructional level is interpretative and adaptive rather than original. And few centers have systematic procedures for gathering and utilizing teachers' expressions of satisfaction and need. Going beyond teachers, our data suggest a passive view of the students' role; as in most of the world, students simply are not regarded as important in determining what they are to study.

There appears to be widespread international agreement regarding what is involved substantively in curriculum work. First, general goals for the educational system are set—in almost all the countries we surveyed, by the Ministry. The curriculum centers seek to make these operational by translating them into more specific goals, there being some effort to make clear what is expected behaviorally of students. Then, units of work are selected and developed, usually within the framework of the established subject disciplines.

Instead of the proposed units and other learning opportunities being selected to fulfill the objectives and then being organized by subjects or some other pattern of curriculum organization, it appears that the separate subject pattern of organization is accepted in advance, as a given. Indeed, one must raise the question of whether goals determine the rest of the curriculum or whether mathematics, the humanities, and the natural and social sciences already are so well established as "the curriculum" that the linear process of first establishing goals and then selecting means to obtain them is simply part of the mythical "should" of curriculum development—an after-the-fact rationalization of what we believe should be but, in practice, is not the way it is. At any rate, Tyler's step of organizing the curriculum consciously and deliberately does not appear to occur. The subject pattern already exists; old units of work are revised and new ones are created within this pattern.

Our respondents were very conscious of the need to evaluate outcomes, presumably through indices of student achievement. But little of such evaluation occurred. Similarly, the need to evaluate the entire curriculum development enterprise was recognized by our respondents but not met in any systematic way. Most of the centers went about their business without the benefit of much empirical data on which to base evaluations of either the curricula produced or their own functioning.

A major conclusion from our survey is that there is considerable agreement between curriculum workers in the United States and personnel of national curriculum centers in other countries on what curriculum workers are supposed to do. Some of the tasks are neglected and there is, in many places, a paucity of well-prepared persons for their accomplishment. But a curriculum maker could move from center to center around the world and find himself very much at home with activities underway in each successive center. He or she would find himself readily commiserating, also, with staffs encountering familiar problems within and without—and especially on the commonly held view that teachers generally are incapable of satisfactorily adopting new curricula.

Clearly, there is developing around the world a field of specialization variously referred to as "curriculum," or "curriculum planning," or "curriculum development" and a need for persons specially trained to be curriculum workers. Many of the persons already in the field have developed the usual means of communicating with one another—through direct correspondence, exchange of visits, case studies released through international organizations such as UNESCO and OECD, journals, and meetings of experts. It is unfortunate that the International Curriculum Organization did not stay alive to expedite these processes and activities, but perhaps the already established organizations will move more rapidly in the years ahead to respond to what is an obvious need for the international exchange of curriculum knowledge and expertise.

NOTES

1. *Report of the International Seminar for Advanced Training in Curriculum Development and Innovation*, held in Gränna, Sweden, July 5–August 14, 1971, International Association for the Evaluation of Educational Achievement, Stockholm, Sweden, 1971.

2. John I. Goodlad (with Maurice N. Richter, Jr.), *The Development of a Conceptual System for Dealing with Problems of Curriculum and Instruction*, Cooperative Research Program USOE, Project No. 454, University of California, Los Angeles, 1966.

3. Ralph W. Tyler, *Basic Principles of Curriculum and Instruction*, University of Chicago Press, Chicago, 1950.

APPENDIX

(Refers specifically to Chapter 11)

QUESTIONNAIRE TO REPRESENTATIVES OF NATIONAL CURRICULUM CENTERS

*A Survey Initiated at the Organizational Meeting of the
International Curriculum Organization
Paris, France, December, 1972*

1. What are the primary purposes, aims or functions stated for your center, if any? (Please send printed statement, if available.)
    Who determines them?
    _____ Members of Parliament or Central Government
    _____ Ministry of Education
    _____ Advisory committees of educators
    _____ Advisory committees composed of educators and lay people
    _____ Ad hoc committees
    _____ Local school councils
    _____ Local school faculties
    _____ Other (please specify)
    How are they determined?
    _____ Governmental law or policy
    _____ Decision by reports to Ministry
    _____ Reports and research by scholars
    _____ Reports by teachers or school inspectors
    _____ Needs assessment of schools
    _____ Other (please specify)

2. Describe the organizational structure of your center, or a coordinated system for curriculum development and research; please include an organizational chart and other explanatory documents (in English, if possible).

3. Are there any other groups or units in your country engaged

in curriculum activities? If so, indicate your relationship to them (working councils, teacher unions, scholarly groups—mathematicians, scientists, etc.—national school administration units other than Ministry of Education, etc.).

4. What individuals or organizations give directives or suggestions to you for curriculum activities?
   _____ Parliament or an equivalent governmental unit
   _____ Ministry makes decisions in agreement with national goals
   _____ National school administration units
   _____ Teacher unions
   _____ Professional educator groups
   _____ Political parties or organizations
   _____ Religious groups
   _____ University personnel
   _____ School inspectors
   _____ Local school faculties
   _____ Suggestions by professional persons other than educators
   _____ Ad hoc committees
   _____ Teachers
   _____ Parents
   _____ Student unions
   _____ None
   _____ Others (please specify)

5. How would you assess the importance of each of these contributors from an overall perspective?

6. What kinds of activities in regard to the curriculum occur at the individual school level?
   _____ None
   _____ Refining Ministry policy
   _____ Selecting among approved courses from Ministry
   _____ Determining own objectives for students
   _____ Determining own learning activities for students
   _____ Organizing the curriculum
   _____ Planning procedures and instruments for evaluating the curriculum
   _____ Planning units and courses
   _____ Complete freedom in curriculum planning and development
   _____ Other (please specify)

7. In what subject areas of the curriculum does planning occur at the individual school level?

_____ All areas

_____ None

_____ Selected areas (please state them—arts, sciences, social sciences, language arts, foreign languages, physical education, archeological sites, environmental studies, etc.)

8. How are the subject areas organized in the curriculum?

_____ Disciplines

_____ Concepts

_____ Processes

_____ Integrative approach

_____ Issues or problems

_____ Other (please specify)

9. How much do each of the following groups contribute to planning at the individual school level?

Rate importance of contributions for each group (5 very important, 1 of least importance)

		5	4	3	2	1
_____	Supervisors	5	4	3	2	1
_____	Inspectors	5	4	3	2	1
_____	Faculty decisions	5	4	3	2	1
_____	Decisions by groups of teachers	5	4	3	2	1
_____	Principal decision	5	4	3	2	1
_____	Decision by individual teachers	5	4	3	2	1
_____	Advisors	5	4	3	2	1
_____	Parents	5	4	3	2	1
_____	Students	5	4	3	2	1

10. What kinds of activities in regard to the curriculum are carried out by the individual teacher?

_____ None

_____ Refinement of Ministry (or equivalent) policy
_____ Determination of own objectives for students
_____ Determining own activities for students
_____ Selecting among approved courses from Ministry (or equivalent)
_____ Organizing the curriculum
_____ Planning and implementing own units and courses
_____ Planning procedures and instruments for evaluating the curriculum
_____ Complete freedom in curriculum planning and development
_____ Other (please specify)

11. What kinds of activities in regard to the curriculum are done by the student?
_____ No decision making about the curriculum
_____ Setting his objectives
_____ Determining learning activities
_____ Preparing own learning materials
_____ Organizing his curriculum
_____ Assisting in evaluating his own progress
_____ Selecting among several units or curricula
_____ Other (please specify)

12. Are there other levels at which activities occur in regard to curricula (e.g., municipal level)? Please state what kind of activities occur at each level named.

13. In what subject areas of the curriculum does your center carry out planning and development?
_____ All areas
_____ None
_____ Selected areas (please state them—arts, sciences, social sciences, language arts, foreign languages, physical education, environmental studies, etc.)

14. Are alternative curricula available to the schools? In what areas? How are they approved?

15. What process, if any, is used by your center to evaluate the curriculum work done?

How often?

_____ Research studies by Ministry   _____
_____ Conferences   _____
_____ Local school studies on pupils   _____
_____ Reports and meetings by teachers   _____

_____ Visits by Ministry officials to schools _____

_____ Examinations of student achievement _____

_____ Committees of scholars (mathematicians, scientists, etc.) and educators _____

_____ Checking on governmental specifi-
cations in laws _____

_____ Questionnaires or polls for reactions
of _____ students _____ teachers _____
parents _____

_____ Data bank test items _____

_____ None _____

*What
percentage in
the country?*

16. How many schools use the results of the
curriculum development in which your center or institute participates? _____
How many teachers use the results of your
curriculum development? _____
How many students use the results of your
curriculum development? _____

17. How often is a curriculum area reviewed and updated within
your center?
_____ Every 1–5 years
_____ Every 10–20 years
_____ Sporadically
_____ Continuously
_____ Other (please specify)
Please give specific examples, if possible, when major subject
areas were updated and what criteria were used in making
the decision to update the curriculum.

18. How many people are on your staff whose major responsibil-
ities are curricular activities?
Professional people (actual number of personnel):
Full time _____
Part time _____
What are their major responsibilities and how many people
are charged with each responsibility?

Support nonprofessionals (actual number of personnel):
Full time _____
Part time _____
Total size of staff concerned with curriculum development:
_____

19. How is your center funded (indicate amounts in U.S. dollars given by each source):

Over what period of time?

_____ Government funds   _____
_____ Grants from other agencies   _____
_____ International agencies   _____
_____ Income from sales of materials developed and published   _____
_____ Other (please specify)   _____

20. What kinds of data about the curricula you develop are collected by your center?

How often?

_____ Teacher reactions about curricula   _____
_____ Achievement test data   _____
_____ Student reactions   _____
_____ Parental reactions   _____
_____ Follow-up studies on student success as adults   _____
_____ Lay council reactions   _____
_____ Critiques and reviews in professional journals
and other publications   _____
_____ Scholars' reactions to curriculum   _____
_____ Needs assessment of schools   _____
_____ Advice from scholars and leading educators about curriculum building   _____
_____ Impact of center upon local schools   _____
_____ Other (please specify)   _____

21. Indicate the activities conducted in your center
_____ Planning of curricular units work
_____ Preparation of teacher materials to achieve objectives set by the Ministry
_____ Preparation of student materials to achieve objectives set by the Ministry

_____ Determination of educational objectives

_____ Refinement of educational objectives

_____ Conduct of educational research

_____ Preparation of tests for students

_____ Collection of curriculum evaluation data

_____ Surveys or needs assessments of local schools

_____ Training of

      _____ own staff

      _____ project staffs

      _____ teachers participating in various try-out stages

      _____ teachers who disseminate materials

      _____ teachers in local schools

_____ Maintain a resource library of materials

_____ Logistics of equipment (in sciences, agriculture, arts and crafts, etc.)

_____ Supervision of implementation of new curricula in pilot schools

_____ Supervision of implementation of new curricula in all schools

_____ Clearinghouse for disseminating information

_____ Coordination of activities in other centers for curriculum development

_____ State any other not in this list

22. In what areas do you most need assistance in training and at what level?

	Ministry Personnel	University Personnel	Center Personnel	National Board of Education Personnel	Teachers	Other (specify)
Subject matter	_____	_____	_____	_____	_____	_____
Curriculum specialists	_____	_____	_____	_____	_____	_____
Teacher training	_____	_____	_____	_____	_____	_____
Research specialists	_____	_____	_____	_____	_____	_____
Evaluation specialists	_____	_____	_____	_____	_____	_____
Other (please specify)	_____	_____	_____	_____	_____	_____

23. How do you provide for the implementation in the classrooms of the curriculum work done in your center?

24. What are the major issues or problems which your center faces now?

25. What are the major issues or problems which your center may face in the future?

26. In what areas of curriculum planning, development, implementation, and evaluation have you been most successful?

27. What criteria did you use to determine that these were areas of success?

28. What changes, if any, need to be made in your center in order to help you more effectively attain your goals or perform your functions?

29. Are the above changes possible for you to achieve in the near future?

30. What are your most immediate professional needs? (Indicate potential sources of help in solving these needs.)

31. What are your long-range needs? (Indicate potential sources of help in solving these needs.)

32. How do you consider your center to be unique from most other curriculum centers?

33. Please record any comments or observations about your center which you believe are important but not included in this questionnaire.

12

Praxiology and Curriculum

ALICJA IWAŃSKA

Two types of activities, expressive and technical, have often been singled out from the history of mankind by sociologists[1] and anthropologists.[2] It has been said that while the expressive activities are ends in themselves (or "good for their own sake"), technical activities serve only as the means for achieving something else; they are tools, or instruments. While art, literature and religion usually have been assigned without much controversy to the category of expressive activities, technology, magic, and science have been most often, but not without controversy,[3] described as technical activities meant to achieve something else, cumulative and improvable.

That cumulative and improvable character of technical activities has been contrasted with the noncumulative and nonimprovable character of expressive activities. It has often been said that while the technological, scientific, and even magical tasks add up, or, so to speak, "progress," and may thus be evaluated as more advanced or less advanced (sometimes we say simply "better" or "worse"), we cannot make such assessments in regard to art, religion, and literature. In the area of expressive activities we have different styles or different value systems rather than cumulative development, and, unlike our evaluation of a 1975 television set as being better than a 1950 set, the evaluation of, say, one religion as being better than another religion lacks the necessary objective criteria.

The objective criteria, in terms of which we evaluate our technical activities, are the criteria of efficiency or good workmanship. We may speak about well-done work or efficient action. And we may speak about better or more poorly done work, or action being more or less efficient. In one form or another the concern with efficiency has been always characteristic of humankind, and so were some ideas about man's technical ingenuity and his technical failures. In fact, at a certain period of history (probably somewhere in the middle of the Industrial Revolution) the preoccupation with efficiency became so great that for some people to do good work became a value in itself, and efficiency, without ceasing to be a technical virtue, became a moral virtue as well. But to acquire the status of a moral value does not mean necessarily to become an unquestioned "absolute." Even in those societies where efficiency is a cherished value, as in the United States today, some people choose to act inefficiently not because "they do not know any better" but because of their concern with other values, such as charity, beauty, respect for tradition, disagreement with the ends to which a given efficient action is to contribute, etc.

A systematic study of the rules of good workmanship or efficient action was started during the last four or five decades by a few scholars who worked for many years independently of each other and who represented such different sciences as economics, engineering, and philosophy. These include Tadeusz Kotarbiński,[4] Georges Hostélet,[5] G. H. Mead,[6] and Richard Von Mises,[7] to mention only a few. The most extensive work in this area was done by the Polish philosopher, Tadeusz Kotarbiński, the author of a number of books and articles on praxiology, as he named this emerging science. Praxiology is defined by Kotarbiński as the general theory of good work (or efficient action) in all areas of human behavior.

Kotarbiński divided praxiology into two branches—the theory of cooperation and the theory of struggle. The praxiologist attempts to clarify and systematize the common-sense generalizations about efficient action in general and then about efficient ways of cooperating and struggling (in some cases only competing) with others. He tried further to bring under a common frame of reference the findings of various writers concerned with efficiency in some specialized areas such as military logistics, scientific organization of work, theories of winning in various games, eristics, etc. And, of course, the praxiologist tries also to observe the behavior of people involved in various types of action and make explicit the implicit assumptions on which their actions rely.

Like other men of action—lawyer, engineer, army officer, and gambler—who have not only to plan their own actions but also to deal with other people, the curriculum maker is constantly involved in three types of decisions:

1. He is involved in making decisions which require individual efficiency (planning his own work).

2. He is involved in decisions involving efficient cooperation with others (for instance, cooperation with other curriculum makers, teachers, administrators, etc.).

3. He is involved in decisions concerned with efficient struggling with some people, if we understand, of course, "struggle" in the large praxiological sense of this word.* He has, for instance, to struggle efficiently with some members of the community who oppose him, sometimes with his own superiors, sometimes with his subordinates.

In spite of the tentative character of the propositions so far formulated by praxiology, some acquaintance with this emerging science may be useful for scholars of different brands and even more so for so-called men of action. Since methodology is just a different name for praxiology of scientific behavior (efficient planning of experiments, good observation, etc.) the value of praxiology for scholarly activity is self-explanatory.

Unlike the scholars who are mainly concerned with deci-

---

*For those disturbed by the term "struggle," we propose "negative collective action," a less shocking term used by Kotarbiński on some occasions.

sions in the realm of ideas, men of action are mainly concerned with decisions involving people and things, to put it very simply. The problem of the most efficient way of arriving at fruitful hypotheses concerned with building a bridge, winning a battle or a game of cards, organizing a mass meeting or planning a school curriculum—these are the common praxiological preoccupations of the scholar, engineer, soldier, card player, politician, and curriculum maker.

In their work, men of action need also, of course, to make some use of ideas, to "apply science," as we call it, and different actions obviously require different amounts of science if they are to be efficient and rational. We may imagine a continuum on which the types of action are placed according to the degree of science they use. And we may imagine another continuum on which the men of action are placed in the order of their use of the systematic reflection necessary, according to them, for the performance of good work. On the left side we will have, say, those men of action who rely very little upon such reflection in their dealings with people and things; on the right side of the continuum we will have those who apply whatever science is available in their dealings with people and things.

The curriculum maker should be placed at the extreme of the scientific right side of the continuum. As an educational planner, he makes decisions involving people as well as decisions involving ideas. Sometimes, it is true, he is either an administrator (i.e., clearly a man of action) or a curriculum expert (i.e., clearly a man of knowledge, a scholar consulting administrators and teachers); but more often he is less specialized and more overworked. Most often, he is a teacher whose job is to make a curriculum and whose job also is to deal not only with students but also with all sorts of people who either support or oppose his activities. In this responsible, difficult, and uncomfortable role, he often has the duties of both man of action and man of knowledge, without the status and privileges of either. In the midst of such difficulties (and often conflicts), it is not easy to make rational decisions and to plan efficient actions. The curriculum maker does not have one loyalty: he usually has many. He is concerned with scholarly values, but he is also concerned with some of the ideals cherished by students or by the community and must pay some attention to those of his superiors before whom he is responsible. He may be dedicated besides to some conception of the school of the future, to a utopian world of one or another type. And the more loyalties, the more ideals involved, the greater the possibility of their conflict with good work or efficient action.

The curriculum maker is a man in charge of planning a school curriculum, whatever school it may be (barbers' college, university, initiation school of a Bantu tribe, or high school). In some countries, he may be an officer in the ministry of education; in some others an expert on curriculum; in others a superintendent of a school or a teacher; in some he may be a tribal chief; still somewhere else he may be a secretary of the Party or an assistant to king or emperor. Whatever his actual role in society, to us he is a curriculum maker as long as he is involved in making curricular decisions.

This chapter presents a few examples of praxiological rules, and a few hypothetical cases of the curriculum maker's dilemmas. Praxiology may help him to clarify some conflicts, may help him see where he stands, and possibly release him from some guilt feelings or from feelings of inadequacy which may trouble him when he gives up efficiency in the name of some other values.

We turn, first, to a general presentation of the technical and practical values of any action (or work) and then pass on to the analysis of more specific problems—those of the rules of successful cooperation (positive collective action), and the rules of successful struggle (negative collective action).

A curriculum maker, like any other man of action, is constantly confronted with planning how to achieve various, more-or-less complex goals, and he is concerned with the understanding of how he achieved them, and with the evaluation as to what extent he managed to achieve them. Like an engineer who, once the bridge is finished, goes back to his blueprint to evaluate his work (i.e., to compare it with the finished product), a curriculum maker at some point in his work should also evaluate his action by comparing his products (for instance the changes achieved in students) with his blueprint (the curriculum).

Any work may have a number of technical or practical values or virtues. One such value is *precision*. The result of our work is more precise in a given respect if in this respect it conforms more to the established or expected standards. A printed page may be more precise according to the accepted standards of the aesthetic features of print, another page more precise so far as spelling is concerned. The result of the work done by a curriculum maker in a liberal arts college may be thus precise in one respect if the graduates of that college show as much sensitivity to other individuals' points of view, as much competence in arts and literature, as much curiosity about different cultures as he planned to develop in them through his curriculum. The results of his work may be evaluated as precise in another respect if as many students of this college as were anticipated in the curriculum plan graduate during some given period, say, five years.

We may also evaluate any work from the point of view of its *purity*. Whatever we are planning to produce we are always able to single out in a given product the positive elements (those we wanted to see in our product) as well as the negative elements (those we wanted to avoid). The qualities of the material from which we produce, as well as the conditions of work, are often responsible for such negative unplanned elements in our product as, for instance, the unpleasant smell of the soap, or a noise interfering with music on the records. To do a pure work means to avoid successfully all accidental negative elements in our product. A curriculum maker who planned in his curriculum to produce graduates with strong character and intellectual curiosity and, indeed, achieved both these characteristics, with, however, a third one, say intolerance—which from his point of view was highly undesirable—did not do a pure work.

Still another virtue of good work is its *economy*, i.e., the ability to achieve the goal with the minimum expenditure of all sorts of investments, costs, casualties, etc. Economy of work may be subdivided into two types: (1) *Economy* in the narrower sense of this word, i.e., the ability to spend the minimum of available resources for achieving a given goal; for example, the ability to prepare a certain number of mechanics during the minimum time available, or the ability to train good acrobats at minimum cost to their health.

(2) *Productivity,* or the ability to prepare better, or more, mechanics during the time available.

We may also evaluate our work from the point of view of its *certainty,* i.e., the ability to predict the results, by which we do not mean, of course, a purely subjective self-assurance which may have no connection whatsoever with a good knowledge of the conditions of a given work, of the characteristics, of material from which we are to make our product, the tools available, etc.

Our work may be evaluated from the point of view of its *coherence*—an important and rare virtue of efficient, intelligent action. To be coherent in action means to organize our particular acts in such a coordinated way that the earlier acts are a preparation for the ones to follow. To use a simple example: such languages as Latin and French are usually disturbing one to another when taught at the same time. The teaching of Latin, however, may be used as a good preparation for teaching French in the succeeding year.

Simplicity is still another important virtue of good work in any area. A car with an automatic transmission is simpler to operate than a car with gears manipulated by hand; an electric clock easier to operate than an old-fashioned clock which had to be wound with a special key. A hierarchically organized group is simpler from the point of view of its leader, though not necessarily the best from an ideological perspective.

Though the above inventory of selected virtues of good work is far from being exhaustive, we turn now to another problem, one of how to achieve these practical values. We will try to answer a question: What are the general methods leading to success in action?

According to Kotarbiński, all methods of efficient action may be divided into three categories: *economization, preparation,* and *instrumentalization.*

Here are examples of two important rules of *economization:*

The rule of minimum intervention can easily be observed in all areas of action. It has been used since time immemorial by loggers who, instead of transporting logs themselves, let the streams or rivers "do the job for them" whenever possible. A physician who at some stage of a cure stops giving his patient medicine and allows the healing to take its own course applies the same rule. Such a minimum intervention should not be mistaken for passivity or the lack of action. Action is not equivalent to activity. A guard, a nurse sitting at a bedside of a patient, a soldier standing at attention are all active (in the sense of being involved in an action) though they may not perform any actual motions. The rule of minimum intervention is also well known to teachers, who often try to arrange a class discussion in such a way that "it runs itself," thus making his or her intervention practically unnecessary.

A curriculum maker will certainly have numerous occasions for using this rule of the economy of work. While planning education on a national scale he may, for instance, prefer to adapt the already existing institutions for the purpose of such planning, rather than to create new institutions.

The rule of potentialization is based on the assumption that it is more costly to act than to show a readiness to act. Warfare provides us probably with the most clear-cut examples of this praxiological rule. The very concept of "cold war" rests upon it—we replace a military action with the threat of military action. The use of the scarecrow is another example of the same principle from the area of man's "warfare" with animals. But the rule of potentialization is a general praxiological rule valid as well in individual planning of action and in cooperation. Payment by check instead of payment in cash is among the common illustrations of this rule. Instead of providing X with certain goods, we give an assurance of providing these goods, on request. Teaching a student the techniques of gathering information instead of providing given pieces of information is a case of the same rule. When an educator proclaims that "it is more important to teach how to think than to teach what to think" (an exclamation often

heard in the contemporary U.S.A.), he is applying the praxiological rule of potentialization to the domain of teaching.
A curriculum maker may also apply this rule to his own job
and, instead of learning "everything" about the social structure of his community or his country, he may provide his
office with a series of books on this topic as well as with
books on the techniques of gathering such information rapidly.

The next area of praxiological inquiry, *the preparation of
actions,* could be guided by Pasteur's saying "Le hasard ne
favorise que des esprits préparés"—good preparation is the
secret of good improvisation. This paradox may be translated
into a praxiological rule saying that the condition of doing
something without immediate preparation is the previous
preparation.

There are four steps of preparing an efficient action, not
necessarily succeeding each other:

1.   Removing the handicaps.
2.   Preliminary shaping of the material (for example, preparation of the prefabricated houses, packaged food, etc.).
3.   Preparation of oneself for action (for instance, to make
oneself "fit" for a tennis match, a panel discussion, a difficult
interview, etc.).
4.   Working out a plan—having some conception, some
"model" as we often say, and then listing the detailed steps
for its realization.

Here are some praxiological virtues of the good plan as
presented by Kotarbiński: first of all, the plan has to be
adapted to the goal in question. For example, the planning
of a trip to visit the Capitol in Washington obviously is not
well-adapted to the goal if the means of transportation selected arrives after the conclusion of the session. Then, a
good plan has to be *feasible* (for example, if we planned
transferring to a plane which left before our plane had arrived
at its destination, our plan obviously was not feasible). A
good plan has to be as *economical* as possible in its construction (i.e., without superfluous elements, or unnecessarily long

expositions) and in the way it may be used (it has to be easy to use—transparent and readable). Last but not least, the good plan has to be *flexible*. It should not recommend a given step where that step depends on circumstances to be known later. And it should be *well-grounded* in knowledge, taking as much as possible into consideration facts which may be necessary or helpful in its realization.

Now, let us imagine a curriculum maker who had a wonderful conception for an experimental curriculum for a high school in a conservative American community but did not want, or did not know, how to prepare it efficiently. He either neglected, or consciously disregarded, some of the rules of preparation described above. First of all, he was so blinded by his enthusiasm that he did not anticipate such handicaps as the opposition of school trustees and some important members of the community to the very name "experimental" he gave to his curriculum. If he was aware of this opposition, maybe he would have changed the name "experimental" to some more neutral name and increased the chances of success. Let us imagine further that the curriculum maker whose experimental curriculum was defeated wrote another curriculum proposal which was, however, so long and so "sophisticated" that no teacher (not to mention trustee) was able to understand it. He did anticipate the fact that the level of curriculum was not adapted to the readers who were to pass judgment, but he valued their sophistication so highly and had such contempt for "lowering the level" that he chose to fail rather than to yield. Unlike the first case, which was an instance of neglect, this was an instance of value resistance. He resisted in the name of his personal values. How often, however, have we seen other men of action (and, no doubt, many curriculum makers among them) choose to act inefficiently not in the name of their personal values but in the name of social values—how many clearly unfeasible plans have been for centuries proposed (and doomed to failure) by ideological groups of all sorts?

Watching this, one cannot fail to remark that human nature, indeed, is more ideological than praxiological, and so must be the nature of the curriculum maker—unless, of course, he has managed to make himself subhuman or superhuman.

The third area of praxiological inquiry—*instrumentalization of actions*—is of limited importance for a curriculum maker and will be only briefly mentioned. Instrumentalization of actions is defined here as the increase in the use of technical apparatus. Among the great concerns of engineers is, for instance, the concern with *operability* of tools. Kotarbiński writes about subjective and objective operability. The ordering, for example, of papers alphabetically or according to dates of arrival increases our *subjective operability*. So does standardization of tools (the word "tool" being used, of course, in the larger, praxiological sense).

Objective operability may be increased in several ways. First of all, in some kinds of work, it may be increased by centralization. The greater the complexity of the apparatus, the greater centralization is needed to make it function efficiently. This view often is held in regard to tools and machines, as well as in regard to working teams or institutions. This rule may be of some use to a curriculum maker involved in the planning of curricula for large schools or constructing programs of education on a national or even an international scale.

Another example of the way of increasing objective operability is provided by automatization of the apparatus. The greater the automatization (independence of a given apparatus from man), the more human effort is saved. Apart from any moral considerations, the saving of human effort for the areas in which machines cannot work as yet is obviously an important praxiological virtue. The curriculum maker (as any man of action) has been faced, and no doubt will be increasingly faced, with numerous dilemmas resulting from the advance of automatization. Nobody has yet invented a machine for curriculum making, but other machines (radio, TV, tape recorder, and even some machines which are supposed to drill students better than any teacher can do in certain subjects) have been creating for decades an unwarranted enthusiasm or unwarranted disturbance among teachers, students, and important citizens who have some say (and the power to back it) in the area of education.

Of the two specialized branches of praxiology—*the theory of cooperation* and the *theory of struggle*—the former is definitely less well-developed, a fact about which it would be interesting to speculate.

Cooperation is defined here as complex, multisubject (i.e., collective) action. Some of the rules, however, for efficient performance of one-subject, complex actions are highly relevant for the *theory of cooperation* as well. We have in mind such rules as the rule of *integration,* i.e., building of the whole from the parts, plus the problem of the maintenance of this whole. We recognize in this rule a particular case of a more general rule of good work—the rule of preparation of action. In order to maintain a whole (whether it is a machine or a college), we have to have a *supply* of the material from which it was built so that in case of damage or disintegration, the repairs may be made as soon as possible. In the case of a college, our supply is, of course, people—we have to have some ideas of where to recruit students in case the predicted registration fails, and we have to have some ideas of which universities are most or least likely to provide us with the faculty we want to have in a given college. The problem of substitution is equally important for the maintenance of the whole, whatever its nature. In case our supplies fail, we have to use substitutes, whether these are substitute parts or substitute teachers.

Another example of such a rule of the efficient performance of one-subject, complex action which is highly relevant for the theory of cooperation is the *rule of coordination.* To coordinate actions means to organize them in such a way that they do not disturb one another and, in addition, to organize them in such a way that they help one another in the achievement of the selected goal. A violinist, for instance, has to coordinate the movements of his right hand, which works in one way, with the movements of his left hand, which works in another. A curriculum maker may be faced with the necessity of coordinating his actions in a somewhat similar manner, which isn't always an easy job, particularly for people who have not been trained since early childhood (as many Americans are) in the art of doing two or more things at the same time. In trying to articulate a curriculum at an improvised meeting with the less well-educated superiors, let's say, the curriculum worker may have to be at the same time a diplomat (using all the difficult tactics of evasion, persuasion, silence, and sudden outbursts of eloquence) and an intensive thinker who cannot afford to lose track of his arguments and the continuity of his thought. The problem of division of labor among the members of a team (the problem of cooperation in the proper sense of this word) is, from a praxiological point of view, only a case of coordination. This is a case of coordination of complex, multisubject actions. Such problems as how to divide work most efficiently in the case of nonrecurrent and recurrent activities (specialization of work) are most relevant for the curriculum maker as they are for any man of action.

Two theories are, according to Kotarbiński, badly needed for the efficient planning of cooperation—a theory of information (communication between subjects) and a theory of centralization (which in the case of human teams means mainly a theory of leadership).

The second specialized branch of praxiology is, as was said before, the *theory of struggle*. Struggle in a praxiological sense is any at least two-subject action in which at least one subject tries (consciously) to disturb another. We may give here as an example a curriculum maker who tries to defend his curriculum against the pressures of the P.T.A. In this case he is obviously on the defensive. The praxiological definitions of "attack" and "defense" may be helpful at this point. X attacks when he tries to cause a change incompatible with the goal of his opponent Y. Y defends himself when he tries to prevent occurrence of this change. Sometimes, in order to prevent the attack of the opponent (for example, the P.T.A.), a curriculum maker may act wisely if he attacks first, this praxiological truth being well-known to less reflective and more aggressive men of action.

It is clear from the definition given above of the praxiological concept of struggle that it should not be identified too closely with its particular case, military struggle. Side by side with military struggle, commercial competition, dispute, playing games, etc. are instances of "struggle" in the most general, praxiological sense of this word.

In one most common and praxiologically most interesting case of struggle, both subjects are trying to achieve contrary goals, both know about it, and in their actions they take into consideration the actions of the opposite side. A dispute between the curriculum maker and some controlling agency over an issue, say of some educational goal (for instance the goal of teaching all high school students Latin) may serve as an example of this type of struggle.

From the examples of the rules of efficient struggle given below, we will see that they often teach us (as do the fables of La Fontaine) that it is wit or intelligence rather than "pure strength" that makes the victory.

We act according to the praxiological *rule of concentration* (and this is again a general rule of efficient action, particularly relevant, however, to the theory of struggle) when we try to achieve a goal by a number of simultaneous actions. The concentration of the army in one place before the attack is an example of the rule of concentration from the area of military struggle. In the case of dispute, for instance, an accumulation of arguments which independently of one another support our thesis is an example of the application of this rule to a case of nonmilitary struggle. A curriculum worker who takes with him to P.T.A. meetings the members of the community (preferably representing different power groups) who are likely to support his thesis against that of an opponent acts according to the praxiological rule of concentration.

Another rule of efficient struggle called the *rule of divide and govern (divide et impera)* is colorfully described in the well-known legend from Ancient Rome about the struggle of three men against three other men of equal strength. From among the first three men, two were killed but one remained untouched. From among the other three men, all survived but were all weakened by wounds. The man from among the first three would certainly have perished, in spite of his good health and strength because he was surrounded by the three wounded ones. Recognizing this, he ran away. The three wounded men followed him but since their strength was less and they did not run with the same speed, the crafty man was able to defeat them one by one.

We may say in a more general way that any inciting of conflict among opponents is an application of the praxiological rule of "divide and govern" and a reliable way of increasing the probability of victory.

It may look at first sight very Machiavellian to recommend such a praxiological rule to a curriculum maker. Against whom is he to use this rule in the country of which he is a loyal citizen, or in the school of which he is a faithful employee? Should he use it against the superintendent of the school? Should he use it against the community's power groups? There is no clear answer to such questions. It all depends on the social and individual values of the curriculum maker in question, on the structure of the society and, finally, on the curriculum maker's intelligence (self-awareness and realistic perception of the situation) and integrity. There are certainly a number of situations, such as in countries invaded by foreign powers or in various colonial or semi-independent countries, where the curriculum maker with intelligence, energy, and integrity will not hesitate to use the praxiological rule of "divide and govern."

But this problem, though maybe most acute in the case of the "divide and govern" rule, is by no means restricted to it. Like electricity, logic, or atomic energy, praxiology can be put to bad or good use, and since the conceptions of good and bad vary from one culture to another and from one individual to another, all we can say to a curriculum maker is that he should be careful and constructive in his use of praxiology—constructive according to the standards he believes in. Since praxiology pertains to human action and conduct, curriculum praxiology necessarily is involved with and affected by human values.

NOTES

1. R. M. MacIver, *Society*, Rinehart and Company, Inc., New York, 1946.

2. Robert Redfield, *The Primitive World View and Its Transformations*, Cornell University Press, Ithaca, New York, 1958.

3. See, for example, the discussion of this problem in Bronislaw Malinowski, *Magic, Science and Religion*, Doubleday & Company, Inc., Garden City, New York, 1954; or in W. L. Warner, *Black Civilization*, Harper and Sons, New York, 1937.

4. Tadeusz Kotarbiński, *Traktat O Dobrej Robocie* (Treatise on Good Work), Zaklad Imienia Ossolińskich we Wroclawiu, Lódz, 1955; *Sprawność i Blad* (Efficiency and Error), Państwowe Zaklady Wydawnictw Szkolnych, Warsaw; 1956; "Principes du bon travail," *Studia Philosophica*, vol. III, 1939–1946; "Les valeurs techniques de l'activité," *Studia Philosophica*, vol. IV, 1951; "La notion de l'action," *Proceedings of the XIth International Congress of Philosophy*, vol. VII, 1953.

5. Georges Hostélet, "Les rapports entre les principes du bon travail et de la methodologie de l'investigation scientifique dans les domaines de l'action," *Studia Philosophica*, 1951; "Aperçu sur les positions des problèmes de l'action," *Revue Philosophique*, vol. 113, Paris, 1932.

6. G. H. Mead, *The Philosophy of the Act*, edited by Charles W. Morris, et al., University of Chicago Press, Chicago, 1938.

7. Ludwig Von Mises, *Human Action: A Treatise on Economics*, Yale University Press, New Haven, Connecticut, 1949.

13

Dialogue Between a Philosopher and a Curriculum Worker

JAMES A. JORDAN

CW (*curriculum worker*). What I'm looking for is a guide, a way of thinking about the problems of curriculum development. I keep having the feeling that curricula are just made-up affairs, and I don't like it.

P (*philosopher*). Well, what do you want with me? I don't know anything about curricula. You know how philosophers are. They spend all their time with the "big questions." What use do you have for an ivory tower kind of fellow like me?

CW. I don't know; maybe none. But I don't think developing a curriculum is unrelated to the so-called big questions. If there is a relationship, I'd like to know about it.

P. Suppose we start with some of your problems and see where this leads us.

CW. Sounds good to me. Why don't we just start with the problem that worries every sensitive curriculum worker at some time. People often say that the curriculum in our schools is too easy. They say that young people coming through the American school system don't know anything; that they spend time on things like flower arrangement and household budgeting. Well, I think they ought to know something, too, and I think household budgeting is important. After all, most of them are marrying by the time they've been out of high school two or three years, and being able to run a household on a limited amount of money is not a skill they just grow up with. Our society is complex, and there are all kinds of things people can throw away their money on without getting any of the things they need. After all, in our society what is more important than being able to handle money?

P. If you don't slow down, we'll have so many problems before us that we'll not even get started, much less find out what you want to know. You've talked about several things— knowing something, what young people need, our complex society, and what's important in courses—with which of these do you want to begin? We can't discuss all of them at once, you know.

CW. Let's talk about the courses. That's what people are always jumping on me about. The courses are too easy or they're not in the right subjects. If we can figure out the courses thing, maybe the rest will come.

P. All right, courses. How do you select the courses you'll offer? I mean how do you determine which courses are going to be part of your curriculum and which courses aren't?

CW. Well, we have a faculty meeting and we talk things over. We find out what the superintendent thinks—if he has any pet ideas he wants to insist on. Generally, we just sit down with the faculty and talk out which courses we ought to offer. Everybody gets a chance to have his say. We're pretty much in agreement, actually. Every now and then there's some argument when you try to start a new course, like family living. We argue about it and listen to the reasons somebody has for wanting a course like family living; then we just decide whether his reasons are good enough and either put it in or leave it out. The whole thing is pretty democratic—the way it ought to be—and ahead of most faculty groups, I think.

P. Let's explore two phrases you used—"courses we ought to offer" and "reasons are good enough." Apparently, you feel that some courses are so important that they ought to be part of a school curriculum, and you feel that whatever courses are part of the school curriculum ought to be part of it for a reason.

CW. Of course, I do. I don't need a philosopher to tell me I think some things ought to be part of the curriculum. Neither does anybody else. Everybody knows, for instance, that English ought to be part of the curriculum. How can anybody get along if he doesn't know how to communicate effectively? And what a poor life he'd lead if he'd never had any contact with the great classics of English literature. As for reasons, you don't just put courses in the curriculum for fun; of course you have a reason.

P. Well, now don't get excited. I'm not trying to tell you anything. I'm just trying to talk with you about the curriculum. Now, tell me, how do you determine the courses you ought to offer?

CW. I told you. We just sit down and talk it over and decide.

P. But how do you decide? What do you use as the basis for decision? How, for instance, a few years ago, did you decide to drop Latin from the curriculum?

CW. We had a long argument about that. I'd almost forgotten it until you mentioned it. Most of us were pretty neutral, I guess. The two who argued most were the language teacher and the family-living teacher. We were going to substitute family living for Latin, but that didn't work out. What we did was add family living and then, a little later, drop Latin. That way, the decisions came a little easier.

P. But what sort of things did the language teacher and the Latin teacher say?

CW. Well, I can't remember exactly, of course, but it went something like this: the language teacher said that Latin not only should not be dropped but should be returned to its place as a requirement. It was good discipline for any mind; helped students learn English; disciplined the mind for strong mental achievement in any field—mathematics, physics, or what have you. Aside from that, Latin was the language used by the people who were, in a way, founders of our civilization. It had been spoken for centuries as the scholarly language even after it died out among the people. All the Romance languages were directly descended from it. She even went so far as to say you couldn't really understand our Western heritage if you didn't know how to read Latin. Of course, most of us couldn't go along with this since we didn't read Latin, but all in all she used some pretty convincing talk. But the family-living teacher really won the day when he kept asking of what use it was to most of our students. He admitted that Latin might be of use to people who planned to become professional scholars, but most of our students don't even go on to college. They end up as white-collar workers—clerks, salesmen, junior business executives in local concerns—that kind of stuff. Most of the girls are housewives by the time they've been out of high school for three years. Somehow, all the Latin teacher said about the beauty of the *Aeneid* in the original and the historical and aesthetic material that was unavailable to those who didn't read Latin just didn't seem to stand up too well against white-collar workers and housewives. The truth of the matter is, most of our kids just didn't need Latin and that's why it was dropped.

P. Then the reason for dropping Latin was that it wasn't "needed" by most of your students, at least in the opinion of most of your faculty?

CW. That's right. After all, what's the use of trying to teach kids something they don't need. It's all we can do to give them what they do need.

P. But how do you decide what they need? Need for what?

CW. Need to get along, of course. Everybody has to get along. And there are certain things you have to know to get along. These are the things they need.

P. But do you just want to teach people to get along? You would concede, wouldn't you, that there might be circumstances that would arise in which you wouldn't want one of your students to get along? For instance, if one of your students found himself caught in a series of shady deals involving his business associates, you wouldn't want him to get along with these circumstances, would you? Wouldn't you want him to pull himself away from such a group, stand alone—in fact, refuse to get along with them?

CW. Of course, we want our students to be honest, first and foremost. Naturally, I didn't mean by "get along" that he should be able to get along with a bunch of crooks. But then, part of getting along is being honest, at least part of getting along with the right people is.

P. For the moment, I'll grant that part of getting along with the right people is being honest. But suppose that it were possible to get along with the right people, in fact, with the best people, without being honest; suppose it were possible to hide the fact that you were dishonest so completely that no one would be able to discover it; and suppose that you had all the other virtues necessary in order to get along; would a person like this need to be honest?

CW. Well, no, I suppose, strictly speaking; he wouldn't need to be honest, but he ought to be honest anyway. Even if it turned out to be true that a person didn't need to be honest, we'd still try to teach our students to be honest.

P. Why?

CW. Why? Because they *ought* to be honest. How could we have a society if people weren't honest? I mean, at least minimally honest? Why, without such honesty, society would soon disintegrate into roving bands of thieves little better than animals.

P. We'll accept that for the moment, but in passing I want to point out that you're not sure why people should be honest. Should they be honest simply because they ought to be or should they be honest because the very existence of society is threatened if they're not? Right now let's see if we can find out whether there are many things other than "need to get along" that help determine what courses should be in your curriculum. Maybe we should even focus upon what you mean by "get along." After all, people get along in various ways. I don't suppose you think we should all get along as well as the Rockefellers, for instance. On the other hand, I suppose you wouldn't think of the people on skid row as "getting along," would you?

CW. Don't be silly. There's almost no chance that any of our students will ever get along as well as the Rockefellers. You know that's not what I meant, and, of course, the folks on skid row aren't getting along. I mean by "get along" just the regular sort of healthy, happy existence that most of the people in our society think of as happiness. Enough to eat, a loving family, friends, a job that offers a little more than just a way to make a living, membership in a community, a hobby of some sort—that sort of thing. Everybody knows what "get along" means. It's sort of a happy adjustment in society.

P. "Get along" seems to mean a sort of modicum adjustment to the more obvious aspects of our environment. But I get the feeling that lurking just beneath the surface of what you're saying is the real reason that justifies placing courses in your curriculum. For instance, if a person can get along perfectly— e.g., he has all of his bodily wants well taken care of, he has a loving family, he has friends, his job enables him to contribute something to the welfare of his community, etc.— is this actual process of getting along the end you have in mind? In other words, do you want a person to be able to get along for a purpose or is getting along a purpose in itself? Should a person have friends just to have friends or is there a reason for having friends? Do you see what I mean?

CW. I think so. I suppose I mean that a person should be able to get along in order to be happy. A person can't be happy if he can't get along. A person can't be happy if he's lonely, hungry, or feels unimportant or worthless. I guess the reason he should do all the things I said is so that he can be happy. Then the things I'm talking about when I talk about the things people need to get along are the things they need to be happy. I see what you're going to ask already. You're going to ask if there is any need for them to be happy. I mean, you'll want to know what makes me think that people need to be happy, right?

P. Well, not just now. I'll accept your statement that you get people's needs from what it takes for them to be happy. But this puts us back to where we were a few minutes ago. Suppose a person could be happy and dishonest, would this suit you? Would you be content to teach people how to be happy if you discovered that it were perfectly possible to be happy and dishonest at the same time? Wouldn't you still want to teach them to be honest?

CW. I certainly would. And there are lots of other things like that. I'd want them to be just, fair-minded, reasonable, kind, and probably a lot of other things that just don't pop into my mind right now. I'd want a person to be all these things, whether he were involved with being happy or not.

P. Now you seem to be pointing to at least two sources or justifications for the kinds of things you put in your curriculum. You seem to be saying that you want those courses in your curriculum that will give a person whatever it takes to be happy, and there are some things you want people to learn (I'm not sure whether they'd learn them from courses) even if these things turned out to be independent of happiness. For the moment, let's turn our attention to your notion of happiness. After all, happiness is a pretty vague term, sometimes known as a catchall with no real meaning at all. I'll not press you to tell me what you mean by happiness right now. Let us assume that there is such a thing as happiness, but there would seem to be, right offhand, many different kinds of happiness. I don't imagine you think that the same things always will make different people happy. Since different things make different people happy, there seem to be different happinesses. Now, suppose that there are different happinesses, do you want to have courses in your curriculum that will enable a person to achieve any kind of happiness? Suppose, for instance, that you discovered, much in the manner in which Aldous Huxley discussed these things in *Brave New World*, that it was perfectly possible to train people to be happy with listening to the cheapest sort of music, reading the most childish sort of comic books, engaging in the freest sort of sexual activity, and working in the dullest, most senseless kind of trade. Suppose you discovered a method of training that was foolproof. No one who went through your method of training failed to be happy with the activities listed. Would you want to train some people to be happy in this sort of way?

CW. Of course not! After all, I'm educating human beings,

not pigs. Besides, society can't afford to have such a non-productive segment dragging on the efforts of the rest. In order to make progress, society must have everyone producing in ways that are beneficial to all, not just in ways that occupy people's time. You must see that not just any sort of happiness will do. There are some kinds of happiness, though I am reluctant to refer to them as happiness, that are just not fitting to human beings.

P. I'll let that pass for the time being; I mean that remark about some kinds of happiness not being fitting to human beings. Let's pursue our imaginary case just a little bit further. Suppose this group of happy human pigs (to modify a phrase of yours) is engaged in the sort of drudgery that exists in any society. Suppose that by degrading their tastes in other respects (music, art, etc.) you can train a segment of your society to be happy in performing the menial tasks that abound. Suppose, in fact, that the rest of society benefits in terms of more happiness because you have been able to train such a group of people. Would you then want to have a group of happy human pigs (using pigs here in a descriptive, not a pejorative sense)?

CW. The question is too hard. Besides, we've strayed too far afield. All I want to know is how to bring a little order to the process of developing a curriculum. I don't want to waste my time with a lot of philosophical speculation.

CW. Perhaps the task is too hard. But didn't we arrive at our question by asking the very question you wanted answered? Didn't we arrive at the difficult question by asking how you determine what courses go into your curriculum? Didn't we discover that people argued for courses to go in a curriculum because they thought the courses would fill the needs of youngsters? Didn't we discover that by needs of youngsters we meant those things that are needed in order to be happy? Are we then to give up our pursuit because of the unpleasant discovery that there are different kinds of happiness? And what of the question that we turned aside earlier? I mean the one about some things that should be in the curriculum even if they turn out to be independent of happiness? We haven't even taken that up. At present we don't seem to know how you go about determining in a rational way what should be in your curriculum. Answer the question now according to your feelings. We needn't be afraid of missing the truth.

CW. I suppose, then, that we have to make some sort of distinction between the happiness of individuals in a society and the happiness of individuals as the aggregate that is the society. I think it makes sense to say that we want to train individuals in such a way that the aggregate contains or enjoys the greatest amount of happiness. But it also makes sense to me to say that we ought not to "sacrifice" the happiness of a group of people to the happiness of the aggregate. I know that you haven't talked about sacrificing the happiness of anybody, but that's what it amounts to when you talk about training a group of happy human pigs.

P. But aren't you overlooking the word "happy" in the phrase "happy human pigs?" After all, their happiness would contribute to the happiness of the aggregate, wouldn't it? You have not ruled out any kind of happiness as noncontributory to the total amount. Why do you speak of sacrificing one group to the aggregate when the sacrificed group is itself not only adding to the happiness of the aggregate by performing the menial tasks necessary to the society, but also adding its own happiness as members of a group, so that the sacrificed group contributes to the happiness of the aggregate of society in two ways?

CW. What you say seems to make sense, but there is something about it I don't like. When you speak of different kinds of happiness, that makes sense. Obviously, individuals regard different things as the necessary ingredients of happiness. But I seem to want to say that some happinesses are better than other happinesses, yet this doesn't seem to make sense. After all, what can a person be more than perfectly happy? Somehow, it seems to me degrading to speak of human beings being happy in the way of pigs. I suppose I want to say that we should educate all human beings toward happiness of the best sort, even if this meant a reduction of the amount of happiness attainable in the aggregate of society.

P. I think we're getting to the point where maybe a

philosopher can be of help. At least, we're pushing toward the sorts of problems some philosophers spend time with. You seem to want happiness; that is, you seem to think that probably the all-justifying goal of human activity is happiness or the pursuit of happiness, to use a hallowed old phrase; but you keep drawing back from just happiness. I mean you don't seem to like some of the possible results of pursuit of happiness. You don't like the idea of happy human pigs, for instance. You also seem to think that there are probably some things that should be taught people whether these things make them happy or not—honesty, for instance, although you, no doubt, think the honest person is more likely to be happy. Now, as far as I can tell, we have three distinct problems here:

1.   If the pursuit of happiness is the all-justifying human goal, we must decide what kind or kinds of happiness can be pursued and whether the individual should seek the greatest happiness for himself or for the greatest number. Whatever else this sort of question is, it is a question always asked by ethics of consequences, that is, every act is judged in terms of its consequences. A thing is good if it contributes to the achievement of whatever kind of happiness we are seeking.

2.   Our second problem grows out of this first. If we decide that there are kinds of happiness, we must decide whether there are some kinds that are unworthy of pursuit by human beings. This will help us with our problem of happy human pigs. If there are some kinds of happiness that are clearly inappropriate for human beings, then the greatest happiness for the greatest number is not what we are seeking but the greatest happiness of a sort that is appropriate for human beings. We are still dealing with questions of consequences, however, since an act is judged good if it contributes toward the achievement of the kind of happiness appropriate to human beings.

3.   Our third question or problem breaks entirely with the other two. The question here is not what is good or what promotes happiness, but what ought to be done. Happiness is secondary, in fact almost inconsequential, here. This is our

question of honesty. Ought a man to be honest in spite of the consequences? You see this is where the third question breaks with the first two: we are not concerned with consequences; we are concerned with whether or not an act falls in the class of acts that ought to be done. I suppose most normally one talks about this problem in terms of moral absolutes. There are some things that ought to be done even in the rare cases where these things seem to lead to a reduction of everybody's happiness. Perhaps we should pause now and be sure these problems are closely related to the curriculum problem we started out with. If they are, then clearly, you have use for a philosopher. If they are not, then we should try to find where we have gone astray in our reasoning.

CW. I think I can see how these things are all related to our curriculum problem. Our curriculum problem was, What courses do we include in a curriculum? Well, we had to find out how one decides what courses belong in and what courses belong out. How do you decide on the basis of what courses lead to the kinds of things you want? These things were: being able to get along, which seemed to lead us directly to happiness; doing some things even when these things didn't lead immediately to getting along, which seemed to lead us, perhaps not so directly, to happy human pigs. Well, these are problems of value and philosophers are supposed to deal with such problems. As soon as you can give me answers, I'll be ready to handle my problems of curriculum.

P. I wish it were that simple. I think you are right. These are problems of value and some decisions about them have to be made before you can rationally solve your curriculum problem. In fact, anybody working with curriculum anywhere must make some decisions about the same things before he can build his curriculum. If he wants to be rational about solving his curriculum problem, he'll give these value decisions a full and deep consideration. What happens most of the time, if the example you gave is any indication, is that people spend their time arguing without ever clearly recognizing that they differ on the level of values. Curriculum decisions are made on the basis of hidden value decisions.

It seems to me that rational curriculum decisions necessitate open and deliberate consideration of the value decisions that lie at their base.

CW. I'm agreed; now let's get with it. I'm ready to consider the value decisions that I have to make. You're not arguing with me. If it's this easy, I don't see why people haven't been building curricula on this basis all along.

P. I see, you've caught me. The truth is that knowing value decisions must be considered and made explicit just opens up the problem; it doesn't solve it. I suppose the reason I was jabbering so just now is that I recognize how extremely difficult a task we're letting ourselves in for.

CW. Oh, you philosophers are all alike. Once you find a problem, you don't want to attack it. You want to sniff around and see which way the wind's blowing and what other problems there might be around and whether there isn't somebody who'll help you. You spend so much time sniffing around the problem, you have no energy or time left for the attack.

P. Hold! I accept your accusation as having some truth. But don't rush me too much against my natural bent. First, let us be sure we couldn't avoid all this difficulty by asking a different curriculum question.If we can possibly get around this value problem, then it makes sense to do it. Perhaps you shouldn't be worrying about what courses should or should not be in your curriculum. Why have courses at all? Perhaps you get into value troubles only when you ask questions that presuppose values. Have you tried asking other curricular questions?

CW. Now wait! I see what you're driving at. All right. Perhaps what courses to offer isn't the question I should be asking. I wouldn't fight you over that right now. But whatever the question you ask—what courses, whether courses, or what have you—you immediately start moving toward where we are when you ask why. What is the justification for whatever we do? This is the question we're really considering. What kinds of justification are there for the things you do in education? Now, I know you can always say you do this because it gets you to that, and you can keep this up for a long time. But, sooner or later, you have to say why you want to get to that in some terms other than it gets you to something else. Sooner or later, you have to talk about something you're trying to get to, which, if you got there, would be justification in itself for all the things you did on the way. Now, it seems to me it doesn't matter what kind of curriculum question you start with, you always have to go back to this question before you can really get started. It seems to me, also, that we've already indicated the broad kinds of answers or justifications that are available. You justify whatever you do by saying it is better than something else. When you talk about "better than," you're already on the treadmill. What we've really been saying is that you do certain things because you think they are good things. How are they good things? You gave three tentative answers. They are good in that they promote the greatest happiness for the greatest number. They are good in that they promote the greatest amount of happiness appropriate to human beings. They are good in that they promote the kind of behavior that human beings ought to display. I don't care what kind of curriculum question you ask, unless you want to play the ostrich, you end up here.

P. Bravo! You may be the better philosopher yet. We are agreed, then, that curriculum questions lead to value questions when you ask for justification of answers. "Justification" is a good word. That's what we're concerned with—justification of goals, justification of values. Now, I can see that we're going to have a little trouble with our three tentative answers because neither of us has managed to phrase them in any sort of precise manner. We want to be sure, also, that we're exhausting the list. How many ways of justifying an action are there? Let us suppose you were instituting a new course in your curriculum. What are the possible justifications for your action, ignoring the step-by-step process you would have to go through before you reached your final justification? Let's just consider the kinds of final justification available to you. In a way, I think we should step right beyond the answer that what you did was a good thing. Let us just assume this. What we really want to know, then, is the justification for thinking it is a good thing. To return to our three tentative answers, you could justify your action by saying that it promoted the greatest happiness of the greatest number. You could justify your action by saying that it promoted an increase in the kind of happiness appropriate to human beings. You could justify your action by saying that it promoted honesty or justness, or righteousness, or some other behavior that ought to be promoted.

Are there any other ways? I can think of several variations of these, but no different justifications. What strikes me about all three of our justifications is the awkward position we would be in if someone were to say, "But why promote the greatest happiness of the greatest number?" I think in each case we would be reduced to saying that you ought to. This lands us right smack in the middle of the knottiest problem in philosophy today. How do you justify statements of obligation, of ought? Once we get to this point, you see, it makes no difference how we talk about the good, whether in terms of greatest happiness, or what have you, because we are now asking, "Why ought I do good, why ought I promote the good, why should I work to increase the amount of good?" In a way, I suppose all three of our tentative answers are now reduced to the third, and our one question to be solved is the question of "ought." Why ought I do anything? What are the possible justifications for saying, "you ought?"

CW. I can't find anything to object to in what you've said, but I confess this question to which everything else has been reduced frightens me a little. It never really occurred to me that someone might question whether or not he should seek the good. I can see how we might argue over whether one thing or another is actually the good. I don't imagine such arguments will ever end, but with one little turn of the screw, you've slipped by these arguments, as if they weren't bad enough, to one which frightens me. It's one thing to argue about the good if at least everybody's agreed that whatever the good is, men ought to seek it. There are vast areas of agreement about what kinds of experiences and things are involved in the good. But when you ask, "Why ought I promote the good?" this leaves me feeling a little empty. Not that this doesn't seem to be the question we've come to, but that not being able to settle this argument seems to carry far more frightening consequences than not being able to settle the question of what is the good. Suppose we can't find a justification for saying "you ought," what then? Suppose we end up saying, "There is no way of determining what a person ought to do?" Somehow, this possibility leaves me feeling very much ill at ease.

P. This question leaves us all feeling ill at ease. That's why so many prefer to ignore it as though the question really weren't pressing at all. One of the favorite ways of ignoring it is to argue that since there are no definite choices available in the field and since no one position seems able to muster support of a respectable majority, one position must be as good as another. Thus active refusal to choose becomes itself a positive choice, especially since one of the positions offered for choice maintains that basically all value choices are matters of preference and one preference is just as good as any other. To refuse to choose is tacitly to align yourself with this position.

CW. You mean that it is incumbent upon people working with a curriculum to make a choice between various value positions? If that is true, then it seems to me that your function is to offer us a clear delineation of the choices available. I'm not a philosopher and I don't know beans about "value positions," as you call them. Of course, I have some notion of what we're talking about when we talk about happiness. I know something about ought, when we say something like "he ought to be honest." And I guess, I know what we mean even when we talk about happiness appropriate to a human being. I'm willing to say something in favor of all three of these things. Is that a possible value position? I mean is it inconsistent or something? I'd hate to think that I can't have all three, at least parts of all three and still be consistent. I see some of the problems involved, even some that we haven't talked about—like whether we should prepare people to seek their own individual happiness, or whether there is some good reason for their seeking the happiness of others, or even whether there is really an antithesis between the individual's long-range happiness and the happiness of others. I'm not sure I felt the full weight of the last question you asked, but it still seems to me that the function of you philosophers is to tell us other folks what the state of things is in value theory. If there are several agreed-upon and consistent theories of value and nobody is able to agree that one of them is better than another, then you philosophers ought to give us a choice among them all.

P. I suppose there might be some reason for a philosopher to try to collect the various value positions together into a sort of symposium so that anyone who wanted to could look them over. But suppose a good friend of yours had several books and he wanted you to choose one of them; suppose, also, that because of the effect any one of the books would have upon you, your friend warned you to be sure to choose the best book. Now what would you think of your friend if, after saying this, he said also that he couldn't help you in any other way than to indicate your choices? You'd want to ask him if he'd read all the books. You'd want to ask him if he thought one was as good as another. You'd want to ask him which one he thought was the best. And you would be more than a little chagrined with him if he said that he had read all of them and he had definite notions about which one was best and he was pretty sure that one wasn't as good as another, but he still wouldn't do anything but indicate your choices. You'd hardly think him a true friend, would you? Now, if there were other friends of yours telling you that one book was really as good as another and it didn't make any difference which one you chose, and your old friend persistently did nothing more than indicate that there were several choices and that you must choose, you would decide, wouldn't you, that either your old friend was no longer your friend (since he wouldn't tell you which book he regarded as best) or if he was your friend, he really thought that it didn't make any difference which book you chose? In other words, either your friend doesn't think the choice you have to make is really important or he will, if he has any friendly regard for your welfare, tell you which choice he thinks is the best.

CW. But are value choices as neatly separated as books? And even if they are, I'm not sure I want my friend telling me which one to choose. After all, I'm a grown man and I can make up my own mind. If my friend is really my friend, he won't try to influence my choice. He will just try to help me make the best choice.

P. Oh, you're leaping ahead again. I didn't say your friend should make your choice for you. I didn't say, "He should tell you which one to choose." I said that if he is your friend, either he doesn't think the choice is a very important one, or he will tell you which one he thinks is best. In other words, he will give you his considered judgment for what it's worth. I quite agree that we don't want our friends making up our minds for us, but we don't want to lose whatever good there is in the wisdom and experience of friends. I never said that you shouldn't consult several friends. I simply said that a real friend would be quite willing to give you the benefit of his experience; that is, to tell you what he thinks. I quite agree, also, that a real friend won't try to influence your choice, in some ways, at least. He'll recognize that you are a grown man, but part of being a grown man, I should think, is being able to assess your friend's testimony properly. Thus, I should think, you would want to consult with several friends who have different opinions, but your friend who thinks that one choice is as good as another wins by default if all your other friends are unwilling to indicate their own choices. After all, free and open debate doesn't mean refusal to take sides.

CW. Well, that makes sense. But I still don't see anything wrong with asking a friend to give me an impartial review of the various choices available to me, especially if my friend happens to be specially qualified in the field I ask him to review. If he knows a great deal about the field and can give me an impartial survey of it, he will do me a great favor. After all, at this point I don't even know the choices available to me. It makes good sense to ask some qualified friend to review the field and give me an impartial survey of the choices, especially since my choice is such an important one. Why shouldn't a friend be willing to do that?

P. You make it very hard for me. Perhaps a friend should be willing to do that, but this is such an important choice that a friend is obligated to do all in his power to see that you make the right choice. I suppose the only way to be sure that you have the best opportunity to make the right choice is to apprise you of the possible choices and insist that you hear each choice argued for before you choose. My feeling of losing by default might be overcome in such a case, since not only would the position that your choice is simply a matter of preference be heard, but all others also—I mean, heard from an ardent supporter. If I were your friend and I knew that you were going to hear each possibility argued before you made up your mind, I think I could regard my duty fulfilled if I simply pointed out each possibility. What we are really concerned to discover is the method that will most likely insure the most rational choice.

CW. I think that is correct. After all, I can't debate about this thing forever. In the long run, this is a practical choice for me. I've got to have something in the curriculum. In fact, something is going to be in the curriculum. The problem is to inject as much rationality as possible into the framework upon which curriculum choices rest. It may be that the pressures of time—that is, the fact that I must have a curriculum ready to offer at the beginning of each school year, whether I've settled all these problems or not—will prevent complete rationality. If this turns out to be the case, then, I suppose, paradoxically enough, what we're trying to find is a way to be rational about the amount of nonrationality that is necessarily a part of my curriculum framework. It seems that the best we can hope for is a maximum reduction of nonrationality. Now, again, I say this is your province and you ought to be able to help me.

P. Now, let's see just what you're cooking up for me. If I understand you, you think I ought to be able to offer you an objective run-down on the possible or, at least, shall we say, respectable value positions, and you think that, since an absolutely rational choice might be impossible because of the limitations of time, I should be able to offer you a way of reducing the amount of nonrationality that infects your choices to a minimum. This last, I think, is a very interesting notion, and I think I just had the faintest glimmer of a thought that might even help us with our first problem. Unless I'm mistaken, we're back to talking about the justifications for decisions. Unless I'm mistaken again, a decision is completely rational if on every level of consideration it is justified. Then what we are concerned to bring about is a way of making decisions that will reduce the lack of justification to a minimum. This is a practical problem, I take it, since we have sort of assumed that if we had an infinite amount of time or at least a lot longer than we do have, we could probably discover a procedure that would make every decision, if not the right decision, at least one arrived at through a completely rational procedure. Now, suppose there are levels of justifications. We might picture the levels of justification like the rungs of a stepladder. A completely rational decision would be one justified on each rung of the ladder. Now, a decision with a minimum of nonrationality would be one justified upon every rung that there was time to consider. This doesn't seem quite accurate because the levels of justification don't seem to be as discrete and independent as the rungs of a ladder. For instance, one would think that there would be some levels of justification that could be justified once and for all, or at least until new evidence were uncovered, whereas there would be some that would have to be reconsidered almost constantly. Although we haven't given these levels or rungs names yet, suppose that on the top level we placed problems like the ones we've been discussing, problems of happiness and ought. Suppose one considered the evidence most fully and made a justified and rational decision at this level. There seems to be little likelihood that this decision would need to be constantly changed even though it might need periodic reconsideration and perhaps reconstruction. Suppose one had made a justified decision that the best final goal of the school was the greatest happiness for the greatest number and had even spelled out some of the ingredients of happiness, such as health, security, aesthetic appreciation, etc. This decision would furnish the justification for any lower-level decision that was correctly calculated to lead to it. Thus the rungs of the ladders are obviously related in the sense of means-ends so that the lower rungs are justified if evidence can be deduced to show that they lead to higher rungs. Obviously if, say, the top three rungs have been related in the proper means-end sense, a justification of any decision is completed if it can be shown to lead to the lowest of the top three rungs. Unfortunately, however, the highest rung probably contains the decision that is most difficult to be completely rational about and any amount of nonrationality allowed at the top rung infects every decision at a level lower. It may still be true that the way to reduce nonrationality to a minimum is to be sure that every decision lower than the top is justified.

CW. I think I see what you're getting at. The problem seems now to be discovering what the rungs of the ladder are, I mean, giving them some kind of name. There must be a sort of cluster of decisions that have to be made at each level. If we can give each cluster a name, then our next problem is to discover which clusters yield the greatest return in justification per unit of time spent. Isn't this right?

P. Right. But we seem to be temporarily stuck with a situation in which the decisions that are the easiest to be rational about contribute the least amount of justification to the total process. For instance, it should be reasonably easy to justify a particular classroom activity on the grounds that it can be demonstrated to produce a certain kind of behavior that we think is good (or that the school ought) to produce. If there is evidence to support the contention that such and such activities produce such and such behavior, then the decision to engage in such and such activities partakes of whatever justification we can claim for the upper rungs of our ladder. You see our problem? We can never claim full justification for our decisions until we can justify the decision at the highest level, and the decision at the highest level is the hardest one to justify. I suppose, to be accurate, I should have said "my problem" because it is my problem to help you justify your highest level decision; your problem is to reduce the lack of justification that necessarily obtains at the highest level to the minimum that time allows so that your total program will have a maximum of rationality. The trouble is, at least so far as your problem is concerned, that you need to have the top-level decision made first so that your lower-level decisions will have some foundation. We seem to have something of another paradox since the top-level decision is the foundation or undergirding of all your other decisions.

CW. I can see that, but what is the justification for spending time with the top-level decision? It seems to me that time should be spent in proportion as it offers us rationality for the total program. If the decision at the top level is as tough as you've indicated, then I'm not sure time spent upon it is well used; but if the total program can never be more rational than this top-level decision, then, obviously, if the program is to have any rationality about it, this top-level decision must have some rationality about it. Still, rationality at all the lower levels isn't automatic, and if I have to spend all my time making the top-level decision, chances are we'll even lose the rationality possible to the lower levels. In other words, I can't spend a lot of time getting started. Just as you said, this is a practical problem. I've got to do something, even if it's wrong. It doesn't really do me any good for you to point out that if I start too quickly, my program will be shot through with unjustified decisions. I have to start quickly, no matter what the consequences. Now, I want to know if you can help me make my program more rational. If you can't, I'll just have to muddle along like I've been doing.

P. I don't blame you for getting a little impatient, but I'm afraid problems like this don't really yield to impatience. Maybe we can take the edge off our impatience if we turn to naming the rungs of the ladder. Surely, we can make some progress here. You've already indicated one cluster of decisions. Somebody at the classroom level has to decide what activities will produce the desired behaviors. At the classroom level, this decision is considerably restricted by the fact that one classroom isn't expected to produce the totality of desired behaviors. Presumably, the behaviors that should be produced in a particular classroom result from a decision made upon a higher level. This higher level would be the level on which the place of the classroom in the school is decided. No matter whether the classrooms are selected on the basis of courses or not, there will be some principle of dividing the activities of the school into units and this level of decision is the level above the classroom. Let us call the level upon which the place of the classroom in the school is decided "the school level." If we follow a similar principle, then, the next level would seem to be the one on which the place of the school in education is decided. Other agencies than the school carry on educational activities and so at this level one expects some goals to be set that involve a selection from among all the agencies in society that carry on education. Presumably there would be some educational goals for which a school would be peculiarly suited. Let us call this level the "societal level." After moving through these three levels, it would seem to me that we are approaching the highest level. If we tried to follow our principle, we would try to say something like this: "The highest level is the one on which the place of education in something is decided." I suppose that, tentatively, we could say that the place of education in the good life is decided at this highest level although we are already aware that this is not quite accurate. It is true, nevertheless, to say that at the highest level, the decision would be made that justified the existence of education. Thus, again, we find education either rational or not depending upon our decision at the highest level.

CW. Wait a minute! Before we get into that again, let me see if I have these levels straight. We have the classroom level, the school level, the societal level, and the "good-life" level. Given the place of the classroom in the school, the decisions at the classroom level are to select or choose those activities that will allow the classroom to fill its place. Doubtless, various classrooms would have different places to fill, but one classroom might be selected to develop skill in, let's say, reading. Then, the classroom decisions to be made in relationship to this goal would involve selecting those activities that led to skill in reading. This is a gross oversimplification, but I think the principle is sound. In order to be completely rational at this level, nothing needs to be considered other than the relationship between the activities introduced into the classroom and the given goal, in this case skill in reading. All our skill at this level (at least insofar as we are trying to be rational) will be directed toward collecting evidence to establish the fact that the activities engaged in do produce skill in reading. Now, I know that there are various kinds of reading skills and various levels of achievement in each kind of skill. Don't try to complicate matters by bringing that up. All I'm trying to establish is the kind of thing we'd have to do in order to be rational at this level. Being rational at this level, in other words, does not involve a consideration of the goals selected by the school for the classroom. That gets us into another level.

P. So far, you sound good to me. Why don't we keep moving up the scale and see what happens?

CW. Then, let's try the school level. Part of the complications has already been introduced. But though the task is complex, it seems to me that the school operates in a similar manner. Given the goals of the school, the decisions to be made at this level involve the classrooms or other subdivisions that will enable the school to achieve its goals. Again, rationality consists in collecting evidence to demonstrate that what goes on in the classrooms in achieving their goals does, in fact, bring about the behaviors selected as the goals of the school. We can be completely rational at this level without considering whether or not the goals of the school are rationally selected, but at the school level, the goals of the classroom must be selected because of some demonstrable connection with the goals of the school. There seems to be some sort of principle operating here. At each level, rationality seems to involve collecting evidence to show that the goals of the lower level (the classroom, for instance), when achieved, do in fact constitute a realization of the goals given by a higher level. Of course, there is nothing in what we've said to prevent there being organizational subdivisions beyond the classroom level. But I don't think we need to get involved in that. Our principle would still hold. At any level, one starts with given goals from a higher level and constructs simpler or smaller goals which, if realized, will constitute the realization of the given goals. The rationality of the process lies in the logic of the goal construction carried on and in the evidence brought forth to establish the hypothesis that the constructed goals do, in fact, when achieved, add up to the larger goals. As a schoolman, I've actually talked about nothing more than what goes on in any alert and forward-looking school. But anticipating the weakness of my experience as we move to another level, I think I'll ask you to move on from here.

P. I think you've done well so far, but, of course, we can both see that our earlier statement is still true. There can be no more rationality in the whole process than there is in the selection of goals or the decisions made at the highest level. This fact makes me feel that perhaps we're fooling ourselves with this more or less careful delineation of rationality on these lower levels. We can see where your principles lead. Society gives goals to the school, but this problem gets a little more troublesome because the relationship between the school and society is not so clear as the relationship between the classroom and the school.

Not only is the school not related to society in the same way that a classroom is related to a school, in some cases it is not even related to society in any direct sense. We can easily imagine private schools—military academies, church schools, colleges, and universities—that have relatively little concern for what society might expect or demand of them. Quite obviously, then, "societal level" seems to be a poor phrase for the level above the school.

CW. But if there is no discernible relationship between the school and some agency above it, our whole scheme falls apart because justification of objectives in each case was possible only if one started with objectives that had come down, so to speak, from above. If the school is given no objectives from society, then the justification for the school and classroom activities is chimerical.

P. Perhaps we shouldn't abandon our little scheme so hastily. I think we still have a central notion about the school in hand. Every school is a dependent agency. In other words, no school exists for itself; it is never its own end. If it never exists as an end in itself, then it must exist for purposes outside itself—that is, whatever agency calls the school into existence must be responsible for the objectives of the school.

Thus, in many cases, the state or society or some other such abstraction that represents a political order does offer the school broad objectives. It calls the school into existence to perform certain duties. It takes no stretch of the imagination to see the truth of this statement.

In a totalitarian state, the school is obviously under tight and closely regulated control. What the school is for is an easy question to settle just as the question of the school's objectives is. The state openly and unashamedly dictates the policies of the school. If you worked in such a state, your task would be greatly simplified. Assuming that the state had full trust in your loyalties and abilities, it could feel safe in dictating the place of the school in the educational processes of the state and in allowing you to implement or establish this place from your own professional competence. In other words, you would deal only with problems relating to the school and the classroom. Whether the school should indeed fill the place dictated by the state is a question you would not trouble yourself with. Of course, you might be called upon to clarify various issues. For instance, if the state said, as it undoubtedly would, that part of the place of the school in education was to furnish pupils with the developed intellectual abilities to be loyal subjects of the state, you might very well have to work with a minister of the state in clarifying just what characteristics a loyal subject of the state would have. Would he need to think for himself? Would he need to know the canons of science and evidence? Should he receive an unbiased picture of the part the state has played in world history? These and many other questions would have to be clarified before you could go about doing your job. But if the state said, "Yes, a loyal citizen should think for himself," presumably, you would draw mainly upon your professional knowledge of the nature of children, the thinking process, etc., to set up a series of experiences that produced children who could think for themselves.

Undoubtedly, the state would hold you responsible for demonstrating that children who had gone through the program you instituted could actually think for themselves. If you were able to make such a demonstration, the state would likely not care what process you used to obtain your results unless the process itself happened to produce other results that conflicted with different objectives given by the state to the school. In a situation like this, obviously our little scheme for the justification of objectives is still intact. Objectives and activities of the school are justified if they can be demonstrated to bring about the results that were demanded of the school by the state. The justification of any part of a curriculum is, ultimately, a demonstration that it performs the task it was given to perform.

CW. Now wait a minute! Not all curricula are formed in such a way. And even if they were, I'm not sure that questions of whether a particular objective ought to be sought is not a question relevant to the curriculum worker. You seem to have done a complete about-face. At the beginning of our talk, you proved to me that the curriculum worker could not avoid considering the question of what ought to be done. Now you seem to be telling me that if the curriculum performs that task it was given to perform, it is justified and, I assume, good. Suppose it is given the task of developing good murderers, as I think I could argue some schools in Nazi Germany were, and it performed this task beautifully, is the curriculum justified?

P. You seem to have overlooked a part of our previous talk. Remember we said that a particular objective at any level can be no more justified than the goals at the levels higher up on which it depends. In the case you bring up, of course, the curriculum was justified, but only to the extent that the goal set for it by the state was justified. That is, if the goal set for the school by the state is to produce good (meaning skilled) murderers, then, of course, the curriculum is justified. But we must insist and always attach this proviso, justified only to the extent that producing good murderers can be justified as a goal for the school. Justifying good murderers as a goal would have to be done in terms of the good life that results for all or some or in terms of the kind of life that ought to be brought about. In other words, the goals the state sets for the school are justified on the basis of the state's notion of what constitutes the good life or of what ought to be done.

As we've said before, no objective can be more justified than this final justification. But we broke our justifications into levels in order that a curriculum might be developed even if the process of justifying objectives at the highest level were not complete. Remember, also, that we were simply trying to reduce to a minimum the amount of nonrationality that must infect a curriculum.

CW. Well, I remember most of what you said. What bothers me is the way you seem to be absolving the curriculum person of any responsibility for objectives at a level higher than the classroom. He seems to be in the position of having to take whatever society or somebody gives him as objectives and start there. This seems to be to be solving the problem by cutting it in half and just throwing one half in the river so you can spend your time working on the other half, which I grant, is difficult enough in itself. But what I'm worrying about is that half that's been thrown in the river. I can't help feeling that I haven't done my duty by it.

P. And justly feeling so! Of course, we haven't done our duty by it yet. But let's not say we just threw it in the river. We divided our problem so that we could direct our attention to attacking its several parts. I wouldn't pretend for a minute that we have solved the problem of justifying the objectives of the school, that is, of justifying the place of the school in education. But let's turn back to a phrase we mentioned earlier: the school is a dependent agency. I would assume that to be dependent implies the need of something else for existence. In other words, if the school is dependent, it cannot exist without something that supports it. This something may be almost anything from a primitive individual to the total political state. But, in any case, something must support the school, for the school cannot get on without such support. If a school is dependent for its very existence upon some agency external to itself, it would seem that this external agency could exercise a certain amount of control over the activities of the school. In other words, there is always available to the external agency a threat to the school's very existence as a means for getting its wishes accomplished since an external agency always has a great deal of control over the school, although it may not use it. Let's call this external agency "the controlling agency," substituting the notion of a controlling agency for what has previously been the societal level. If there is some agency that can (mind you, I don't say that it must, but simply that it can) threaten a school's existence if the school refuses to comply with its wishes, I would say that this agency has quite a bit of control over the school. In fact, it seems to me that something like this is always the case with schools. There is always some controlling agency that has within its power the ability to take away the school's existence if it wishes. The only exceptions are cases in which the controlling agency has deliberately given its power away. One can imagine, for instance, a university's board of trustees delegating its policy-making power to some arm of the university, thus making the university its own controlling agency. But such cases would be an exception rather than the rule.

CW. But why do you speak of policy-making power? If a controlling agency, as you call it, really has the power you seem to think, why can't the controlling agency dictate everything the school does? What's the need for a curriculum worker or anything else, for that matter—that is, anything else that thinks? With the amount of control you're giving the controlling agency, it could control every single activity that goes on in a school. Why stop with policies?

P. You're exactly right. And the truth of the matter is that by setting the policies, or, let's say, goals, of the school, this is exactly what the controlling agency intends to do, in a sense. In practice, however, and I suppose I'm getting out of character when I talk about practice, the controlling agency isn't interested in controlling anything but ends, although some may seek to dictate everything. Beyond goals, it is interested in efficiency. This, I think, points to the necessity for a curriculum worker. Perhaps I can draw an analogy from another field. In business, one generally finds a manufacturer, wholesaler, and retailer. Each has functions to perform. Now, there is nothing in the nature of the case that prevents the manufacturer from also being the wholesaler and retailer. But if he is, he must, in spite of himself, perform those functions that are usually performed by the wholesaler. He must contact outlets, distribute goods, maintain an efficient transportation system, etc. You see, there are certain things that must be done before a manufactured article reaches the hands of a customer. It doesn't really matter who does them. What we look for in such cases is efficiency.

I think the same is true in education. There are specific things that must be done before certain objectives of a school can be accomplished. These specifics must be clarified, broken down into an organized sequence of activities, with such and such materials and activities, etc. This is not a process that automatically takes place. To say that a school should give each student the tools and skills necessary for a comfortable adjustment to society doesn't really say very much. Somebody has to decide what this means. Somebody has to decide what experiences will most efficiently do what it means. The controlling agency, for that matter, could do this. But it would be like the manufacturer assuming the functions of the wholesaler. It would have to develop the skills, knowledge, and techniques that are normally supposed to belong to, in this case, the educator. The educator is a specialist. Supposedly, he knows what experiences are likely to produce what results. He knows what is likely to result from a proposed series of activities. He knows what help and hindrance he can expect from the growth patterns and emotional structures of children. Now, there is nothing to prevent the controlling agency from finding out all these things and performing the functions that are normally performed by the educator, but as a matter of efficiency, it normally doesn't do it.

The truth of the matter is that the controlling agency is only interested in results. Whenever it dabbles in procedures, it does this not because it has any particular interest in procedures but because it connects certain procedures with certain results. After all, the controlling agency sets the school up because it is interested in certain ends, not because it just likes schools. Schools are thought to furnish the most efficient medium for accomplishing the controlling agency's goals.

CW. I think I see what you're driving at, and I think I'm

willing to grant that no school exists without some sort of controlling agency upon which it depends. But I'm not sure this relieves the curriculum worker of any of his problems. For instance, it doesn't mean much to propose as the objective of a school that it prepare students for a comfortable adjustment to society. Since this is vague, and since somebody has to work out what it means, and since this somebody, you seemed to think, is going to be the educator, that is, the curriculum worker, then what has the concept done for us? The curriculum worker still has the problem of deciding what the proper objectives for his school are even though now we say he is only clarifying what certain general goals mean. I don't see that the controlling agency has helped him very much. Any school boy could tell us that a school ought to prepare good people to live in a good society.

P. You may be right, but I think we've moved a little closer to pinpointing the proper concerns of the educator with curriculum. I think you are focusing upon a very important fact: normally, the controlling agency doesn't perform its functions. If a controlling agency is not going to give the school a clear notion of what its ends ought to be, then the controlling agency hasn't helped. I think this calls for clarifying the role of the controlling agency, however, not abandoning the notion that there is one. As a matter of fact, I would argue that a controlling agency normally specifies in rather indirect ways what it regards as the proper ends of the school. It functions, I think, as a kind of limiting idea. In other words, the controlling agency, because of its distance from the actual activities and experiences going on in the school, is never quite sure whether the school is carrying out its functions properly or not. But when the school is clearly, or at least in the eyes of the controlling agency clearly, neglecting its functions, then the controlling agency objects. These objections take various forms, depending upon the nature of the controlling agency. A board of trustees might call in the president of a university and issue a few directives for changes. A minister of education might call in a district superintendent and suggest different procedures. Each of these, if the educator only interprets them rightly, is an attempt on the part of the controlling agency to give a clearer specification of just what it regards as the proper end of the school. I think this points to one of the biggest problems in education today, if not the biggest, and that is the problem of channels of communication between the controlling agency and the educator. The educator cannot really do his work efficiently unless he has a rather clear and specific notion of just what is wanted by the controlling agency. A controlling agency cannot do its work efficiently if it has no clear notion of just what kinds of ends the activities of the school are actually leading to. This plunks us right down again, I think, into the middle of the relationship of the school to society.

CW. If I interpret you correctly, you are saying that one of the biggest problems facing the educator today is setting up some means of identifying the controlling agency of his school and of finding out clearly and specifically what ends the controlling agency thinks ought to be the ends of the school. I gather, then, that you mean by the relationship of the school to society, the relationship of those schools that are related to a society that is functioning as a controlling agent. The problem of the educator is not whether or not there is a controlling agency, but what to do in order to get the controlling agency to function as it should so that the educator can function as he should. It would seem that the natural thing to happen when the controlling agency abdicates its functions is for the educator to try to perform both his own role and that of this controlling agency. I take it this would be justifiable only if both roles can be more efficiently performed by one person or one agency.

P. Actually, I don't think it's a matter of whether one person can do the whole business efficiently or not. It doesn't seem to me to matter who actually makes the decisions at the various levels. The problem is one of having the school function in terms of its dependency. By this I mean the problem is having the school actually seek to carry out those purposes that are the purposes of its controlling agency. How one discovers what the purposes of the controlling agency are isn't important so long as one does find out what they are. The difficulties of having one person, the educator, for example, make decisions at both levels stem from the inveterate tendency of that person to make decisions primarily from his own standpoint. Thus, after a period of time, the demands of the controlling agency fall into the background.

CW. Let's take the most difficult case and push it through a little. You said the most difficult relationship between the school and its controlling agency was likely to occur if the controlling agency were society. I take it this difficulty arises out of the somewhat nebulous nature of society's control. I mean, rather, not that the society doesn't have the power to abolish the school, but that society has great difficulty making up its mind about just what it wants. In fact, it is likely to want some things at one minute and others at another. What can the educator do then?

P. We must be perfectly clear, in the first place, that we are not talking about all societies. Some societies might have administrative machinery set up for precisely the purpose of spelling out the proper function of the school in that particular society. You are obviously thinking of a somewhat open, democratic society—that is, one in which there is no central agency responsible for the functioning of the schools. Schools grow up under the aegis of many controlling agencies, but you are thinking of what in this country would be called the public schools. Other schools presumably would have less trouble identifying the controlling agency and its purposes for the school. Whatever the role of the educator in relationship to the public schools, it would be essentially the same in other situations, though simpler.

CW. Yes, this seems to me accurate. If the curriculum worker, in all cases, must find out the purposes or objectives of his school from some controlling agency, then it seems to me that it would be most instructive to consider the most difficult case, which happens to be the case of the curriculum worker in relationship to society as controlling agent in a democracy.

P. Then let's begin. It will always be the case that most of the objectives that the society holds out for the school are either one or all of the following: unformulated, deceptively vague, disguised completely, ambiguous, or supported by ambivalent feelings in many groups found in the society at large. Now, if this is true, and if there is no group or body specifically designated by the society to check upon the school and determine whether or not its activities are acceptable, then it would seem that the educator has almost a free hand to set the objectives that he regards as proper for the school in view of his own notion of the good life and the proper place of the school in bringing it about. After all, the society neither knows what it wants nor has any way of getting it done if it did.

CW. Well, lo and behold! We're back where we were in the very beginning. The curriculum worker is going to form a curriculum with only a glance in the direction of the superintendent and a bit of consultation with the teachers of the school and never mind anybody else.

P. It does sound that way, doesn't it? But the situation has changed a little bit. Now, the curriculum worker knows that his school has a controlling agency that by all rights should set the purposes or objectives of the school. If he is an educator of integrity, he does not even want to conduct his school in any way that obscures from society what he is trying to do. In fact, he wants his school to be conducted in full view of society so that the society can check what is being done against what it thinks ought to be done. In other words, the educator wants to detail the activities of his school and the objectives these imply so that they can be critically reviewed by society. It is his purpose now to find out the limits of toleration that his controlling agency sets. His integrity forces him to respond only to what he can discover as the real wishes of the society to which he is responsible, not to vocal pressure groups or special-interest cliques. His integrity also forces him to abandon a situation in which his own beliefs and values prevent him from honestly seeking to carry out what seem to be the wishes of his controlling agency. Thus, almost paradoxically, he is in the position of trying to find out exactly what his society desires so that he can press it from his own professional position toward what he thinks it ought to desire. His only pressure is his integrity, his refusal to be engaged with a school of a certain sort. This is the sense in which the educator is a leader in a community. He is always a reformer. But with any sense of integrity, he cannot reform surreptitiously. He can only press his controlling agency to re-examine its own position because it conflicts with his. Its respect for him as an individual is all he has to expand its beliefs with.

CW. Things are coming a little fast for me. The educator, as a leader, wants to find out the boundaries set by his controlling agency, but he doesn't want to do this so that it will be easy for him to remain within, but so that he can, while remaining within, stretch these to include more and more. I know, I'm speaking metaphorically, but I'm not sure I can do otherwise. The educator is a leader in the sense that he is always reconstructing his own position in the light of new evidence and new thinking. You think this is likely to put him ahead of society. But he shouldn't use the fact that he is ahead of society to do things surreptitiously that society would disapprove of, even though he thinks these things would be for society's own good. He should, in fact, argue from his vantage point and press society to re-examine its own position because of its conflict with his. His integrity, then, operates in two ways. It prevents him from doing things that conflict with what he knows is the real viewpoint of his controlling agency, and it prevents him from operating under a controlling agency whose viewpoint is in serious conflict with his own. Preferably, however, it furnishes him with a prod to society; that is, because he must refuse to operate under certain circumstances, he can constantly prod society either to modify its position or to dispense with him. Somehow, this sounds a little foolish. It sounds as if the curriculum worker sits around and threatens to quit if society doesn't see that what it really wants is what he thinks it ought to want. I have a feeling that society would just let him quit.

P. You have a rather disconcerting way of taking what I've said and pressing it just a little too far. But there is some sense in what you've said. It does sound as if the educator has as his only weapon his willingness to quit, and it does sound as if I've said he should use this weapon to lead society toward a continually expanding viewpoint. Taken with a grain of common sense, this is what I mean. Of course, the educator shouldn't quit because the controlling agency won't accede to his every demand, but there should be some principles and beliefs the curriculum worker holds so strongly that he is willing to resign if he discovers the wishes of his controlling agency are unalterably opposed to them. What we're searching for here is a theory of social action. I'm afraid I don't have one ready at hand. I think, to be truthful, that there are probably better people to turn to for one than the philosopher. The sociologist or the anthropologist might be of some help here.

CW. I can see that. What I can't see is what happened to our scheme for justifying objectives and what help the philosopher can be to the educator. See if you can pick these up for me.

P. Our scheme for justifying objectives called for justifying them at various levels of decision. The final justification for any series of objectives was to have been furnished by the choices and decisions made at the level of the good life. It is still true, I think, that a series of objectives is only justified to the extent that the value position upon which it rests is justified. We started at the bottom. Classroom objectives were justified in terms of school objectives. School objectives, according to our discussion, are justified in terms of the objectives of the controlling agency. The objectives of the controlling agency are justified in terms of a conception of the good life.

Where does the curriculum worker fit in? According to our discussion, he is a specialist in education who should be most effective at translating into pupil experiences the objectives offered by the controlling agency for the school. But he does more than this. He operates as a sort of gadfly, constantly prodding, clarifying, suggesting to the controlling agency new roles for the school. His work on the practical level is a work of finding out just what the objectives set by the controlling agency mean in terms of school activities. In relation to the controlling agency, he is always trying to find out what it wants and to improve the quality of what it wants. He does this by constantly prodding the limits of the controlling agency's thinking.

But in spite of all this extremely complex activity on the part of the curriculum worker, the goals of the school are justified to the extent that their realization would actually achieve the real purposes of the controlling agency. In other words, the goals of the school are justified to the extent that they allow the school to fill the place allotted to it by the controlling agency. It seems to me that we have two roles operating here, both calling for the proficiency of experts. On the one hand, there is the curriculum worker translating the objectives given to the school into activities and experiences that will most efficiently realize them. On the other hand, there is someone, let's call him an educational planner, giving the school objectives formulated in terms of their efficacy in bringing about the good life.

The significance of these two roles is not that two people should fill them, but that different kinds of things are taken into consideration when performing one or the other of them. The curriculum worker is concerned that the objectives he receives for the school be such that he can utilize his knowledge about the nature of learning, subject matter, and children to translate these objectives into pupil experiences. He is also concerned that the objectives be clear, represent the real wishes of the controlling agency, and be such that he can strive for them with integrity. His integrity is the prod he uses to get the educational planner to do the controlling agency's work well. The educational planner, by contrast, is concerned to formulate objectives that accurately express the controlling agency's idea of the good life and the place of the school in its achievement. His sources are all those disciplines with ideas that bear upon a conception of the good life. His decision is that one notion of the good life is better than others. Once this decision is made, his struggle is to formulate the place of education and the school in the achievement of this good life. The justification for his conception of the place of the school and education in the good life is that, if a school and education are accorded the place he reserves for them, then the life that results is indeed good. In other words, the educational planner bets on one conception of the good life. He stakes his whole educational system on the belief that his conception of the good life is, in fact, the best one, and he invites those curriculum workers who have a similar notion of the good life to join him in translating the notion of the good life into an actual fact through education.

CW. Then, the curriculum worker's concern with philosophy is a personal concern involving his integrity; correct? He is not a specialist in philosophy and so he joins the educational planner, who, I assume, is something of a specialist in philosophy, and who advocates a system of education based on a concept of values that offers no serious conflict with the personal philosophy of the curriculum worker. If I understand you, the curriculum worker and the educational planner work together toward the clarification of concepts. The curriculum worker stretches the educational planner by probing for the limits placed on pupil experiences by the objectives offered to the school. The educational planner stretches the curriculum worker by demanding evidence that the experiences offered in the schools do, in fact, achieve the goals set for the school by the controlling agency. They stretch each other constantly in their concern over whether or not the objectives drawn for the school by the educational planner are, in fact, the best objectives for the realization of the good life. The educational planner is *professionally* concerned to see that the conception of the good life upon which he relies is the best that is currently available; the curriculum worker is *personally* concerned over the same matter.

P. Philosophy, in such a set-up, is one of the sources to which the educational planner turns in considering various conceptions of the good life. Philosophy can offer much help as a source, but the educational planner must make his choice finally upon the basis of his own examination and must determine the objectives of the school on the basis of his conclusions. Since any discipline or person that offers a value position for a consideration becomes automatically a possible source of ideas for the educational planner, the curriculum worker as a thinking individual may also be a source for the educational planner. In fact, since the educational planner is likely to be something like the board of education instead of an individual, many pressure groups are likely to try to influence his choices in favor of their own conception of the good life. His decision, however, insofar as he is a good educational planner, must be based upon a reasoned consideration of the evidence available to him. After making a reasoned choice, there is not much else he can do other than keep his choice open to continuous re-examination.

CW. There is one lurking difficulty. As we've already agreed, in many cases there is no educational planner operating for the controlling agency which is likely to be unaware even that it is a controlling agency in some cases. I'm not sure this analysis helps us in cases where the controlling agency is a community, state, county, or what have you, in which the community has no formal process for determining what it thinks is the good life, much less what it thinks its notion of the good life dictates in terms of the place of the school in education.

P. I think this is only an apparent difficulty. As long as we don't hypostatize our terms, we're all right. What we've been talking about are roles that must be occupied, or better, clusters of decisions that must be made in trying to make a curriculum rational. We found that many of these decisions were quite beyond the curriculum itself, but were, nonetheless, decisions that furnished a foundation upon which a curriculum must be built. Our clusters of decisions, I think, reside in the levels of justification we have already discussed. The highest involves a specification of just what the good life is. The next involves a specification of the place of education in this good life. The next involves a specification of the place of the school in education. The next involves a specification of the place of the classroom in the school. Of course, these levels are not as clear-cut as we make them seem, nor are they all the levels that one might reasonably suggest. We placed the curriculum worker at the level of the school looking up to the controlling agency for a specification of the school's objectives and down at the classroom to which he offered objectives. We placed the educational planner at the level of the controlling agency where, as its representative, he chose the concept of the good life that was to be pursued, the place of education in its pursuit, and the place of the school in education. Clearly, the kinds of decisions that have to be made by the educational planner call for a different kind of expertness and knowledge from the kind required of the curriculum worker. That these kinds of decisions normally are made by someone who is unprepared to make them means no more than that they are likely to be poorly made. They must still be made. If the curriculum worker is forced to make them because other folks have abdicated their responsibilities, then either he must develop the skills that will enable him to make them well, or he must make them the best way he can. I would venture to say that it would be very difficult for one person to combine the knowledge and skill necessary to be both an expert educational planner and an expert curriculum worker. I would also venture to say that one of the skills necessary to be an expert educational planner is skill in philosophical analysis and thinking. I wouldn't go as far as to say that the educational planner ought to be a philosopher, but it would help.

CW. I believe you're falling into your own trap. Here you are talking as though the educational planner were somebody, when you just warned me not to hypostatize our terms. The problem is not that I can't conceive of the difference in the kind of decisions that are to be made by our two types of folks, but that in a democratic society there is no such thing as an educational planner and no likelihood that a philosopher would be chosen to act as one even if the difference in the kinds of decisions to be made were clearly understood by the controlling agency, in this case the community. What community do you know that is even halfway articulate in specifying what it believes to be the good life? And even if it were articulate, what community do you know that has agreed upon its concept? And if the community hasn't agreed and isn't likely to, how can even a philosopher make decisions that would represent what the community really believed about the good life and really thought was the place of the schools in education? And in the absence of such decisions, how can a curriculum worker go about his job in a rational way? In this case, it seems to me that we don't need a philosopher; we need some way of finding out what the community really believes and some way of constantly improving upon these beliefs. Perhaps our notion of the curriculum worker stretching the community by attempting to find the limits of toleration set by the community and by threatening too narrow limits with his resignation is as good as we've got. But even here, the curriculum worker doesn't have the qualifications he needs. He needs some help just to determine what too narrow limits are. If some way isn't found for decisions at the level of the educational planner to be made with more consideration of the possibilities, the evidence available, and the canons of logic and reason, I don't see how curriculum building can ever become a rational process, that is, a process in which effort has been made to reduce the amount of nonrationality to a minimum.

P. I can only agree.

14

Coda: The Conceptual System for Curriculum Revisited

JOHN I. GOODLAD

SOME MODIFICATIONS AND REFINEMENTS

All of the preceding chapters deal with various aspects of the practice and study of curriculum. Their scope and variety are mind-boggling. One might conclude, after reading such widely disparate material, that the proper study of curriculum is humankind.

The temptation is to narrow the scope by defining the field narrowly; for example, to what is learned or to be learned. But this helps only if one is myopic to the point of ignoring such questions as: "As perceived by whom?" or "How did what is being taught get there?" or "What is the best way to deliver what is to be learned?" What begins as a rather pure substantive concern quickly moves into the arena of socio-political and technical concerns. Are these to be ignored because they were not even hinted at in the definition? It would appear that, whatever one's definition of the word "curriculum," the practice of curriculum embraces a vast universe. Consequently, the study of curriculum, too, must embrace a great deal.

It would be difficult to argue that any of the foregoing chapters is not about some aspect of curriculum, whatever else it may include. All chapters imply the importance of something to be taught or learned; most get involved with social and political issues; several give considerable attention to the technical-professional. As stated in the first paragraph of Chapter 1, the curriculum field, comprehensively and realistically conceived, includes three kinds of phenomena: substantive, political-social and technical-professional. A conceptualization of practice and, therefore, of what curriculum inquiry entails likewise includes all three.

This volume set out to report the use (particularly for research and inquiry) of a conceptualization, published in 1966, developed by Goodlad in collaboration with Ammons, Iwańska, Jordan, and Richter. Each chapter illuminates and usually refines or elaborates some part of that conceptualization. The major elements were shown to exist even in relatively simple societies. The relative importance of the so-called "levels" of decision making was shown to vary from country to country, in part because of centralization or decentralization of authority over substantive matters of ends and means. Rather uniformly in practice, the institutional level appears to be weak or inadequately developed; societal decisions are directed to teachers (the instructional level). Likewise, the needs, interests, and feelings of students receive a good deal of lip-service but little attention in curriculum practice. All levels are heavily influenced and complicated by processes of human interaction and persuasion.

In summary, the conceptualization of curriculum in its original form and as abbreviated in Chapter 1 provides a reasonably accurate identification of the major components or elements of curriculum practice in complex, industrialized settings such as the United States. However, by appearing to give equal weight to all of the assumed levels of decision making, the conceptual system does not adequately reflect practice. Taken prescriptively, the system points to what may be elements of practice badly in need of attention. Clearly, this conceptualization succeeded in stimulating inquiry into itself and into the domains and processes the system sought to identify and illuminate.

In our initial work at the University of Chicago years ago, my four colleagues and I began with an almost exclusive interest in the substantive phenomena of curriculum. We quickly found ourselves into questions of who makes and who should make curriculum decisions. My subsequent experience with the curriculum development activities described by Wilson (Chapter 9) and with the University Elementary School (Chapters 5, 6, and 7) impressed me with the appropriateness of this earlier, somewhat academic awareness. Sociopolitical processes are inextricably part and parcel of the practice and study of curriculum. So far as study is concerned, they have been too long neglected.

While these chapters and the years of study and inquiry they report or reflect do not fundamentally change in my mind the initial conceptualization referred to above, they certainly suggest some modifications and a number of caveats regarding interpreting and using it. Three modifications are of rather major significance.

The first already has been taken care of in Chapter 1. For decades, I have worked in a close, collegial relationship with Frances Klein and Louise Tyler. They brought to my attention what appeared to them to be a static rather than dynamic place for students or learners in the initial formulation and focused attention on what they named the "personal" level or domain.[1] In recent years, also, several of that diverse group of curriculumists who sometimes refer to themselves as "reconceptualists" have brought increased attention to students as potential generators and not merely passive recipients of curricular ends and means.[2] Responding to these and other influences, I have endeavored to give at least equivalent attention to the personal or experiential as a decision-making level in the conceptual system (see Figure 1.1). This reduces the descriptive accuracy of the conceptualization but draws attention to a relatively neglected domain for development and research.

The second major modification pertains to the place of values. Although it is possible to formulate a set of values or assumptions about the good person in the good society as a beginning point in curriculum development, this happens in only a few, rather sharply circumscribed situations. Even when such are stated in the form of a philosophy (e.g., a set of religious beliefs in a church-related school), they usually serve rhetorical more than curricular ends.

Values are pervasive and express themselves in the form of personal or group interests at all levels and in all decisions of curriculum making even when we believe these decisions to be very "scientific."[3] As Macdonald points out, knowledge cannot be divorced from human interest: "My basic proposition then about curriculum is that at all levels and specifically at what I called the structural perspectives and rational values level (curriculum theory and design), the basic phenomenon which underlies all activity is the existence of human interest which precedes and channels the activity of curriculum thinking."[4]

Chapter 13 contributes significantly to our understanding of where and how value perspectives enter into curriculum thought and practice. Even after getting back to so-called "first premises," the curriculum worker's life is fraught with conflict and choice as new interests intrude into the decisions to be made. Circular thinking and poor communication often result. As Macdonald points out, curriculum theorists and designers have done little to sort out and clarify the problems of value.[5]

Over the years, it has become increasingly clear to me that identification of a level of values in the conceptual system is simply too neat and rational. It was done initially to draw attention to the fact that one comes from or with values to the selection of curricular ends and means (in contrast to Tyler's use of values as a "screen" to be used after a preliminary set of goals has been selected[6]). But one is never done with values. That initial formulation might have appeared to some interpreters as a simplistic way of disposing of them simply by stating all value premises at the outset.

Consequently, in my present, updated formulation of a conceptual system for the practice and study of curriculum (Figure 14.1), I have removed the "values level" and included values or their equivalent in the surrounding milieu out of which come all of these expressions of interest which affect curricula. In a way, this is avoidance behavior—avoidance of a more precise delineation of the role of values—but this new depiction is a more accurately descriptive one than that previously presented.

The third major modification of the conceptual system is a more general opening up of each level of decision making to the surrounding milieu. The initial formulation showed, in one of two representations,[7] two-way arrows extending to funded knowledge on one hand and conventional wisdom on the other. Figure 1.1 in Chapter 1 of this volume identifies, further, an interpretative role of clarifying what funded knowledge means for the curriculum and also what people want or expect. The process implied is a very rational one and appears to ignore the sociopolitical, transactional ones in which interests and interest groups seek to affect curricula. The school principal and the teachers engage regularly in these processes, just as the board does. Consequently, the new depiction provides for such transactions at all levels.

Three refinements are of somewhat lesser import only because they are elaborations more than revisions of the initial conceptualization. The first pertains to the further elaboration of the several levels into five domains—ideological, formal, perceived, operational, and experiential—where tangible curricula exist and may be observed and examined (Chapter 2). The least easily observed is the experiential; deductions must be drawn, in large part, from student effects or reactions to on-going practices. Likewise, finding out about the perceived curriculum entails identification of whose perceptions are sought and then probing through interviews and questionnaires. We found this refinement of the original conceptualization into more categories to be a useful operationalization for research purposes.

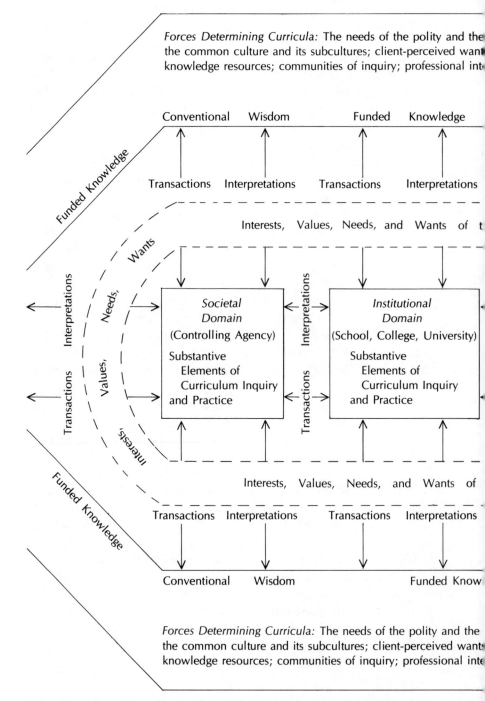

Figure 14.1. A conceptualization for guiding curriculum practice and inquiry

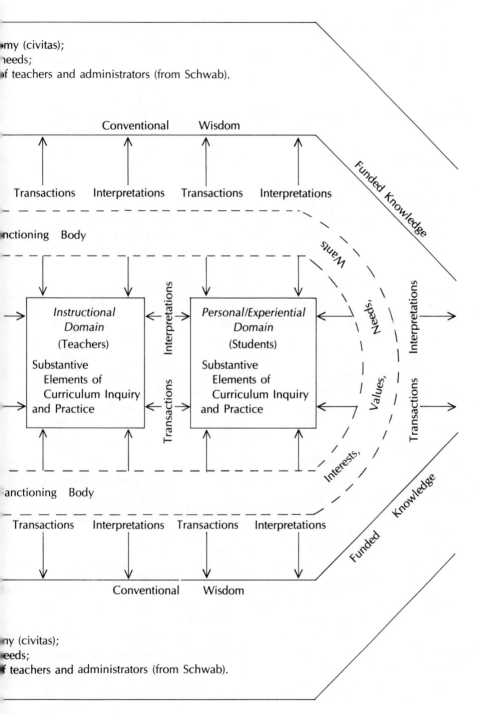

•my (civitas);
ʼeeds;
ʼf teachers and administrators (from Schwab).

Conventional   Wisdom

Transactions   Interpretations   Transactions   Interpretations

Funded Knowledge

ʼnctioning   Body

Instructional
Domain
(Teachers)

Substantive
Elements of
Curriculum Inquiry
and Practice

Interpretations

Personal/Experiential
Domain
(Students)

Substantive
Elements of
Curriculum Inquiry
and Practice

Transactions

Wants,

Needs,

Values,

Interests,

Interpretations

Transactions

ʼanctioning   Body

Transactions   Interpretations   Transactions   Interpretations

Funded   Knowledge

Conventional   Wisdom

ny (civitas);
ʼeeds;
ʼteachers and administrators (from Schwab).

It should be pointed out that the few levels depicted in both Figure 1.1 and Figure 14.1 constitute a relatively gross categorization. Many refinements within this general framework are possible. For example, societal can be broken down into federal, state, and local, and each of these can be subdivided to differentiate between an elected body such as Congress or a state legislature and various appointed bodies. And, in this country, there are variations from state to state in regard to whether certain decision-making individuals or groups are elected or appointed. For example, the commissioner of education is appointed at the federal level but sometimes elected and sometimes appointed at the state level. Nonetheless, all fit within the "societal" level of the conceptual system. Similar refinements and distinctions can be made throughout the conceptualization.

Another refinement is of similar nature. The rectangles used to identify relatively discrete levels or domains of decision making are both separated and linked by two-way arrows depicting, on one hand, a process of interpreting substantive decisions from one level to another and, on the other hand, a sociopolitical process of transacting agreements and ground rules. Of course, the two are intertwined, as in teachers' negotiations of a contract; the point is that both kinds of processes always are involved. However, the conceptual system could be modified to reveal a considerable range and variety of classifiable refinements of both interlevel and intralevel interpretations and transactions. For example, the superintendent negotiates with the board (societal level) and then frequently represents these societal-level agreements in negotiating institutional agreements with school principals. Then, there are sublevels of interpretation and transaction within each individual institution. Again, however, these are refinements in, rather than basic modifications of, the initial conceptualization.

A third refinement pertains to the milieu within which curriculum development at all levels proceeds. In the original, I attempted to make a distinction between funded knowledge as a data source and virtually everything else (which I overgeneralized as conventional wisdom). But knowledge is not pure; much of what passes as knowledge today is soon to become conventional wisdom or discredited or both. Interests push some "knowledge" to the forefront and discredit other knowledge that often has more to commend it. Again, the substantive and the sociopolitical become intertwined. Curriculum theorists have done little to untangle them or to provide insight into how these things and not those become essential rather than peripheral in curricula.

Schwab has identified six "forces" which, he claims, determine the overwhelming bulk of the curriculum.[8] These are:

1. Civil interest (civitas) or the needs of the polity and the economy.

2. The common culture and its subcultures (morals and manners, prevailing beliefs and loyalties, recreations widely enjoyed, etc.).

3. Client-perceived wants and needs (e.g., vocational training).

4. Knowledge resources (conventionally recognized "fields" of knowledge and organized bodies of experience and behavior).

5. Communities of inquiry (research and scholarship).

6. "Professional" interests of teachers, administrators, etc. (both self-interests and in others' welfare).

How these function and serve to influence provides promising turf for investigation.

In Figure 14.1, I have expanded on the elements of the context within which curricula are planned and operate, primarily to suggest once again the complexity of the processes rather than to sort out and organize the influences. Since most of these same forces influence human activity extending far beyond curriculum development, I have drawn a dotted line to separate and contain the latter somewhat. The solid lines around each level suggest more distinct and identifiable domains where curriculum practices can be studied and improved. Most curriculum writing and research concentrates on what lies within the rectangles, particularly those encompassing the institutional and instructional levels. The interactive terrain between levels and between the levels and the surrounding milieu is relatively barren of sustained research and inquiry.

THE ELEMENTS OF A CONCEPTUAL SYSTEM
FOR CURRICULUM

The revised conceptual system for dealing with the practice and study of curriculum emerging on previous pages and charted here is designed to serve both descriptive and prescriptive functions. In earlier chapters, we have seen its use for identifying the extent and kinds of curriculum activity at several assumed decision-making levels (Chapter 3); for portraying difficulties in conducting sustained institutional curriculum development (Chapter 5); for guiding institutional and instructional processes (Chapters 6 and 9); and for inquiring into questions such as who should make what curriculum decisions (Chapter 4). We have had a glimpse, also, into how such a conceptualization, combined with a value position regarding "good" curriculum work, could serve to develop praxiological principles and theories of curriculum construction (Chapter 12).

As a descriptive tool, this conceptualization does not reflect ongoing practice in a balanced way. That is, its use for inquiry will reveal in practice the omission or near-omission of entire domains or levels of decisions. But such findings may then be used for evaluative purposes. Is it good or desirable that the institutional or personal receives so little attention in practice? The conceptual system may now be used for analytical and even prescriptive purposes.

When one turns to the conceptualization for prescriptive guidance, however, one's values and preferences enter heavily into what to use or not use, stress or not stress. For example, one could take the position that teachers should be *the* curriculum makers and the further position that parents should have a choice among teachers but no further voice in what is taught. Such a position appears to render meaningless and irrelevant all other levels and potential levels of decision making. However, descriptive use of the conceptual level might reveal, depending on the culture, that a national curriculum center, with governmental support, is busy making curricula and that teachers in public schools behaving autonomously soon will be in rough water. Further, prescriptive use would soon reveal many other possible positions and suggest to the person taking the autonomous-teacher position the need for arguments and tactics to fend off impending attack. In brief, by having some awareness of a conceptual whole which, in turn, reflects the real world to some degree, one is then more able to see the relevance and implications of whatever value positions one chooses to adopt.

One might prefer to rearrange the elements to reflect more accurately one's beliefs and knowledge about curriculum practice before setting out to do further research and inquiry. And one might prefer an entirely different conceptualization for prescriptive purposes. I encourage and applaud both. It is my personal conviction, however, that the elements comprising the curriculum field, be it practice or inquiry, remain more or less the same, regardless of how they are manipulated and ultimately organized in one's mind. For example, there has been much debate over the desirability of building curricula by stating objectives and then selecting activities to achieve the former. Regardless of one's position on this issue, however, one cannot even engage in the debate without dealing with the question of ends and means.

In bringing this volume to conclusion, then, I shall attempt to identify those elements which must somehow be encompassed and dealt with in any effort to conceptualize the field of curriculum. I believe that all the major elements have been identified, implicitly or explicitly, somewhere on preceding pages and so what follows is a summary. Needless to say, the list is incomplete and comprises, at best, only "minimum essentials." Each set of elements and subelements is discussed only briefly below.

Substantive Elements

One would have to conclude, if forced to choose, that the substantive elements of curriculum are the most important since they have to do, ultimately, with what is to be learned in or through a curriculum. They probably are the easiest to identify and define; they have been most often the subject of inquiry. Tyler identified four major elements or common-places—goals, learning experiences or activities, organization, and evaluation—and broke down several of these into subelements (e.g., scope, sequence, and integration under the general element of organization). He also provided principles or criteria for selecting and ordering these elements.

One does not need to begin, in developing or studying curricula, with goals; there are alternative approaches and orientations. For example, one might begin with the question of what knowledge is of most worth and, therefore, worth learning, and then grapple with questions of its suitability for students of a given age. Or, one could begin with inquiry into the kinds of activities most appropriate for human beings and then determine what goals will assure student partici-pation in them. But this is not the time or place to argue for any particular alternative; the issues involved are extensively dealt with in the literature.

The essential point to be made here is that these and probably other substantive elements are common to any discourse—that is, they are curriculum commonplaces. The orientation to them depends on one's interests or values. A conceptual system for curriculum must include these com-monplaces and virtually invite various approaches to, and interpretation of, them. A major criterion for judging a cur-riculum plan is whether that plan includes attention to many—or only a few—commonplaces. Another is whether the plan took account of alternative approaches to any given commonplace and whether only a few commonplaces, in one pattern of ordering, were naïvely or blindly addressed.

Encompassing only the substantive elements of activities, organization, evaluation, and goals in a conceptual system for curriculum provides the practitioner with a substantial guide to decision making and the researcher with extensive terrain for inquiry. Even with this arbitrary narrowing, how-ever, the problems and issues are so formidable that little systematic ordering of the field has occurred. Tyler's concep-tualization is one of the few available. Unfortunately, perhaps more energy has gone into criticizing it than into creating others. 'Tis a pity.

Whether or not one agrees with Tyler's rationale, his *Basic Principles of Curriculum and Instruction* provides a concise, comprehensive identification and ordering of substantive elements and subelements. The conceptualization provided in this volume reveals that there are at least five major domains of curriculum decision making where these elements are addressed. Four of these are encompassed in the rectangles of Figure 14.1: societal, institutional, instructional, and experiential. The making of curricular decisions in these several domains draws our attention to the sociopolitical elements of curriculum—that is, the human processes inevitably involved in any decision about activities, goals, evaluation, or organization (see below).

The fifth domain—the ideological—is not included in Figure 14.1 because it is largely divorced or protected from the sociopolitical aspects of curriculum development the conceptualization seeks to include. That is, the ideological domain is purely substantive or nearly so. In a way, too, the ideological parallels each of the other four domains. Ideological or ideaistic curricular plans can be developed for any or all of the other domains. In practice, however, any preconceived plans for the institutional or any other domain invariably are modified in practice either deliberately or through the inadvertent intrusion of personal interpretations. Consequently, there often is an extraordinary difference between a science curriculum developed in a university and a teacher's instructional use of that curriculum. Nonetheless, both the staff of the university curriculum project and that teacher deal with essentially the same curricular commonplaces. A comprehensive conceptualization of the field of curriculum— more comprehensive than the one sketched here—necessarily identifies and arranges these commonplaces in some reasonably clear and understandable way.

Political-Social Elements

There are at least three different types of political-social processes to be encompassed by a conceptual system in curriculum. First, there are those internal to a domain such as the institutional. Second, there are those between domains such as the institutional and the societal. Third, there are processes conducted between a domain such as the institutional and individuals (e.g., parents) or groups (e.g., Local Citizens for Better Schools) located outside of that domain. Actually, there is a fourth set of processes which might be described as the general debate over education and educational institutions. But this doesn't affect any existing curriculum until some resolution, however temporary, of that debate finds its way into one of the curriculum domains. For all practical purposes, then, this fourth type of political-social process is a variation on or extension of the third.

While the existence of political-social phenomena in curriculum is self-evident, there has been little documentation of them and virtually no efforts to classify them. There probably are enough empirical studies in fields such as political science, social psychology, management, and education to suggest the elements to be taken into account in a conceptualization of the curriculum field—even though few of the studies have been in curriculum.

For example, there are studies, particularly in higher education, into the political processes at work when faculty members (institutional domain) seek to arrive at agreements on requirements for graduation. Unfortunately, these processes are guided more by hidden agendas than *Robert's Rules of Order* and so are not easily described and classified. And, of course, what goes on in a particular institution depends on the actors. Nonetheless, there probably are patterns that repeat themselves sufficiently to warrant some conceptualizing of the common elements and, perhaps, even some theory-based predictions of how political-social processes observed in certain types of institutions might proceed in other samples of the same types. Further, we probably know enough now about what facilitates and what derails faculty processes of curriculum planning to be able to put together quite useful prescriptions for faculty behavior.

The interdomain elements of the political-social in curriculum development have come to the fore recently in public education with the rise of collective bargaining. The substantive elements of curriculum are at least optional components of the bargaining process in many states. A reasonable prediction is that the curriculum will become more rather than less a topic for arbitration between teacher groups and state and local boards of education.

With or without collective bargaining, however, there always are transactions of one kind or another between curricular domains. Figure 14.1 shows two sets of two-way arrows between domains. One of these is named "interpretations"; it is substantive rather than political-social. Teachers, for example, seek to interpret or translate the meaning of some societal or institutional directive for their instructional behavior. But unless they challenge the directive and perhaps seek to establish an alternative, political-social negotiations are not involved.

The second set of arrows in Figure 14.1 is labeled "transactions" and clearly identifies in the conceptual system elements of curriculum which are social or political. The transactions might be between third-grade teachers and the principal or a school's policy committee; or between a committee of teachers and the school board; or between a superintendent of schools and a state or local board of education, etc. And, of course, a great deal of transactional activity transpires between students (experiential domain) and their teachers (instructional domain). Indeed, if all the curriculum work in a school or school district were added up, the political-social aspects probably would outweigh the substantive.

Figure 14.1 suggests a much more rational and orderly world of curriculum development than exists in practice, reflecting the more predictable substantive elements rather than the less predictable political-social ones. For example, the domain-to-domain transactions are not always between two adjacent domains such as the experiential and the instructional. Sometimes, a domain is "jumped," as when teachers transact the instructional curriculum with some societal agency or group. In fact, the research of Griffin (Chapter 3) and Hill (Chapter 4) suggests that there may be more sociopolitical activity between the instructional and societal domains than between the instructional and institutional. One is tempted, therefore, to draw arrows between the instructional and the societal, arrows that simply bypass the institutional domain. However, there are so many avenues of political and social interaction that it is perhaps better simply to note that many possibilities for deviating from Figure 14.1 exist. To attempt to include them carries the obligation to be all-inclusive. But our present state of knowledge is such that the implied precision and detail simply are impossible.

This problem of multiple possibilities is compounded when we come to those political-social processes that obtain between a domain and its milieu. Figure 1.1 kept things neat and tidy simply by including only the largely substantive problem of seeking to pay attention to conventional wisdom while drawing upon funded knowledge as a prime data source in all curricular decisions. The first section of this chapter states the need for a major revision of the conceptual system in this particular aspect.

The direction of the needed revision is toward greater recognition of political-social elements, particularly those involving transactions between individuals and groups associated with or responsible for educational institutions and various other individuals and groups in the community.

Figure 14.1 attempts to include the needed revision. Each of the substantive domains of curriculum is linked to each of the others through the dual processes of translation or interpretation (substantive) and transaction (political-social) as shown in Figures 1.1. and 14.1. But each also is loosely or quite firmly linked to elements of the surrounding culture, social system, or community. Some schools, for example, probably pay far more attention to the prevailing moods of parents and communities than to directives from the societal domain of formal decision making. It is almost certain that school board members (societal domain) are more tuned in to the electorate than to school employees and, as a consequence, stimulate the emergence of teachers' unions.

In various, largely unchartered ways, teachers and educational institutions are alert and respond (both negatively and positively) to people and ideas in the surrounding society. Teachers carry with them into their classrooms aspects of funded knowledge, pieces of conventional wisdom, the expectations and wishes of this group or that. Through other than regularized processes of curriculum planning, the hopes, aspirations, and expectations of various individuals and groups find their way into classrooms. The programs of educational institutions and the teaching of teachers are influenced and determined by much more than the directives of societal agencies and school officials responsible for educational programs. Not only is the educational system an open one, whatever its degree of autonomy, each level or domain also is open to the surrounding milieu. No wonder much state legislation intended for schools and teachers never reaches its mark or is distorted en route to the target.

To attempt to classify all the varied influences and to arrange these classifications in some ascending or descending order of importance or impact is premature. As stated earlier in this chapter, however, I find Schwab's six forces[9] to be useful and so have placed them outside of the dotted ellipse in Figure 14.1 as a way of suggesting that the elements constituting the milieu can be identified and ordered through systematic inquiry. The two-way arrows passing through the dotted ellipse suggest the kinds of interpretative and transactional processes that continuously link educational institutions with their surrounding culture. To repeat, these links sometimes are very close and strong, sometimes loose and weak. Because Schwab's "forces" are all part of the total sanctioning body, I have attempted to depict them in Figure 14.1 as components of the latter.

Technical-Professional Elements

Chapter 1 emphasized the importance of specialized knowledge and skills in the curriculum planning process. No separate identification of these technical-professional elements appears in Figure 14.1 simply because they are an integral part of all other elements in all domains. What needs to be made clear, however, is that the need for utilizing relevant knowledge and skills is not confined to the instructional level. We assume that there is useful lore for teachers but tend to ignore the fact that the need for specialized knowledge and for using it is at least as great for the societal and institutional domains. School boards, for example, rarely go beyond the conventional wisdom of their members in making decisions that have great impact for students in schools.

Badly needed, first, is a descriptive conceptualization of the kinds of curricular decisions made by state and local school boards, what kinds of data they employ, where they get their data and how they arrive at decisions. Scattered studies of such phenomena exist.[10] Likewise, we need more studies of institutional processes that would suggest the kinds of technical and professional abilities required. The instructional domain is the most studied; the experiential probably has received the least attention, in spite of its obvious importance.

It appears that the conceptualization depicted in Figure 14.1 is sufficiently comprehensive to guide the detailed work involved. In effect, what is needed is a detailed account of the kinds of technical and professional knowledge and skills required for all aspects of curriculum planning. Then, empirical work is necessary to determine what is praxiologically sound. Ultimately, it should be possible to create some middle-range theories regarding "what works" for selected purposes in particular situations. But for the present, Figure 14.1 is sufficiently comprehensive to suggest the elements to be studied, described, and tested.

CONCLUDING COMMENTS

As the conceptual system for curriculum is depicted in Figure 1.1, it differs little from the original that first appeared in print in 1966. The refinements made in the latter and included in Figure 1.1 were intended largely for the purpose of clearing up some problems of interpretation. The major elaboration is the naming and greater emphasis accorded the experiential or personal domain. And virtually all of the refinements and elaborations addressed substantive elements. It is the conceptualization of Figure 1.1 that was known to the several authors of this volume and to a degree guided the work reported in preceding chapters.

The most striking difference between Figure 1.1 and Figure 14.1 pertains to political-social elements. The revisions and elaborations in this area are quite marked. This suggests two observations. First, the more one stays with ideological or ideaistic curriculum inquiry, with little involvement in or attention to the "stuff" of ongoing practice, the less need one senses for a conceptual depiction of anything other than substantive curricular elements. This probably was why the initial work of the Chicago group, reported earlier, paid relatively little attention to the social and political, while still recognizing its existence.

Many of the preceding chapters are based on experience with situations where those involved had a stake in the outcomes. It was curriculum planning that affected people's lives. The major sources of data and reasons were not necessarily "what research says." They were more likely what interested or affected the participants. Consequently, my simultaneous or subsequent reflection on the conceptual system led rather naturally to recognition of deficiencies or inadequacies in the system's inclusion of political-social considerations. Figure 14.1 emerges, as a result, substantially changed in these respects from Figure 1.1, and much better balanced, I believe, with respect to the political-social dimension.

The second observation that comes to mind in reflecting on this shift is that we have been, for at least a decade, in a period when political and social considerations have dominated all aspects of education and schooling. Congress, state legislatures, and the courts have been the prime movers. Minority rights, women's rights, and, most recently, children's rights have been at the forefront of change. When representatives of organizations interested or potentially interested in curriculum matters were asked to identify the most pressing curricular issues, substantive ones were scarcely mentioned.[11] Political issues of involvement, representation, and who should make curriculum decisions far outnumbered the classic ones of what should be taught or how curricula should be organized. Education, schooling, politics, and human rights have been intimately entwined in recent years.

Students of a field are not as detached from the currents of their milieu as they would like to believe. Indeed, they often fail to realize that what their life's work reflects usually is little more than a series of passing phases and episodes and that the work of this phase will be outdated in a decade or less. Difficult as it is to escape from this temporal parochialism, it is better to be aware of, rather than oblivious to, it. Scholarly fashions change—sometimes almost as quickly as *haute couture*.

There is little doubt in my mind that the greater emphasis on the political and social represented in Figure 14.1 is a reflection of recognized imbalance in the original made more acute by curricular emphases of the past ten years. Interestingly, there now appears to be some resurgence of interest in the classic questions and issues of curriculum—that is, largely substantive matters. It soon will be fashionable to talk once more about scope, sequence, and integration.

Interestingly, I find my own interests returning to the matters my colleagues and I discussed at the University of Chicago years ago in seeking to come up with a conceptual ordering of the field. Consequently, I feel sure that any revision of Figure 14.1 attempted by me a decade from now will reflect an ongoing effort to elaborate and clarify the substantive more than the political-social elements comprising the practice and study of curriculum.

Finally, it is necessary to comment on the use of conceptual systems for both descriptive and prescriptive purposes. I am comfortable now with the conclusion that one system can be used for both purposes—up to a point. Used descriptively, a comprehensive conceptual system points to the questions to be asked about ongoing practice: What goals are being pursued? To what extent do students, teachers, and parents agree on what the goals should be? What variety exists in the individual programs of students taking courses labeled science? Does the use of time accurately reflect teachers' stated priorities? What evaluative procedures are being used?

Used prescriptively, a conceptual system might well focus attention on the same matters, but the verbs "is" and "are" change to "should" or "ought." What should the goals be? How should time be spent? What kinds of evaluative criteria should be used? A single conceptualization can serve both research and practice.

What must be understood is that the use of a conceptual system for descriptive purposes does not provide a prescription. That is, finding out what exists does not answer the question of what should be. One ponders the factual data, makes judgments about them, and, perhaps, recommends a highly divergent alternative.

The critical question to ask of a conceptual system designed for inquiry into practice is whether it draws attention to the "proper" phenomena to be studied. The critical question to ask of a conceptual system designed to guide practice is whether it draws attention to the "proper" questions to be answered. The former use is designed to tell us what now exists. The latter is designed to help us decide what should be. Curriculum planning, development, and improvement require both.

NOTES

1. Louise L. Tyler and M. Frances Klein, "Not Either-Or," Paper delivered at the Annual Meeting of the American Educational Research Association, New Orleans, February 25, 1973.

2. For a useful bibliography of relevant writing, see B. J. Benham, *Curriculum Theory in the 1970's: The Reconceptualist Movement, 50 Annotated Sources*, Texas Tech University, Lubbock, Texas, 1977.

3. John I. Goodlad, "Program Development: Identification and Formulation of Desirable Educational Goals," in Jack Blaney, Jan Housego, and Gordon McIntosh (eds.), *Program Development in Education*, Morriss Printing Company Ltd., Victoria, B.C., 1974, pp. 56–57.

4. James B. Macdonald, "Curriculum and Human Interests," Virgil E. Herrick Memorial Lecture, University of Wisconsin, 1972, p. 5.

5. Ibid, p. 2.

6. Ralph W. Tyler, *Basic Principles of Curriculum and Instruction*, University of Chicago Press, Chicago, 1950.

7. John I. Goodlad (with Maurice N. Richter, Jr.), *The Development of a Conceptual System for Dealing with Problems of Curriculum and Instruction*, Cooperative Research Program, USOE, Project No. 454, University of California, Los Angeles, 1966, Figure 3, p. 65.

8. Joseph J. Schwab, "What 'Drives' the Schools?" Paper prepared for the Curriculum Development Task Force, National Institute of Education, 1976 (10 pp, mimeo).

9. Ibid.

10. For example, see Kenneth A. Tye, "A Conceptual Framework for Political Analysis, Public Demands, and School Board Decisions," Unpublished doctoral dissertation, University of California, Los Angeles, 1968.

11. *Curriculum Issues, Problems and Concerns in Curriculum Development*, Report of the National Institute of Education, Curriculum Task Force to the National Council on Educational Research, The National Institute of Education, Washington, D.C., January 15, 1976, 80 pp.

Index